Scandal Nation

Scandal Nation

LAW AND AUTHORSHIP IN BRITAIN, 1750–1832

Kathryn Temple

Cornell University Press

Ithaca and London

First published 2003 by Cornell University Press

Printed in the United States of America

Library of Congress Cataloging-in-Publication Data

Temple, Kathryn, 1955–
  Scandal nation : law and authorship in Britain, 1750–1832 / Kathryn Temple.
    p. cm.
Includes bibliographical references and index.
  ISBN 0-8014-4042-4 (cloth : alk. paper)
  1. Authors and publishers—Great Britain—History.   2. Libel and slander—Great Britain—History.   3. Piracy (Copyright)—Great Britain—History.   4. Copyright infringement—Great Britain—History.   5. Literary forgeries and mystifications—History.   6. Authorship—History.   7. Scandals—Great Britain—History.   I. Title.
  KD1340 .T46 2003
  346.4104'82—dc21   2002010658

Part of chapter 1 was published in *Novel: A Forum on Fiction* 33. 2 (spring 2000), copyright NOVEL Corp. © 2000. Reprinted by permission. An earlier version of chapter 2 was published as "Johnson and Macpherson: Cultural Identity and the Construction of Literary Property." Reprinted by permission of *The Yale Journal of Law & the Humanities* 5 (1993): 355–87. Portions of chapter 3 were published in "'Manly Composition': Hume and the *History of England*," in *Feminist Interpretations of David Hume,* ed. Nancy Tuana (University Park: Penn State University Press, 1999), 194–211, 273–80. Copyright © 1999 by The Pennsylvania State University. Reproduced by permission of the publisher.

Cornell University Press strives to use environmentally responsible suppliers and materials to the fullest extent possible in the publishing of its books. Such materials include vegetable-based, low-VOC inks and acid-free papers that are recycled, totally chlorine-free, or partly composed of nonwood fibers. For further information, visit our website at www.cornellpress.cornell.edu.

Cloth printing   10 9 8 7 6 5 4 3 2 1

Contents

Illustrations

Acknowledgments

Like most academic projects, this one has been completed over a number of years and in many venues. Throughout the process, my colleagues and friends at Georgetown University have been unfailingly helpful and supportive. I thank particularly Anton Trinidad, Angelyn Mitchell, Dennis Todd, Alvaro Ribeiro, Paul Betz, Joe Sitterson, Michael Ragussis, Bruce Smith, Lindsay Kaplan, Jason Rosenblatt, Gay Cima, Matthew Tinkcom, John Glavin, and Gerry Mara. Penn Szittya intervened at a moment crucial to the success of the project. Friends both in and out of the academy have also contributed more than I can say. Donna and Nathaniel Floyd, the Pavco-Giaccia family, especially Olivia, Helen Lydon, Mary Mahoney, Yumei Bruce, Larkin Postles, Michele Madison, Nicole Droog, and Carol, Keith, Marissa, and Tommy Kurtz, were all instrumental to my peace and happiness while I worked. I first met Patricia Meyer Spacks at the University of Virginia, where I was a graduate student. Unfailingly supportive, she has been a rigorous, invigorating reader from the very beginning of the project right up to the end. That she turned into a friend along the way has been one of life's wonderful surprises. Other colleagues, including Deborah Kaplan, Mary Pat Martin, Janet Sorensen, Paula McDowell, J. Paul Hunter, John Radner, Barbara Schnorrenberg, Peter Jaszi, Joan Williams, Nancy Armstrong, and Cynthia Wall, not only provided a supportive intellectual community but also read portions of the manuscript and offered generous and helpful comments. Among these, I could not have finished the book without the support of Sonja Foss. Kristina Straub and Joseph Bartolomeo, who read the manuscript for Cornell University Press, gave generously of their time and expertise. Bernhard Kendler at Cornell University Press offered his experience and advice and could not have been more helpful. My parents, Donald and Louise Streever, my siblings Kristyn Greaves and Bill Streever, and my niece Margaret Greaves, all writers themselves, urged me on at important moments. My husband, James Slevin, always good in a crisis, sustained me, and our daughter, Lucy Slevin, supplied energy, liveliness, and a sense of purpose. Without them I would lead a dull life indeed.

I also thank those teachers at Chesterbrook Montessori School, Judy Balcazar-Mercill, Marion Paulson, Bernadette Bretana, and Olga Cordova, who made it possible for me to finish this book in the knowledge that my daughter was safe and happy.

The American Council of Learned Societies, the National Endowment for the Humanities, the Graduate School of Georgetown University, and the Georgetown University English Department all provided funding for this project, and I thank them. Through the Georgetown Undergraduate Research Opportunities Program, I received invaluable help from Elizabeth Carten, Elizabeth Pender, Christina Morin, and Allison Foley, charming and accomplished undergraduate students who became enthusiastic, supportive colleagues. I also thank the librarians at the Folger Shakespeare Library and at the interlibrary loan department of the Joseph Mark Lauinger Library at Georgetown University. Jill Hollingsworth of the reference staff was unfailingly helpful, as were librarians at the University of Virginia main campus and law school.

Scandal Nation

Introduction

The National Print Spectacle

I began this project with a simple question: Why did eighteenth-century writers and readers argue with such intensity and tenacity about transgressive literary acts like book piracy, literary forgery, copyright violations, and libel? In pursuing this question, I found that the scandals of eighteenth-century Grub Street were not limited to literary issues nor confined to literary venues. Instead, they fulfilled a public function, forming sites where national identity was negotiated, mediated, and defined.[1] Writers often staged such scandals publicly as if to invite general comment; indeed, such staging is at work in the well-known story of Samuel Johnson's feud with the Scottish literary forger, James Macpherson. In that tale, the aging Johnson, already beginning to be celebrated as a representative of English literature was depicted as preparing to defend himself against the much younger Macpherson, a Highland poet who claimed to have discovered an ancient Scottish tradition fit to rival English traditions. John Hawkins suggested that after receiving a threatening letter from Macpherson, Johnson armed himself carefully:

---

1. Benedict Anderson's sophisticated understanding of nation, articulated in full in *Imagined Communities*, offered literary and cultural critics a tremendously helpful and malleable model for understanding national identity. See Katherine Verdery and Anderson in *Mapping the Nation* for a recent survey of the field. For representative feminist critiques, see the special issue "Nationalisms and National Identities" of *Feminist Review* 44 (1993), especially McClintock, "Family Feuds." See also the special issue on nation of *Gender and History* 5.2 (summer 1993). While Anderson's influence on all contemporary work on nation is impossible to overstate, my understanding of nation has been helpfully complicated by Homi Bhabha, Lauren Berlant, Linda Colley, Katie Trumpener, and Richard Helgerson, and by Julia Kristeva's *Strangers to Ourselves*.

Whether Johnson . . . meant to shew all who came to see him that he stood upon his guard, he provided himself with a weapon, both of the offensive and defensive kind. It was an oak-plant of a tremendous size; a plant, I say, and not a shoot or branch, for it had a root, which being trimmed to the size of a larger orange, became the head of it. Its height was upwards of six feet, and from about an inch in diameter at the lower end, increased to near three: this he kept in his bed-chamber, so near the chair in which he constantly sat, as to be within reach. (491)

If Johnson wanted "to shew all who came to see him that he stood upon his guard," he succeeded, for the story has been repeated in almost every account of Johnson's life.

Meant perhaps to demonstrate Johnson's manliness, though also suggesting manliness at risk, the story reveals the ludicrously phallic and violent side of what had begun as a scholarly debate among the literati. But it also makes manifest the political stakes in literary disputes. To defend English tradition, Johnson chose a piece of quintessentially English oak, kept not simply close at hand, but "in his bedchamber, so near the chair in which he constantly sat," at the very center of his domestic and literary life.[2] The "tremendous plant" with its root-turned-head figures the rootedness and antiquity of the English tradition, a tradition Johnson wields from the psychic center of the nation as he protects domestic boundaries and fends off a Celtic fringe come dangerously close to the heart of English life. Simultaneously, Johnson's weapon speaks to the huge transformation in authorship effected during his lifetime. No longer would authorship be owned by the aristocratic patron. Replacing his pen with a sturdy oak staff rather than an aristocratic sword, Johnson signals his willingness to defend with violence what he imagined as a particularly English form of authorship, one oriented to the nation as a whole, as sympathetic to Joseph Andrews as to the king in his royal library, as attuned to the crowd looking in the print shop window as to an elite circle of Cambridge scholars.[3]

As Adrian Johns has suggested, the search "for instances when the principles that are to us most essential to print were in fact in dispute" offers

2. Schama 153–74, historicizes the associations between the English oak and the English nation. As Schama points out, publications such as *Essay on Planting* (1758) and *Heart of Oak: The British Bulwark* (1763) suggest the currency of the connection during the second half of the century. The oak was such an English cliché by the time of Johnson's journey to Scotland that English readers could have been expected to guffaw each time Johnson gibed Boswell by mentioning Scotland's lack of hardwood forests. See Johnson, *A Journey to the Western Islands of Scotland* and Boswell, *The Journal of a Tour to the Hebrides*.

3. I am indebted to Kristina Straub for this idea. Alvin Kernan details Johnson's visits to the King's Library and discusses the library's cultural significance.

a crucial way to explore print culture (325). For this book, exploring print culture at the moments when its principles were being formed also means exploring larger cultural movements. Modern studies of eighteenth-century authorship reveal that the literary transgressions we call piracy, forgery, theft (or more technically, copyright violation), and libel were not limited to "hacks" or other marginal writers. They were legion at the time, their very ubiquity demanding the investigation they are currently receiving. Laurence Sterne, Samuel Johnson, and Samuel Richardson—even Alexander Pope, so critical of writerly misbehavior in the *Dunciad*—bent and broke the rules, yet avoided the consequences meted out to Chatterton, Macpherson, and other more unfortunate transgressors. As an expanding print culture demanded new ways of thinking about doing business and doing art, disputes involving literary transgression generated outraged public commentary. Examining such moments of disputation reveals their imbrication with national imaginings. James Ralph's 1758 claim that "if Heroes and Patriots constitute the first Column of national Glory, Authors of Genius constitute the second," expressed a sentiment widespread by the 1750s (3).

Complex efforts to constitute English national authorship—or intervene strategically in its constitution—drive the scandalous print spectacles I have singled out here. My material spans a little more than a half century and is organized around the threats to Englishness presented by the Irish, the Scots, by women and "the feminine," and by empire. Beginning in chapter 1 with the 1753 Irish piracy of Samuel Richardson's novel *Sir Charles Grandison,* I shift in chapter 2 to the controversy over James Macpherson's forgery of the Scottish Ossian poems. Chapter 3 brings to the foreground issues of gender—latent in the two preceding chapters—in a discussion of the 1770s controversy prompted by the misappropriation of Catherine Macaulay's private letters. The book ends with a reading of the libel cases that turned Mary Prince's 1831 slave narrative into a public relations tool. While these events have much to tell us about England's relationship with the periphery, with gender, and with its own imperial desires, they also allow the examination of a number of English identity claims—to a privileged relationship with juridical legitimacy, to a seamless historical and literary tradition and to literacy itself—at the very moment of their construction.

Because these scandalous print spectacles straddled multiple forms of culture, they offer particularly useful sites for investigating the operations of nationhood. They originated in affronts to the newly emergent "middling" print culture of London, the very print culture that theorists of nationalism, most famously Benedict Anderson, think crucial to the development of national identity. Concurrently, they drew on discourse from the law and thus connected literary transgression to the English legal system, to "official culture," and to what Lauren Berlant calls the "national symbolic."[4] Surprisingly, given the elite legal and technical issues involved, print spectacles also embraced the "low" and the popular. They drew on images of criminality, the carnivalesque, the body, violence, and sexuality, quite literally making a spectacle of themselves not only in courts but also in popular venues such as the theater and in consumables such as broadsides, satirical prints, porcelain collectibles, and wax museum displays. Of course, they did not exhibit a uniform involvement of and with the people. As nationalist antiquarians and other spin doctors know, the success of the national symbolic rests not so much on the actual participation of "the people" as on the credible representation of their participation. The earlier print spectacles I discuss in this book rely more on incorporating images and motifs suggestive of the people's involvement than on actual wide public participation, while in the later "case" of Mary Prince, we can more readily see the immediate engagement of a wide spectrum of the population. Although national identity would come to be imagined around the sort of "middling" culture implied by Johnson's oak weapon, Richardson, Johnson, and Macaulay also attempted to suggest the involvement of the nation as a whole in disputes most likely of interest only to the literate elite. Their attempts had unexpected results. Consumers of popular culture reached "up," not merely because they were interested in images and rhetoric meant to engage them, but because they were eager to contribute to the ongoing debates that made authorship central to national identity.[5] Complicating simple hierarchical models of high and low, print spectacles reached "out" to Britain's Celtic periphery, as well as "down" to its least elite and wealthy members, creating public mainstream identity formations as well as all sorts of resistance to them. Thus print spectacles represented disruptions not only to the normative economic channels associated with the London print industry but also to the restricted version of official culture imagined by the London "center." In these scandals, both highs and lows, centers and peripheries came together to work out meanings of Englishness and Britishness.

That these scandals encompassed both print and spectacle suggests a

4. See Berlant 9–12 and 20 for discussions of the relationship between official culture and the national symbolic.

5. The arguments involving the bifurcation of high from "popular" culture have been aptly summarized by Tim Harris and Jonathan Barry in the collection *Popular Culture in England, c. 1500–1800.*

response to the long-running argument among scholars of nationalism over whether the two are mutually incompatible. Most theorists have identified print as crucial to the formation of national identity. But as Anne McClintock points out, print is an elite form, accessible even in modern times only to a small minority of a nation's population, its impenetrability at odds with the very idea of nation as lateral and democratic. Thus, McClintock disregards print almost entirely, arguing instead that the nation is experienced primarily through spectacles attended by the masses (*Imperial Leather* 374). But while an emphasis on spectacle may be the necessary corrective to the overemphasis on print, the bifurcation of print and spectacle is unnecessarily limiting. A printed work can in itself, if it is long enough or odd enough, become spectacular, while spectacles, such as that of Johnson wandering through the Hebrides, can emanate from print culture. The old story about public readings of *Pamela* that culminated in the ringing of the village church bell proves the point. In communities characterized by both oral and literate subcultures, print and spectacle work together to unite those on the oral-literate continuum.

As "national" as any flag or military uniform, print scandals drew on nationalism's passionate affect and its border-protecting plotting. But unlike flags and uniforms—which reflect and disseminate comparatively static views of "England" or "Britain"—they revealed the nation as a work in progress. Enacting the complex process of conflicted consolidation that vexed efforts to imagine Britain either as sovereign empire or as unified under the sign of Englishness, print scandals revealed Britishness and Englishness to be volatile cultural and discursive constructions, invoked for both exclusionary and inclusive purposes.[6] Equally likely to be desired as attacked, neither "England" nor "Britain" appears here as the powerful "given" that both would become in the nineteenth century; they appear, rather, as sign systems buffeted by conflicting hopes and fears. One of those hopes was represented by the idea of Englishness, an idea powerful for its unifying role, but as I discuss in detail in chapter 1, even more use-

6. Linda Colley argues that "England" had given way to a superimposed "Great Britain" by the 1750s. In *Britons,* she suggests in opposition to Tom Nairn and Michael Hechter that the superimposed "Britain" left peripheral cultures intact. Colley's model thus elides the power of "Englishness" to control the cultural meaning of "Great Britain" while also neglecting the real impact of peripheral cultures on the core. Adopting what has been called a "four nations" or sometimes a "three nations" approach to British identity both informs and complicates Colley's thesis. For a brief synopsis of this debate going back to J. G. A. Pocock's groundbreaking 1975 essay "British History: A Plea for a New Subject," see Bradshaw and Roberts's introduction to *British Consciousness and Identity,* 1–7. See also Gerald Newman's underappreciated study. For an introduction to British historiography's role in constructing national and regional identities, see Murdoch, *British History.*

[5]

ful when mobilized for international export in arenas that emphasized cosmopolitan exchange.

Reinterpreting print scandals as sites for identity formation calls for a shift in our thinking about literature and politics. As Simon Gikandi reminds us, we are in error if we think that national ideology emanates from "a body of stable value and shared experiences," from, in literary terms, a canon (xvii). The story told by print scandals is one of instability, one in which figures who would eventually become canonical are uncertain of their status, where attacks on cultural and canonical authority contribute as much to national identity as any "body of stable value" itself. Each scandalous event I address involves an act that transgressed juridical norms, a discrete instance identified as literary forgery, piracy, copyright invasion, or libel. But these transgressive acts were incorporated into, and in significant ways structured, much larger textual networks consisting only partly of texts traditionally associated with literary and national traditions, and including as well a multiplicity of canonical and non-canonical works, popular tracts, legal treatises, proclamations of aesthetic theory, and spectacles of all kinds.

Spectacle and scandal converge and collapse into each other in the publicity surrounding these transgressive acts. London's print culture constructed as scandalous those events that offended its sensibilities, or even worse, disrupted its normative channels of distribution and exchange.[7] To imply scandal marked certain events, common in the print industry, as extraordinary and singled them out for a heightened level of scrutiny. In the Middle Ages, "scandal" implied religious transgression, but by the mid-eighteenth century it had obtained a more general meaning, suggesting conduct that constituted a "gross disgrace to . . . class, country, position, or the like" or transgressed any system of cultural authority.[8] Scandal was imagined as something that could shock the sensibilities of the public at large. In his *Dictionary,* Samuel Johnson emphasized scandal's public aspects: the scandalous encompassed the "disgraceful," the "shameful," and the "openly vile" to "a degree that gives publick offence." Johnson's choice of illustrative quotation from the Book of Daniel, "thou do'st appear to scandalize / The publick right, and common cause of kings," suggests not only that scandal must work to undermine public authority, but also that it must do so through "appearance," public display, in short, spectacle.

Because it was connected to "low" popular discourses like gossip,

7. Clare Brant's remark that "scandal is not just a matter of events, but the discourses through which those events are constructed as transgressive" (246) has proved helpful here.
8. *OED* (1971 ed.), s.v. "scandal."

broadsheets, news, and hearsay, shaping an event as scandalous was one of the many ways print spectacles implied the participation of the people. But "scandal" gained its cultural and historical weight from the law. As a technical legal term, "scandal" denoted an "indecency introduced into a pleading to the derogation of the dignity of the court."[9] Etymologically identical to "slander," "scandal" was and still is used in law as a synonym for defamation and libel. Such usage probably derived from medieval statutes developed after 1275 that prohibited *scandalum magnatum* or the dissemination of "false news" about the king and other high officials. By 1662, *scandalum magnatum* was defined as "a slander of the State, as to report any thing about the Affairs thereof that is false, and may be to the prejudice of it" (Hamburger 668, quoted at 700). Thus the word subliminally links literary transgression to legal transgression and suggests the possible national import of what might in other contexts be construed as simply gossip. The least familiar modern meaning of the term is also its most suggestive for our purposes here. While the Greek associations of the word with "to spring a trap" had no doubt faded by the eighteenth century, "scandal" remained not merely a noun but an active verb (Johnson, *Dictionary*). "To scandal" meant, in addition to all else, "to charge falsely with faults."[10] Thus the word has a special applicability to events that were often not truly scandalous in themselves but were *constructed* as scandals for purposes both personal and national. The eighteenth-century print spectacles investigated here scandalized in part because that was what they were constructed to do; but if they were traps, they were complicated ones, as likely to catch those who set them as those they were set against.

Clustering the events I consider in this book means taking acts usually considered separately, such as forgery and copyright violation, and grouping them together. It also means reading them as intertextual or perhaps *trans-textual* texts,[11] as interactive and mutually constitutive groupings of related writings, events, and displays. Both types of clusters challenge the Enlightenment categories and disciplinary boundaries crucial to our

9. Ibid.

10. *Dictionary of the English Language*, s.v. "scandal."

11. I use the term "trans-text" in association with the "transnational" and against "intertextual" as it is commonly understood in literary studies. Both intertextual and international perspectives imply an acceptance and reinscription of boundaries. This is perhaps why much "intertextual" scholarship resembles traditional source and influence studies. For this last point, and for a general discussion of intertextuality, see Godard. Like "transnational," "trans-textual" rejects the web imagery of "international" and "intertextual," implying not a web of sign systems or sources but a transformation of many texts into one. It is used speculatively here, as part of an attempt to read across boundaries and to explore the uses an enlarged understanding of text might play for cultural historians.

understanding of the workings of eighteenth-century culture.[12] In the context of literary transgression, the relevant categories include public and private, legal regulation and social regulation, high and low, elite and popular, literate and oral, and legitimate and illegitimate authorship. Challenging such boundaries by considering, for example, legal treatises, newspaper accounts, and broadsides together makes sense, given a period in which both law and culture were disseminated not so much through formal reports but through many different venues. I am not suggesting, of course, that we flatten all categories, but instead that we denaturalize them and foreground their workings in order to examine how they functioned to separate the study of what came to be defined as literary from nonliterary texts, literary from nonliterary issues, and thus to obscure the connections among texts that make visible the national work these print scandals performed.

Contextualizing print spectacles within their larger textual networks allows a more accurate rendering and even a greater appreciation of certain eighteenth-century literary texts. A focus on the textual network rather than on the "work" as traditionally defined destabilizes genre, removing poems, plays, novels, and aesthetic tracts from their traditional generic categories and from traditional accounts of literary history, and resituating them in what might be called, following William Warner, a history of media events. Thus it offers particular advantages for a project interested in both literary studies and cultural studies, allowing an escape from the discourse of canonicity and making possible new readings of texts largely dismissed by conventional criticism. For example, I read *Sir Charles Grandison* neither as a failed novel, insignificant to the "history of the novel," nor as a work that must be "recovered" and incorporated into the canon. By treating it as an informing text embedded in its larger spectacular frame, it can be understood as a highly popular work in its own time— popular in part because it engaged concerns about cultural as well as literary piracy and yet allowed readers a comfortable, domestic place to work out their understandings of "nation." Similarly recontextualizing Macpherson's *Poems of Ossian,* Macaulay's *History of England,* and Mary Prince's autobiography allows us to understand the eighteenth-century interest in these texts and relieves us from the peculiar duty of as-

12. John Bender's influential essay offers one of the most convincing and sophisticated explanations for the resistance of American eighteenth-century studies to New Historicist and cultural materialist approaches. He suggests that traditional eighteenth-century studies have "proceeded largely within deep-rooted postulates—within a frame of reference—that fundamentally reproduced Enlightenment assumptions themselves and therefore yielded recapitulation rather than the knowledge produced by critical analysis" (63).

serting our own aesthetic judgments against, for instance, Jane Austen's affection for *Grandison,* Thomas Jefferson's admiration for Macaulay's *History of England,* or the general public fascination with the slave narratives of the 1820s and early 1830s.

I take seriously the philosopher John Anderson's oft-quoted suggestion that we ask not what ends a social institution serves but rather "of what conflicts is it the scene" (quoted in J. Rose 149). Thus, it seems important to begin by setting my own work in the context of the conflicts that inform the institution of the history and criticism of print transgression. Many scholars have relegated print spectacles to the narrow margins of biography, reducing them to episodic moments, illustrative of eccentricity, neurosis, or moral weakness. Samuel Johnson's biographer W. Jackson Bate, for instance, literalizes this approach when he refers to the Macpherson controversy as an "episode," perhaps building on J. S. Smart's 1905 analysis of Macpherson in *James Macpherson: An Episode in Literature.* Others, like Thomas Chatterton's biographers, take such "episodes" quite seriously yet remove them from their cultural context by reading them individualistically and diagnostically as psychiatric indicators in a Freudian psychology.

A review of the twentieth-century histories of authorial transgression reveals both normative and constructionist trajectories. Major studies of the history of literary transgression have worked against the tendency to trivialize print spectacles by emphasizing what literary transgression has to tell us about ethics and morality. From H. M. Paull's 1929 study, with its insistence that "forgery stamps the age in which it is a common practice" (19), to Alexander Lindey's 1952 assertion that "the theft of a product of the mind is . . . a moral wrong" (231), critics have tended to demonize literary transgression more than historicize it.[13] Anthony Grafton's broad study of forgery, published in 1990, operates in this tradition as well. Although Grafton describes the cultural pressures that lead to forgery, in particular the ways in which the destruction of culture leads to the "exuberant desire to see the ruined past made whole again," his assessment is charged with moral fervor. Forgers exert a "malevolent influence" on culture; they experience "sadistic pleasure" in the act of tricking the public. He ends by drawing a moral boundary between criticism and forgery, arguing that "the exercise of criticism is a sign of health and virtue

---

13. Harold Ogden White's *Plagiarism and Imitation during the English Renaissance* offers an exception. White argues that Renaissance imitators and copyists were not moral monsters but simply writers working within certain historical and cultural constraints. He find this position hard to sustain, however, at one point referring to transgressors as "thieving scribblers" (127).

in a civilization; the prevalence of forgery is a sign of illness and vice" (*Forgers* 36–38, 127). This preoccupation with ethics as normative rather than situational limits the kinds of conversations we can have about the cultural work such transgressions perform. For instance, Grafton cuts short what might have been a more interesting discussion when he privatizes the behavior of forgers by labeling them "sadistic." People do not become literary sadists in a historical and cultural vacuum, but Grafton's terms prevent him from exploring the roots of such sadism, roots that might be found in the cultural equivalent of early trauma—perhaps in the traumatic destruction of a cultural identity. The destruction of cultural identity is, of course, a form of sadism itself.

A different but intersecting strain of criticism informs this book. Studies on authorship have complicated the radical Marxist stance adopted by Stewart Home in association with the "Festival of Plagiarism" in 1988. In the manifesto published after that conference, Home and his colleagues argued that literary transgression reveals more about the constructed nature of normative behavior than about "right" and "wrong." Plagiarism, which they see as an invention of eighteenth-century British capitalism, is a necessary corollary to a culture obsessed with protecting its investment in privilege, in individualism, and in originality. While the objectives of the Festival of Plagiarism may not have been wholeheartedly adopted by subsequent critics, by calling attention to plagiarism's role in defining legitimate authorship, Home's slim pamphlet raised a number of questions that have informed later work in the field. Since 1988, critics such as Susan Stewart, Mark Rose, Martha Woodmansee, Wendy Wall, and Laura Rosenthal have denaturalized authorship and with it literary transgression, exploring the construction of modern authorship by examining the intersections of legal and literary developments.[14] My book joins this critical conversation, offering a very specific way of contextualizing certain of its premises by focusing on various converging and diverging "British" and "English" constructions of authorship. How does authorship in both its legitimate and transgressive forms intersect with nation? Why does it take on such an important role at the very moment when the concept of nation was becoming the organizing principle of communities? What is its relationship to patriotism, to international relations, and to the emergence of empire?

14. Martha Woodmansee, Peter Jaszi, and the Society for Critical Exchange should be credited with spurring much work in this field by sponsoring and organizing the 1991 conference Intellectual Property and the Construction of Authorship. For the collection of essays that resulted, see Woodmansee and Jaszi. For important studies that bear on eighteenth-century British constructions of authorship, see Baines; Stewart, *Crimes of Writing;* Rosenthal; and Rose, *Authors and Owners.*

Like Rose, Woodmansee, and other constructionists, I see the intersections between the literary and the legal as crucial to understanding modern authorship. But here I take up the law both in its specifics, as a system of cases and legislative regulations with cultural implications, and in a larger sense, as a nation-builder in its own right—particularly in its interactions with literary transgression. As early as the fourteenth century, the English were mythologizing their legal system as special, different, and a source of local pride.[15] By the sixteenth century, writers relied on the power of law to define and reinforce claims to a unique Englishness. Comparisons between the English and French legal systems gathered force with Coke's magisterial assertions of the superiority of English law to French legal tyranny. While doubt vexed this position during the Elizabethan era (What if English laws were *too* different? What if this difference signified a national failure of intellectual development?), by the mid-eighteenth century those doubts were being laid to rest.

Those who wrote about print spectacles used the law, drawing on legal terms, legal metaphors, and criminal discourse to lend their positions a national authority and sensationalize the acts of their adversaries. Never the culturally independent system that it claimed to be, law formed a powerful hinge that connected print spectacles and their discussions of authorship and ownership to questions of national identity. Though representative of high or "official" culture, the law reached down to touch everyday life; its mere invocation linked the high with the low. As Linda Gowing and James A. Sharpe suggest, the law tended to interest everyone, even those with no direct link to this "mystical intellectual system." People from the "lower to the middling ranks" both participated in the law and were fascinated by it (Sharpe 244–47).[16] They also felt entitled by it: that the common, even the illiterate person could resort to law when in trouble reinforced the claims of English law to be "common law." Thus, what Pierre Bourdieu refers to as a "chain of legitimation" connected high legal theory to the most localized invocation of law, creating networks of protected juridical acts and of people both inside and outside the juridical circle.

English law carefully avoided acts that might seem arbitrary and singular. Highly influenced by its desire to define itself against French tyranny, it insisted on its lengthy and linear discursive history, in part to offset suggestions that it offered simply an excuse for the exercise of force. Its insistence that it had been in place since "time immemorial" and thus

15. Richard Helgerson's *Forms of Nationhood* has informed this argument.
16. See Gowing's *Domestic Dangers* for many examples of the ability of law to respond to the concerns of "the people."

knew no origins was an attempt to elide the tyrannical exercise of force that lies at the originating point of every legal system. Since English identity relied on the rejection of tyranny and arbitrary rule, the law became particularly defensive in encounters that brought it close to its own origins, which lay buried in the oral culture of barely remembered case law and ancient statutes.[17] Complicating the picture, the print industry of the late seventeenth and early eighteenth centuries transformed law from an oral to a written culture, and in doing so heightened all the anxieties around orality and literacy that had plagued English law since the earliest legal treatises had seen print.[18] As writing became more and more important to legal practice and judicial decision making, the oral origins of the law were mythologized and distanced. Meanwhile, the ever-accumulating body of legal writing required continual reinterpretation and exegesis. It was an impossible situation: print itself implied an artificial and modern technology rather than a natural system rooted in the immemorial customs of common people. How could law seem "common" and natural if only the most sophisticated and literate minds were capable of parsing its intricate history? One way law avoided facing this internal contradiction was by distancing itself from problems of writing involving legitimacy, interpretive difficulties, and issues of origination. It created a regulatory wall between juridical culture and print culture, but in doing so it drew suggestively close to issues that could easily undermine its authority.[19]

Law attempted to distance itself from the problems writing presented in part by pretending that copyright, the system most often encountered by the average author and thus the one most often encountered in this book, was value-free and apolitical, a simple matter of regulating economic exchange. But copyright emerged as nation emerged; it reflected the shift from kingdom to nation that was gradually being consolidated around the turn of the century. Before 1695 the government controlled the press through licensing laws which required printers to apply for and receive a license before printing a work. This system of prepublication censorship was hierarchical, reminding every printer at least metaphorically that the Crown controlled what would be published. Those who took metaphors too lightly were reminded of the force of law through

---

17. See Ross, "Memorial Culture" and "Commoning of the Common Law," and Goodrich, "Poor Illiterate Reason" and *Oedipus Lex,* for theorized approaches to legal historiography.

18. See Ross, "Commoning of the Common Law," and Johns 321–22.

19. I am indebted to Stewart, *Crimes of Writing* 18–19, for her helpful discussion of this problem.

what we would today consider brutal shows of force, draconian punish-
ments in public venues. Early efforts to do away with the licensing laws
emerged directly from Protestant-Catholic tensions of the late 1670s,
from the Crown's attempt to use the licensing acts to control anti-Catholic
exclusionist publications (Hamburger 670). When the laws were allowed
to lapse in 1695, it was partly because they were still associated with anti-
English ideas involving tyranny and Catholicism: prepublication censorship had come to be thought of as not-English. Replacing the licensing
acts was a complex affair that shifted governmental focus from printers
to authors, from prosecution, with its political associations, to a supposedly apolitical ownership. While the legislature invented the copyright
system from the remnants of seventeenth-century licensing, the courts remade the sedition laws to fill the gap left by the end of prepublication censorship. The Act of Anne of 1710, the first copyright statute, inserted the
word "author" into the law for the first time, as many critics have pointed
out, but it also suggested that economic control of writing had been newly
divided from political prosecution, a division reinscribed in countless volumes of scholarship and legal history.[20] Eighteenth-century authors knew
better: they applied similar arguments to both systems and thus revealed
the political subtext that drove them.

Both copyright and seditious libel law offered the potential for controlling social unrest and regulating the national conversation. John How,
writing in 1709 immediately before the passage of the copyright act, argued that the copyright statute (not criminal laws regulating seditious libel as one might expect) would curtail the publication of works that were
"a Scandal to the Country, and . . . a prejudice to the Publick" (quoted in
Moore 168). Even more striking are Joseph Addison's comments on authorship, comments which connect both copyright and seditious libel law
to the national good. Addison, who was instrumental in passing the Act
of Anne, speaks in *Tatler* 101 of what he calls "the zeal of an author," and
comes out soundly on the side of what Mark Rose has called proprietary

---

20. For the history of copyright, see Patterson, Ransom, Feather, and Rose. Ransom
points out that the Act of Anne is often dated 1709 because it was amended and passed before March 25, the crucial date when the year changed in official records. See Moore 171
and more generally for the history and significance of the division between prosecutorial
and economic control of writing. Legal historians tend to take this view even further by
claiming that copyright regulations had nothing to do with the construction of authorship.
Perhaps true in a purely legal sense (the law does not care much who holds a copyright), this
view ignores authorial interest in the Act of Anne and its successors. That authors such as
Addison and Johnson, not to mention Wordsworth and Dickens, were intensely interested
in interpretations of the act suggests not so much their personal greed as their realization of
the cultural impact copyright has on authorship.

authorship. Here authorship is set against "a set of Wretches we Authors call Pirates" in support of the imposition of the new copyright act. The essay is peopled with authors he presents as public men; his major concern is the possibility that without copyright protection the biography of Sir William Temple might be reduced to the level of England's anonymously written "Tom Thumbs." In *Spectator* 451, an essay attacking libelers written less than three years later, he also places authorship under national pressure. Uncontrolled libel would send the wrong message internationally: "Should a foreigner . . . form to himself a notion of the greatest men of all sides in the British Nation . . . from the characters which are given them in some or other of those abominable writings which are daily published among us, what a nation of monsters must we appear" (4:88).

Addison's remarks reveal the discursive working out of an emerging version of national authorship. Like seditious and civil libel law, which I discuss in chapter 4, the first copyright act became a controlling emblem of "official" identity, one that attempted to define authorship (and thus subjectivity), text (and thus culture), and ownership (and thus insider and outsider positions) in ways that supported English norms and undermined the legitimacy of alternative identities. After 1710, the Act of Anne faced any number of challenges emanating particularly, as will be discussed in chapters 1 and 2, from the Irish and the Scots. The Celtic periphery challenged the tight bond that copyright established between author and text, interrupting it through the issuance of unauthorized reprints. While the booksellers in possession of copyrights wanted to retain them forever, competitors believed that copyright should end after a period of years so that works could be placed back into circulation on the open market. The conflict set authorial rights against the rights of the larger community. On the one hand, if authors could control the dissemination of their works perpetually, then the larger community would never have access to them for collections, abridgments, and revisionary texts. On the other hand, if authors had no control, they would not be motivated to expend the time and energy necessary to produce a nationally respectable canon. As we shall see in chapter 3, the problem came to a head in the 1770s as Scottish booksellers moved aggressively to appropriate English-authored and printed works and reprint them. After much national name-calling, the English formally accepted that authorial ownership would have to be limited: authorial rights would persist for a period of years, at which point works would enter what came to be called the "public domain" where they were free to be used by any taker. A widely imagined public domain was a democratizing force; it increased the availability of cheap reprints and allowed more economically marginal printers to stay in business. In its support of what the eighteenth century would call leveling and we might call lateralization, it helped turn kingdom into nation.[21]

Like most cultural critics pursuing the questions surrounding national identity, I have been strongly influenced by Benedict Anderson's *Imagined Communities,* not least by his references to affect. When Anderson suggests that nationalism, like "love," requires a gloss provided by the imagination, he joins a long list of writers interested in the relationship between national identity and affect, and between affect and narrative (154).[22] Of course, neither affect nor narrative need be positive. Most scholars more explicitly relate nationalism to pain than to love. Ernest Renan sees it as rooted in communal suffering, Max Weber in a painful struggle for superiority, Michael Herzfeld in the recognition of communal transgression and embarrassment, scholars and theorists as different as Linda Colley and Julia Kristeva in the hate and fear sparked by difference. Even Anderson, though often criticized for an unrealistically positive view of "nation," refers too frequently to death and grief as constitutive forces for us to dismiss him as a utopian narrator.

And yet I too find some room for optimism. Scandalous print spectacles, though no doubt contributing to the mystifications that made nationalism so attractive, generally elided the physical violence that often accompanies national fervor. That Henry Sacheverell's 1710 prosecution for seditious libel contained mob violence through one of the century's most extravagant displays of judicial attention suggests what power discourse has to transform actual violence into rituals of representation. They provided public spectacles that offered outlets for nationalist expression and tested its power but discouraged mob violence. While scholars such as Helen Hok-Sze Leung have pointed out that national imaginings are generally backed by threats of punitive action, the narrativized nation can also be seen as an attempt to *avoid* recourse to violence. The very features that made scandalous print spectacles so successful in consolidating and displacing difference worked to translate what in other contexts might have become violent action into nonviolent discussion. Perhaps these events played a role in containing violence because they

21. Aravamudan suggests that the English literary tradition was prompted by the creation of the public domain (233). The increased circulation allowed by public domain allowed the reprinting of a selection of works in collected editions and thus their institutionalization. Yet public domain also allowed a more democratic explosion of print as all sorts of works could be reprinted in varied, sometimes cheap editions.
22. See Kristeva, Jacqueline Rose, and Berlant for work on the affective nature of the allegiance to nation.

were constituted as processes rather than products. Unlike national costumes or religions, print spectacles resisted representation in the static signs that so often seem imposed on a people rather than imagined by them. Thus they seemed impervious to hierarchical top-down forms of juridical control. As ever-unfolding textual networks comprising multiple cultural and social domains, print spectacles were always in process and thus created at least the illusion that anyone, any member of the "public," could intervene, introduce, and test diverse ideas about British and English identity. While no one would define their production process as democratic in the strict sense of the word, these scandals took part in the shift toward democratization, a shift that, as Kevin Sharpe and Steven Zwicker point out, involves "not simply the history of the enlargement of the franchise" but rather "the dispersal of authority and agency, the diffusion of power into the public imagination, even a public capacity to conceive itself as a political actor" (19).

This book, while recognizing the role of official culture in controlling nation formation, encompasses resistant alternatives as well. Thus, it represents British identity as always complicated and in some ways actively constituted by simultaneous claims to Englishness *and* Britishness, by Scottish, Irish, and colonial resistance to assimilation, and by populist attacks that ironically undermined the rhetoric of liberty and "the people" on which so many claims of English and British superiority were based. Such complexity suggests that no simple thesis will be forthcoming here. Indeed, what I hope to show is that within the unfolding textual networks of print spectacles, formulations of what it meant to be a "nation" were not constructed solely by elite groups nor with elite materials, but were part of a complex process of dispute and negotiation among numerous competing identity groups.

The chapters that follow map certain identity categories—the Irish, the Scottish, British women, the enslaved colonial subject—onto British identity in light of intellectual and legal history. Yet they emphasize as well the complexity of multiple identities and sub-identities that influenced ideas of what it meant to be English in the British context. Thus in chapter 1, when I examine Samuel Richardson's construction of Irish literary piracy and the Irish reaction to that construction, my discussion of the piracy of *Sir Charles Grandison* takes up the relationship between the heterosocial and the homosocial, the legitimate citizen and the criminal, masculinized authorship and feminized collaboration, as well as the role English "tolerance" played in marketing Englishness to an international audience. In his battle with the Irish, Richardson mobilized piracy discourse (with all its social, legal, and cultural implications) and thus criminalized a legal activity, meanwhile constructing a link between print and popular culture. His effort to distinguish between piracy and privateering denoted a newly *national* version of sovereignty. In legitimating some forms of authorship and textual dissemination—particularly his own—and criminalizing others, Richardson created a print spectacle meant to bolster a middle-class, heterosexual model of national sovereignty and colonial acculturation. Simultaneously, as my reading of *Sir Charles Grandison* shows, he struggled unsuccessfully to resolve a central problem in imagining the nation, that of preserving an insular national identity while putting it to use internationally.

Chapter 2 investigates English-Scottish relations at the height of the Scottish Enlightenment, yet finds the scandal surrounding James Macpherson's Ossian forgeries to be packed with a number of other identity issues as well. What many saw as Macpherson's forgeries inspired any number of popular paintings, operas, and ballads, as well as arousing sustained and agitated commentary by such luminaries as Johnson. Macpherson's popularization of Ossian pointed to submerged conflicts between literate and oral culture, and between the culture of centralized London and that of outlying communities. Moreover, when seen as a Scottish attack on a more limited English construction of authorship, one focusing on literacy rather than on oral culture, the Ossian works reveal the problems England faced in structuring subjectivity around literate notions of individual authorship and private ownership. Scotland's Ossian stood for a truly collaborative form of authorship, and thus for a collaborative form of British identity, one that the Scots put forward repeatedly throughout the century. Even English copyright law was not immune to Ossian's influence. Ossianic authorship posed multiple threats to the English constructions of authorship and text promulgated in the Act of Anne and worked out in court cases throughout the 1770s. But my reading of the interaction between Scottish and English law suggests that the English could not completely ignore Ossianic collaboration. As I show at the end of the chapter, the Scots invented English copyright law, and Ossian collaborated in that invention.

Through a discussion of the first woman historian of England, a celebrity in her own time within Britain, in France, and in the American colonies, my chapter on Catherine Macaulay foregrounds gender as crucial to understanding the construction of the multiple identities discussed in this book. In her *History of England*, Macaulay problematized linear history, a form meant to suggest continuity between national origins and recent events. Like other mid-eighteenth-century historians, she "Englished" history by rejecting the genre of secret history, with its private letters and salacious details. The misappropriation and circulation of her own private letters—letters explaining what her contemporaries felt to be an "indecent" marriage—thus undermined not only her virtuous public image but her claims to national history as well. In revealing how easily her own reputation could be dismantled, the stolen letters represented what her national history had tried to hide. The scandal brought to the surface the efforts of national history to hide its own contingent and arbitrary nature.

My chapter on Mary Prince's slave narrative brings print spectacles into the modern era, suggesting their eventual emergence as important public relations tools. Prince's published narrative brought home to England an account of racism and slavery that called into question British claims to ideal domesticity. Although other slave narratives had been threatened with legal action, in this case Prince's owner sued her amanuensis and editor, Thomas Pringle, alleging that Pringle had libeled him by recording his cruelty against Prince. The resulting affidavits, court appearances, and newspaper accounts created a large collective text that struggled to control a complex challenge to British national and imperial ideology. Partly because it told the story of her importation to London and her treatment there, partly because it challenged the domestic virtue represented by the English household, Prince's narrative attacked the foundational system of checks and balances that domesticated "liberty" and "rights" through recourse to a settled and ordered narrative of familial relations. That Prince's story was vexed by notions of class and by her own self-identification as a worker rather than a slave suggests, too, how her complicated and repeated conflation of supposedly disparate images (literacy versus orality, white editor versus black speaker, choice versus compulsion, economic difference versus racial difference, domestic versus foreign) deconstructed the always unstable integration of the colonial project into British identity.

My account of the national work performed by scandalous print spectacles necessarily leaves out much. Readers may wonder how I might interpret George Psalmanazar's widely believed construction of a "Formosan" foreign identity or Thomas Percy's collecting of ancient ballads. When one asks why Psalmanazar was forced into public repentance while Percy became famous, one returns to questions typical of those investigated here. What is the place of difference in fantasies of national unification? What impact did these complex, in some ways successful, in some ways failed transgressions make on the collective understanding of national identity? While I assume that easy answers are no answers at all, my discussion of particular cases suggests that authorial transgressions, even when treated as scandals and thus in part contained, brought the margins to the center. The texts of those as different as Scottish forgers and African slaves can thus be seen to have influenced national fantasies of unity and identity in perhaps more subtle but no less important ways than the authority of Britain's Samuel Johnson.

[1]

Printing like a Postcolonialist:
The Irish Piracy of *Sir Charles Grandison*

> A postcolonial reading is not one that inscribes
> the temporal and spatial distance between metropolis
> and colony but one that reinstitutes their mutual
> imbrication at that moment of rupture (decolonization),
> when they were supposed to have been finally separated.
>
> SIMON GIKANDI, *Maps of Englishness*

> Every generation gets the pirates it deserves.
>
> JANICE THOMSON, *Mercenaries, Pirates,*
> *and Sovereigns,* quoting Robert I. Burns

During the London printing of Samuel Richardson's influential *History of Sir Charles Grandison,* the novel was pirated by Irish printers.[1] In August 1753, a Dublin printer bribed Richardson's own employees to ship the first six volumes and portions of the seventh to Ireland, where the book was quickly reproduced and sold. In response, Richardson produced two sensationalist tracts that drew on the popular machinery of piracy to vilify the Irish booksellers and vindicate his own virtuous construction of authorship. The tracts—one of which he later appended to the novel—positioned the dispute firmly within the internal colonial politics

1. See Barker for an account of how *Grandison*'s influence on Jane Austen and subsequent novelists has been forgotten and rediscovered a number of times. That we neglect it now says more about modern sensibility than about the novel's impact in its own time. As Jocelyn Harris points out in her introduction to the novel, it was extremely popular, selling 6,500 copies in its first year (xii). I rely here on Harris's 1986 World's Classics version, based on Richardson's first edition. Although this edition goes in and out of print, it is still the only widely available edition of *Grandison.*

[20]

of the 1750s.[2] Although the Irish claimed that English overreaching had prompted a perfectly legal reprinting of *Grandison*, Richardson, by branding them "pirates," thus transformed a commercial matter into a highly politicized dispute involving crimes against the nation.[3] Treating this print spectacle as a major cultural event rather than a footnote to print history reveals the potential of print piracy for shaping understandings of authorship and of nation. As I argue throughout this chapter, Richardson and *Grandison* offered an appealingly safe and integrated version of an anglicized Britain to the international world. The Irish piracy interrupted that idealization. As an event implicating a number of cultural fields and divergent texts, it condensed wide-ranging issues of nation and empire, issues that involve the interaction of center and periphery, assimilation and acculturation, and the unexpected role "tolerance" plays in solidifying an insular and exclusionary understanding of the nation.

Curiously, *Grandison* criticism has more or less ignored the Irishness of the Irish piracy even though Richardson appended one of his anti-Irish tracts to a number of subsequent editions of the novel and complained bitterly that the piracy had delayed and disturbed his writing of *Grandison*.[4] Integral to a literary history that focuses on the eighteenth-century novel's interiority at the expense of its production and circulation, this critical elision cooperates with the novel's effort to disown imperialism, to see England as independent of its colonialist past. Prompted by the Irish printers who resisted English ways of reading the conflict, I offer here a resistant reading of *Sir Charles Grandison* that interprets the piracy as a sophisticated political and cultural move, a challenge to the novel's construction of a version of English authorship suitable for international export.

Richardson's construction of authorship, one that both informs *Grandison* and is constituted by it, celebrates an insular originality and individuality. Yet at the same time it appropriates cosmopolitanism and remakes it in the context of the middle-class English virtues of tolerance

---

2. Richardson appended the second tract to the last volume of *Grandison* under the theory that this would make it impossible for the Dublin printers to pirate that volume. Instead, they simply omitted those pages when they reprinted volume 7. See Sale, *Bibliographical Record* 69.

3. See Tierney for an account of the impact of Richardson's tracts both on the immediate perception of the Dublin trade and on historical accounts of it. Tierney's research suggests that Dublin printers worked collaboratively with London printers as often as not.

4. See Fysh for a discussion of the piracy focusing on normative ethical values rather than political relationships. Chung's work on nation does not deal with the Irish piracy. See Cole 72–74 and Pollard 88–90 for accounts of the incident and for discussions of the Irish print industry.

and inclusion which he had been inventing throughout his career.[5] My reading—specifically postcolonial in Simon Gikandi's sense in that it describes the "mutual imbrication" (228) of the colonies with Englishness during a period of eighteenth-century symbolic decolonization—brings Richardson's tracts, and the issues of internal colonization they evoke, from the literal appendix to the interpretive center of the text. Turning novel and production process, center and periphery against each other reveals England as profoundly implicated in the violent history of internal colonialism at a moment of its attempted erasure.

Both *Grandison*'s national preoccupations and the Englishness of its eponymous hero have been the objects of critical attention since the novel's publication.[6] Almost immediately the novel itself became an emblem of the English nation; it was the *only* novel held by the newly national library at Cambridge between 1740 and 1780 (Oates 65).[7] Richardson positioned Grandison—who advocates Protestantism and proclaims the virtues of Englishness at every turn—no less carefully.[8] But critical observations regarding Grandison's Englishness have come at the expense of any real analysis of *Grandison*'s role in constructing a place for Englishness—as constituted through the authority of authorship and its textual productions—in the context of *interpenetrating* international and internal colonial relations. In part this reflects a larger critical tendency in eighteenth-century studies to focus on nation at the expense of extranational relations—a tendency lately under revision, given Michael Hardt and Antonio Negri's *Empire*.[9] Perhaps critics have also underemphasized

5. Although Richardson was influenced by Locke, Grandisonian tolerance draws more on cosmopolitan Enlightenment models while proclaiming the centrality of Protestantism. That it assumes an English center that "endures," "suffers," and "allows" difference is consistent with Johnson's *Dictionary* entry for the word. For a discussion that reveals both the similarities and differences between Grandison's position and a cosmopolitan one, see Schlereth 73–96.

6. For eighteenth-century reactions to *Grandison*'s publication, see in particular "Critical Remarks on Sir Charles Grandison" and "A Candid Examination of the History of Sir Charles Grandison." For contemporary critical responses, see among others, Doody, *Natural Passion;* Gwilliam; Harris, *Samuel Richardson;* and Marks. For a work that focuses on *Grandison*'s Englishness, see Chung.

7. I describe Cambridge's library as "newly national" because it had become one of the national depository libraries with the copyright act of 1710. For a discussion of the holdings of the library and a reference to *Grandison,* see Oates.

8. Margaret Anne Doody suggested in 1974 that Grandison Hall represents "in miniature English life, its tradition and its future" (*Natural Passion* 349). More recently, Peter Sabor has remarked that the novel "firmly delineates the boundary between England and Abroad," and that Grandison "passes as citizen of the world but is at heart John Bull" (168).

9. As Maura O'Connor remarked in her work on English-Italian relations, "If we think of nation making as a historical process of frequent reinvention and negotiation from both inside and outside diplomatic borders, then crossing national boundaries should be at the

the issue of internal colonialism in *Grandison* because, while Richardson registers his concerns with intra-British relations in hackneyed stereotypes that bolster Englishness by juxtaposing Grandison to infantilized Welshmen, brutal Irish, and frenchified Scots, he consistently subjects Englishness to a more appealingly complex threat in the international context. It was the Italian theme, rather than the references to the British periphery, that drew all the early critical fire. From the moment the book was published, the too-friendly relationship Richardson constructed between Grandison and Catholic Italy evoked criticism from anti-Papists, who argued that a loyal son of Britain should never adopt "foreign fashion," much less consider marrying outside the Protestant faith (quoted in Eaves and Kimpel 404). Contemporary critics have similarly focused on English interiority as defined against an Italian "other" while ignoring internal colonialism. But limiting critical concerns to English-Italian relations is in itself a continuing symptom of internal colonialism, a ratification of *Grandison*'s direction of attention away from internal colonial strife and toward a sanitized version of international European relations. *Grandison*'s internationalism must have been deeply comforting to English readers eager to exoticize, displace, and thus distance the violent past of English oppression and the renewed vexation presented by a resurgence of Irish resistance in the 1750s. For critics today, the novel similarly affirms a powerful fantasy of English tolerance, inclusiveness, and legitimacy. To both the eighteenth-century and present-day reader uncomfortable with the messiness of internal colonial strife, today exacerbated by the breakdown of national allegiances, *Grandison* offers an already achieved transcendent internationalism that trivializes, even erases, local concerns with the British colonies.

Because *Grandison* foregrounded internationalism and tolerance, the novel worked particularly well in the international context. As Brett Levinson argues, the nation is dependent on borders, both metaphorical and actual: "For a nation to come into being . . . it must already be in touch with another, since borders are precisely this being-in-touch: not enclosure but a foundational exposure of one nation to a different one." Exposure rather than enclosure typifies borders. National imaginings that depend on the simplistic displacement of the self's rejected elements onto an "other" are subject to immediate dissolution, given that national identity can occur

---

heart of our study of nation making, yet, historiographically speaking, it is not" (9). See also Hall, *National Collective Identity* 8–11. Immanuel Wallerstein points out that "one of the persisting themes of the history of the modern world is the seesaw between 'nationalism' and 'internationalism'" (1:225). At the time this book went to press, Hardt and Negri's *Empire* was just making itself felt in studies of national identity.

only in the context of "liminality, exposure, relationality" (146). In *Grandison,* Richardson associates tolerance with Englishness and assigns intolerance to Italy, an act that seems at first glance to fall into the category of simplistic displacement. But by choosing tolerance—an attribute imaginable only if directed toward another—as a way of defining English difference, he put the simple displacement model to work in the liminal context of boundaries and borders. Claims of tolerance may be as necessary to imperialism as the continual reassertion of difference. While cultural nationalism imagines an insular national identity impervious to foreign taint, cultural imperialism—because it always involves contamination—not only compromises that insularity but suggests its original impossibility as well. To survive intact, the nation must simultaneously enlist in and resist the lesson that cultural imperialism teaches: that all identities are subject to diffusion when they encounter the "other" and that no identity has pure, impermeable boundaries. This is the conundrum that Richardson attempts to manage under the rubric of "tolerance." Adopting tolerance as a specifically English trait offers a powerful way of negotiating boundaries and bolstering Englishness at the moment of its exposure to the other.

Concerns with the complex relationship between nation and the international world represented by Europe structured Richardson's representation of authorship. As I demonstrate at length later in this chapter, his authorial production process relied on large collaborative and assimilative networks. Despite such practices, he made vigorous claims of individual and original production in the anti-piracy tracts: "Never was work more the property of any man, than *this* is his. The Copy never was in any other Hand: He borrows not from any Author: The paper, the printing, entirely at his own expence" ("Case" 2).[10] That Richardson located these seemingly apolitical assertions of abstract rights within the xenophobic anti-Irish tracts makes clear their connection to questions of international and internal colonial relations. Emerging not in Edward Young's "Conjectures on Original Composition" (which Richardson collaborated on after the piracy, in 1756 and 1757), nor in the lonely garrets of romantic or even "pre-romantic" poets, originary individualized authorship arose out of internal colonial turmoil.[11] Claims to originality went hand in hand

10. See Meltzer 54–55 and Fysh 100–101 for discussions of the application of John Locke's theory of property to literary property.

11. Young consulted closely with Richardson while writing "Conjectures on Original Composition." In 1757, Richardson suggested deletions, added paragraphs, and made a number of editorial suggestions, all in all causing Young to remark, "What masterly assistance you have given" (Pettit 452). Despite their vigorous claims to originality, both Young *and* Richardson provided embodied responses to Young's famous lament, "Born originals, how comes it to pass that we die copies?"

with those of English national identity as Richardson and other mid-century authors pressed authorship into service to link nation and text. To construct authorship in terms of originality coincided conveniently with England's claim to "liberty" as a central value: English texts like Richardson's, as he made clear in every preface, were bound to no tradition but instead were totally new, free from the strictures demanded by imitative models current earlier in the century.[12] But interruptions and challenges to English authorship, such as that Richardson experienced when his work was pirated, raised both the stakes and the claims of the stakeholders. Irish pirates may not have invented English authorship, but their intervention put English authors on the defensive, forcing them to make stronger claims for the value of individualized authorship than actual production processes could support.

Such exaggerated claims were immediately subject to destabilization. If authorship was to serve Englishness, then originality—as personified in the highly individualized figure of the author—had to fulfill a representative function in order to stand for the unity and integrity of the national community in international and internal colonial contexts. The elevation of the individual author served to locate the text physically and genetically, linking text to nation through the author's body—an originating body firmly grounded in a particular national location. Richardson's reaction to the Irish piracy made the conflict between individualized authorship and its representative function legible precisely because *Sir Charles Grandison* was such a collaborative work, a novel that both thematized and enacted community, meant to represent the cohesiveness of Englishness. The investment in originality, manifested in authorial claims to a "liberty" that included a freedom from sources and an independence from the labor of others, conflicted with Richardson's commitment to the tolerant inclusion of the very sources—the romance as well as a large community of collaborators—that allowed the novel to represent the national community. When abstract claims of originality collided with Irish resistance, their intensity increased. On one level, the piracy demanded an extensive rethinking of collectivity, interrupting the closed circle of Englishness that Richardson produced in the novel and exposing it to dissemination and cultural diffusion. On another, it suggested that the

12. The power of liberty as a sign for Englishness has frequently been discussed. In a book-length study of the political functions of liberty, J. C. D. Clark argues that it was well established by the mid-eighteenth century. In *English Literature in History*, John Barrell discusses "the tradition by which the English were seen as, *by nature,* the most tenacious of liberty among all civilized nations." He quotes William Blackstone, who reaffirmed the connection between liberty and Englishness in the *Commentaries:* "The spirit of liberty is . . . deeply implanted in our constitutions, and rooted even in our very soil" (119).

binding of author, text, and nation was always subject to dissolution. Finally, the reaction that the piracy evoked revealed the limits of national authorship's inclusivity, uncloaking the brutality that underlay Richardson's version of cosmopolitan tolerance. Richardson's angry demand that his authorship be respected, inflected through the larger culture in the various newspaper stories and tracts that swirled around the controversy, compensated for the instability of his originality claims while revealing the symbolic violence behind claims for "natural" rights.

Richardson and National Allegory: The Genius of Albion

Reception history as well as *Grandison*'s preoccupations with international relations and English identity suggest that we should read both Richardson's life and work as a national allegory, an intervention in both international and internal colonial relations. True, in the 1754 ode "On Reading Mr. Richardson's History of Sir Charles Grandison" William Cowper had subsumed immediate national concerns to a more universalized version of Grandison. His Grandison—though opposed to tyranny in the standard English way—was a "guardian of mankind," "deriv'd from heaven alone" (53). But we are offered a glimpse of a more politicized understanding of Grandison in a poem published in 1758, significantly enough, not in London but in colonial Maryland. Addressing himself to "Mr. Richardson in London," and praising him as "the Genius of Albion," the Reverend James Sterling titled this work "On the Invention of Letters and the Art of Printing" and published it in the *American Magazine and Monthly Chronicle for the British Colonies*. Unlikely as it seems, given Richardson's retiring nature and almost antiheroic persona, the novelist is here lionized in Grandisonian terms:

> See, for his country obstinately brave,
> He still persists, nor yet despairs to save,
> Men, whom as man he loves, he wishes saints;
> And lives himself the *Grandison* he paints.

The poem links printing, authorship, and national heroism, suggesting that "To shine first printer is his lowest sphere: / While the good man and author all revere," and making of Richardson a national model held out to the colonies for admiration and emulation (quoted in McKillop 216–17).

Richardson intended the novel to reach beyond England; he wanted it to have an internal colonial and an international, particularly a European, career. During its writing he not only arranged for publication in Ireland but also developed several intense epistolary relationships with Europeans and pursued various projects to have his works translated and so read on the Continent. His Dutch and German translators seem to have revered him, but his French translator, Prévost, famous in his own right, thought Richardson's national references neither incidental nor innocent. Prévost's introduction to the French translation made it clear that he had omitted rude references to the French and other "remains of the ancient British coarseness" (quoted in Eaves and Kimpel 416). Although the French may not have been impressed with Richardson's national fervor, subsequent English generations celebrated his impact on Europe: Thomas Babington Macaulay, in particular, praised him for increasing "the fame of English genius in foreign countries" (quoted in Eaves and Kimpel 588).[13]

To claim that *Grandison* operated as a national allegory as I do here is to appropriate a term from the heated debate Fredric Jameson initiated in 1986. When Jameson first coined the term "national allegory" to describe *all* "third-world cultural productions," he provoked a vigorous critique from postcolonial writers and theorists. His categorization of a wide range of different cultures as similarly invested in and able to produce only one narrative, the narrative of nation, was thought to offer an egregious example of high-handed Western theorizing. Worse, he had reproduced a narrative of progress in which "third world" countries were placed in the historical past, doomed to endlessly reproduce nation. "First world" countries, by contrast, had forged ahead, developing a sensitivity for psychological interiority that third world countries were apparently still to experience. Oddly, the notion suggested that interiority itself could not operate as allegory. More broadly, Jameson's narrative of progress aligned difference along a progressive continuum. As Franco Moretti has commented, in such narratives "the 'Alongside' becomes a 'Before-and-After,' and geography is rewritten as history" (51–52). Jameson's approach suffered as well from the reductionism symptomatic of traditional allegorical readings; it seemed to put into motion a machinery of one-to-one correspondences, a charge he raised at the time but was not able to put to rest. Yet the allegorical reading—understood in a larger tropological sense—has much to offer eighteenth-century studies.[14] Putting aside Jameson's totalizing approach to the third world and applying his argument to a novel written in the chronological past rather than in Jameson's

13. For *Clarissa*'s influence in Europe, see Beebee.
14. See Brown, "Tom Jones," for a helpful discussion of allegorical methods of interpretation.

imagined past suggests that the national allegory can be as symptomatic of and as useful to the colonizer as the colonized. Such an allegorical reading offers a rich understanding not only of *Grandison* but also of Richardson. As a writer who struggled to remedy what Katie Trumpener has called "the underdevelopment of Englishness" in his life, his printing career, and his novels, he collapsed life and work into a single allegory (14).

Jameson theorizes that in the West, capitalism bifurcated private and public experience, while in the third world, the "story of the private individual destiny is always an allegory of the embattled situation of the public third world culture and society" (69). Richardson's own "private individual destiny" seems as tailored to illustrate Jameson's remarks as does any account from third world culture: perhaps no "private" history is more easily read in "public" terms than his.[15] By birth and background he was particularly rootless, a man with no "natural" identity to draw on. Although his great-great-grandparents had been farmers, his own father was sent to London to become a joiner, then left for Derbyshire, where Richardson was born. His mother's parents died when she was a child. By the time Richardson was two, he was back in London again, but the family environment was hardly one to inspire loyalty. The area surrounding Mouse Alley was poverty-ridden, dangerous, and dirty; the area north of the Tower, where the family eventually moved, was not much better. Richardson's letters to his Dutch friend and publisher Johannes Stinstra, the only source for his early life, sanitize this background and in doing so reveal his efforts to construct a definitive "middling" authorial identity from his fragmented past and education. Particularly important is the famous "autobiographical" letter written in 1753, when Richardson was immersed in *Grandison,* but before the Irish piracy. Although it contains a number of incidents that may have been calculated to demonstrate an early gift for fiction, it suggests as well a poignant desire to "fit in," a drive to create insider groups that he could join, even dominate. In one anecdote, Richardson claims that at eleven, he wrote a letter pretending to be "a Person in Years" in order to calm a woman who was disrupting the community by "continually fomenting Quarrels and Disturbances, by Backbiting and Scandal." In another, he characterizes himself as the center of a circle of women who sought his aid in pursuing romances. In all of the early examples of his writing ability, that writing places him at the center of what may be seen as model communities, for example, of groups of "mothers and daughters," or of five schoolboys who "delighted to single me out" (Slattery 26–27). The autobiographical letter, written to the

15. I rely on Eaves and Kimpel's authoritative biography and Doody's *Natural Passion* for the details of Richardson's early life.

Dutch Stinstra as part of a larger international work of translation, can be read as an extension of Richardson's Grandisonian project, as partaking in the effort to advertise a unified, cohesive Englishness to a larger international audience.

Richardson's fantasies of communities closely knit around a central authorial figure conflicted with early circumstances that must have repeatedly disappointed his desire for stability. Unlike other major authors of mid-century, who emerged from the university culture of scholarly classicism, Richardson had little education. Born during a particularly low point in his family's fortunes, he was apprenticed to a printer rather than educated for the clergy as he and his father had planned. His cultural heritage consisted of romances, fables, and broadsides rather than the history and philosophy and law that informed the work of authors such as Samuel Johnson. With no education in Englishness and no ties to the land, or to any particular part of the city of London, Richardson must have been hard-pressed to develop any sense of place, history, or identity.

For Richardson, Englishness seems to have offered a stable frame in an unstable, inhospitable material world.[16] It is perhaps "natural," then, that he became a homespun "middling" version of the "encyclopedic" author associated with the rise of national sentiment.[17] Though he seems an apt example of Gramsci's organic intellectual so crucial to class struggles, as writer and printer he played a role as invested in nation as it was in class.[18] Having suffered from class destabilization himself, almost falling out of the "middling" into the street culture of London's poor neighborhoods, he knew that he operated within a system of class constraints that offered him only a limited amount of authority. But in Richardson's world, class conversed with nation. His investment in nation helped level the playing field, suggesting a radical critique of class hierarchy even as it offered a place for every citizen. This does not mean that national identity cloaked the supposedly hidden operations of class as the traditional

16. Homi Bhaba articulates this idea more abstractly when he argues that "the nation fills the void left in the uprooting of communities and kin, and turns that loss into the language of metaphor" (*Location of Culture* 139).

17. See Moretti quoting Edward Mendelson: "Each major national culture in the West, as it becomes aware of itself as a separate entity, produces an encyclopedic author, one whose work attends to the whole social and linguistic range of his nation, who makes use of all the literary styles and conventions known to his countrymen . . . and who becomes the focus of a large and persistent exegetic and textual industry comparable to the industry founded upon the Bible" (4).

18. Terry Eagleton helpfully describes Gramsci's organic intellectuals as those "writers, political leaders and theoreticians who are themselves products of the rising social class rather than remnants of the old" and whose works are "instruments which help to constitute social interests rather than lenses which reflect them" (2, 4).

Marxist formulation holds. Richardson could not have been more painfully aware of class operations. Instead, he represented national identity as rooted in middling behavior, authorized by claims to the higher authority of the landed classes and of didactic value to those below the "middling" sort. Nation thus spanned and integrated class identities, offering, as Rodney Hall has argued, "implications for behavior within and between societies every bit as 'real' as the equally novel construct of socioeconomic class" (24).[19]

The print industry, of course, is often credited with inventing the nation, most famously by Benedict Anderson. As Karl Deutsch posited in the early 1950s, the primary facilitator of national identity is a form of "communicative efficiency" consisting in the most effective "storage, recall, transmission, recombination, and re-application of relatively wide ranges of information" (96). Although Richardson had only begun to participate in the later phenomenon Anderson invokes when he speaks of "the newspaper reader, observing replicas of his own paper being consumed by his subway, barbershop, or residential neighbors" (*Imagined Communities* 35), he nevertheless helped bring the daily national newspaper into being and thus participated in the invention of a national public sphere. As one of the few large printers in London, charged with the responsibility for printing national records, Richardson developed this version of efficiency on a national level. Rewritten as a national printer's progress, an account of his printing career starts with periodicals, advances to the records of the House of Commons, and ends with the prestigious patent to print the common and statutory law of the land. During the early stages of his career, he published a number of different daily, weekly, and semiweekly papers (Sale, *Master Printer* 53, 68). Even then, he was deeply immersed in the consolidation of community. More than what we think of today as a "printer," he solicited writers, read submissions, and organized networks of publications that reinforced one another as well. His publication choices—from opposition newspapers to those that accommodated Walpole—suggest a shift from the support of factionalized communities to the support of a larger national conversation, evidenced by the fact that even the most astute Richardson biographers find it hard to pin down his politics.[20] Whatever Richardson's momentary political allegiances, the larger picture reveals a commitment to exchange and accommodation. As Margaret Doody points out, Richardson put into the fictitious spokesman Mr. B's mouth his own thoughts on En-

19. See Hall for a more developed version of this argument.
20. See Doody, "Richardson's Politics," and Dussinger for speculations regarding Richardson's political position.

gland's need for "openness, argument, conflict and difference; there is a 'Necessity of an Opposition' and the existence of opposition is the only real preservative of the Constitution" ("Richardson's Politics" 120–21). To this end, he created a diverse collective of newspaper printers, writers, and readers who advertised one another's books, read one another's papers, and developed a complex fabric of competing and yet complementary publications that constantly invoked as well as provoked one another. Such an understanding of the public sphere contained conflict within a larger coherent and unified frame.

In the 1740s, coincidentally at the same time he began to publish his novels, Richardson's fortunes turned officially national with the contract to print the records of the House of Commons. Typically, he immersed himself in these duties, spending he said at least "Half a Day every Day" on work that not only brought him into contact with the House of Commons, the center of the nation's political life, but with the periphery as well (Sale, *Master Printer* 76). Many of the bills were related to what William Merritt Sale calls "the moral life of the country," and often they took up issues in distant and rural areas (*Master Printer* 79–80). No mere replicator, Richardson adopted a collaborative process similar to the one he eventually adapted for *Grandison*. He printed bills under consideration on paper with wide margins, distributed them for further deliberation and comments, and then later reprinted them with the notes of various agreements in the margins. In the last year of his life, Richardson cemented his relationship with the nation by buying half the patent for publishing English law (*Master Printer* 76, 135–36). This acquisition capped a career devoted to the collaborative construction of the official version of the nation through print.

In his poem, James Sterling had urged readers to see Richardson as "Printer, author, *and* Good Man." When he argued that Richardson was "Himself the Grandison he Paints," he merged England's "first printer" and the "genius of Albion" with the heroic Grandison. As Sterling recognized, divorcing the novels from the print career decontextualizes Richardson's fiction, particularly if one focuses on Richardson's production of "nation" as a sort of lifelong work inflected in all of his textual productions.[21] To take this one step further and argue that *Grandison* is autobiographical, as Sterling's verse suggests, may seem almost comic, a ratification of Richardson's grandiosity as much as a literary insight. But Sterling points to an underlying truth about the novel: Grandison may not represent Richardson, but as an "author" Grandison realizes easily what

21. Stephanie Fysh provides a compelling analysis of some of the intersections between Richardson's print career and his novels.

Richardson gained only through the most anxious and sustained struggle. Whereas Richardson had built an audience laboriously and developed a "circle" only by teasing, pleading with, and cajoling his many correspondents, Grandison simply writes. Despite his relaxed disinterest in their dissemination, his letters are "published," passed around in packets to an audience composed of English ladies who read with fascination and approbation. Like Pamela, Clarissa, and Lovelace, Grandison is constantly writing and being read; unlike them, he develops a much wider communication network. His letters bring Italy to England, the international world to the national center. Grandison offers an idealization of Richardson's model for national authorship in an international world.

Perhaps Richardson was able to imagine a less insular world for *Grandison*'s (and Grandison's) operations because he wrote at a moment of relative international security, given that the War of Austrian Succession had ended in 1748 and the Seven Years' War was not to start until 1756. There is, of course, no moment at which nation does not feel threatened by its others; fears of incursion serve a stabilizing function even while suggesting the possibility of destabilization. But to categorize *Grandison*'s cultural moment as particularly subject to such fears seems wrong. Richardson's own feelings at the time were conciliatory. As he wrote in 1755, he regretted "national misunderstandings": "To what narrow bounds to those confine their Love, their Humanity, let me say, who make it merely *National*. An *Universal* Philanthropy . . . can be only worthy of an enlarged Mind" (quoted in Eaves and Kimpel 548). In advocating all forms of English tolerance, including tolerance of Catholic difference, he operated on the cusp of an important transition in attitude, part of the movement that led to the more generalized tolerance of Catholic difference which would typify England by the 1760s.[22]

Richardson constructed Grandison as a capacious, umbrella-like figure, benevolent and tolerant. Grandison thus offers a new version of English authorship, one that rejects the authoritarian top-down models that typified patronage and its methodological cousins, classical imitation and the formal constraints of "Augustan Age" writing. Like the capacious novel itself, Grandison reaches "out" as much as "down." Such efforts to embrace everything have led critics to challenge both the novel's and the character's emptiness. The negative aesthetic evaluations began almost the moment the novel was published, with even Richardson's fan Lady Echlin reporting that "some people" had complained about its "tedious

22. See Haydon 166–68; Black, *British* 213; and Bartlett, *Fall and Rise* 67–71 for discussions of shifts in the English attitude toward Catholics.

repetition" and "prolixity" (Barbauld 5:3).[23] While attempts have been made to defend the novel, arguing on the one hand that *Grandison* is boring because of Grandison and on the other that *Grandison* is interesting despite Grandison, these have led to a critical dead end, distracting us from the ways in which being boring lends both *Grandison* and Grandison a powerful normalizing presence.

The Grandison character is boring because he is an unmarked placeholder, "a blank where a character ought to be," as Jocelyn Harris remarks (*Samuel Richardson* 133). As such, he performs as a typical sign of nation, the absence and silence that often forms its center. Contentless except for clichés, Grandison—like the Tomb of the Unknown Soldier or the idea of "the people"—allows readers a uniformity of assumptions in the absence of content.[24] Not only is no particular representation necessary; such particularity would also be counterproductive, the very thing that designates individuals as "other," as Welsh, Irish, French, or Italian, as workers or servants or women. Grandison's disengagement signifies the ideal gentleman, one who could "comprehend" everything that made up Englishness, but nothing so well as to threaten his universality and objectivity or to link him to particular forms of difference (Barrell, *English Literature* 32–33).

Yet both Grandison and *Grandison* balance this enabling absence of content with a strong commitment to national roots. Too often the novel tells us that Grandison represents Englishness. Mrs. Beaumont, for instance, remarks, "His country has not in this age sent abroad a private man who has done it more credit" (3:169). He teaches the Italians Milton's English and imports English specialists to treat Italian disorders.[25]

---

23. See also "Candid Examination," whose author remarked, "Pity some of his Friends don't shew him how much he fails in his Labours, by incumbering his Writings with unnecessary Repetitions, tedious Narratives of very immaterial Circumstances" (35). Alan McKillop details these reactions (*Samuel Richardson* 221–23). Jane Austen, who claimed the novel as one of her favorite works, nevertheless lampooned its verbosity in her abridgment, whose humor relies on numerous references to the novel's length. Much of the modern criticism focuses on Richardson's didacticism, a feature of considerable interest to eighteenth-century readers. Elizabeth Brophy summarizes the reaction: "The failure of *Pamela II* and *Sir Charles Grandison* is often linked to Richardson's didacticism. In trying to be a moralist, it is felt, he simply became a bore" (89). Carol Flynn sadly admits, "There is very little room for the imagination in Richardson's last novel, a prosaic domestication of the world of fantasy: moral overwhelms myth" (186). Indeed, even as Juliet McMaster attempts to redeem the novel by focusing on its sexuality, she finds herself setting up Harriet's sexual yearning as a foil to Grandison's didacticism.

24. Lawrence Needham's comments at the 1998 Midwest Modern Language Association conference prompted this analysis.

25. I am indebted to Jocelyn Harris's and Ewha Chung's discussions of this aspect of Grandison's characterization.

As if having read Linda Colley, he conflates Protestantism and Englishness, calling out "Oh my religion and my country!" when pressured to convert to Catholicism (3:177). Despite such fervor, his character, not so much "flat" as empty, seems able to accommodate and contain almost any instance of difference. The family he constructs, one that expands exponentially over the course of the novel, represents the nation, but a version of it that moves in and out of an international community, in the last volume even gathering that community into its expansive boundaries. What William Hazlitt saw as "an increase of kindred" extended beyond national boundaries, as Grandison collected not only the usual Welsh and Scots (but not Irish) "types" but Italians as well (quoted in Eaves and Kimpel 390).

Grandison's character seems particularly well suited to contain an oft-noted conflict in national identity, that of the desire of each nation to be "new" while nevertheless drawing on a timeless (though invented) historical tradition. An "original," Grandison embodies the contradictions between the "newness" supplied by that word's commonly accepted meaning and the search for origins that the word also implies. While he draws his authority from idiosyncrasy (he proudly rejects almost everyone else's way of doing things and in doing so becomes Richardson's new "man of true honor" [4]), he seeks Englishness in the English past, leapfrogging back beyond his father's rakish European ways to a previous generation of Lockean values that emphasized a newly made world—and, significantly, a profoundly English one—grounded in tolerance. Merging Lockean and cosmopolitan tolerance authorizes Grandison to accommodate and integrate all of the differences that will have to cohere in a national Britain. The conflicts Grandison bridges as he attempts to mediate international differences coalesce in a "new" (though perhaps boring) man who is nevertheless made of "old" materials. Original and copy, independent and interdependent, authoritative and tolerant, English and cosmopolitan, Grandison embodies what it means to be national in an international context.

Heightened claims to connectedness take place in a context of connectedness under threat. Why would one constantly reiterate what everyone accepts as a given? The novel reflects English insecurity in that it repeatedly subjects its center to destabilization. Having famously designated his characters "men," "women" (both implicitly English), or "Italians" in the apparatus, thus naturalizing Englishness and gender in one stroke, in the novel itself Richardson places national categories under stress, in part by drawing on well-worn clichés about the Grand Tour. In sending Grandison on a Grand Tour, he drew on an appropriately national nexus of discussions about the relationship between cosmopolitanism and xenophobia.[26] The more sanitized accounts of the tour emphasized its benefit to the nation. As one young man's bearleader (common slang for the guides who accompanied young men on the tour) wrote in 1738, "The chief thing for a gentleman to attend to anywhere abroad, is the laws and constitution, the polity and temper of the nation he is in; its good, and its bad institutions." A young man was supposed to "make some appearance in our Parliament; and all these things may be of use to him" (Black, *British* 221). Such a didactic plan was idealistic: actual Grand Tour experiences were more likely to involve drinking, womanizing, and the dangers of conversion to Catholicism, or even worse, intermarriage with a Catholic family (Black, *British* 202–204). Around the time that Richardson was writing *Grandison,* the painter Joshua Reynolds depicted a typical Grand Tour scene in which the aesthetic glories of Italy are ignored while drunkenness and raillery prevail. Even more applicable to *Grandison*'s plot, the *London Post* of 1757 slammed British travelers in Rome for "kissing . . . the Pope's toe, and receiving his absolution for the parricide waste of Britannia's portion on foreign wines and foreign whores" (quoted in Black, *British* 297–98).

While Grandison never kisses the pope's toe, his national claims struggle with a cosmopolitanism so vast and comprehensive as to tend toward categorical collapse. As a member of Harriet's circle remarks, "Sir Charles hinted, that he should soon be obliged to go to France. Seas are nothing to him. Dr. Bartlett said, that he considers all nations as joined on the same continent; and doubted not but if he had a call he would undertake a journey to Constantinople or Pekin, with as little difficulty as some other would . . . to Land's End" (3:30). Given the range of travel options, Richardson's decision to send Grandison to Italy, a less threatening version of the more immediate difficulties France represented, seems significant. There Grandison encounters those sexual lures so often associated with the Grand Tour. Those few who have read the novel know that its driving force is Grandison's "divided love": he is drawn to his ideological twin, the quintessentially English Harriet, but that love is threatened by his prior commitment to the Italian Catholic Clementina. As most critics have noted, Clementina dominates the novel. Readers of many generations have preferred her interestingly hysterical exoticism to Harriet's commonplace good nature. The major engine driving the novel's plot, she threatens Grandison's allegiance to Englishness. Harriet's fear that Gran-

26. See Black's two book-length studies and Chaney's work on England and Italy for detailed discussions of letters, diaries, and other accounts of the Grand Tour.

dison has "mistaken some gay weeds for fine flowers, and pick'd them up, and brought them with him to England" (1:194) serves to frame his letters from Italy. The novel translates the fascination that all of elite England felt for Italy's "gay weeds" into tension: "Sir Charles has so much anxiety. . . . I wish this ugly word *foreign* were blotted out of my vocabulary; out of my memory, rather." Here Harriet—underscoring and thus emphasizing the "foreign" as much as the desire to erase it—expresses an ambivalence central to the text, one that explains why learning to control the "foreign" rather than "blot it out" dominates Grandison's account of events in Italy and on his return.

Much of the struggle over assimilation focuses on Catholicism, with the possibility of a marriage between an English Protestant and an Italian Catholic standing in for the threat of a larger cultural merger. As Benedict Anderson has remarked, nation operates affiliatively, drawing on fraternal and sororal metaphors. Both Grandison and the Italians make use of the extended family metaphor, the Italians embedding threats of familial appropriation in a Catholic theme. "I really look upon you . . . as my fourth brother: I should be glad that *all* my brothers were of one religion," suggests Clementina (3:154). From the Italian point of view, marriage to an unconverted Protestant is the equivalent of letting "a foreigner, an Englishman, carry her off" (3:197), while from the English point of view Grandison's conversion would come dangerously close to treason. Negotiating these differences, remaining composed in the face of revisionary efforts, consumes much of Grandison's time and energy. As he puts it, "I labored, I studied for a compromise" (3:130). Hopes for such a compromise lie in tolerance and persuasion rather than furious debate, in acculturation rather than forced colonization. In one exemplary scene, Richardson places acculturation in a medicinal rather than a political frame, "curing" Clementina's brother Jeronymo, hitherto the victim of his own violent character as well as of European physicians, by exporting English medicine to Italy. His English doctor "suggested an alteration in their method, but in so easy and gentle a manner as if he doubted not, but *such* was their intention when the state of the wounds would admit of that method of treatment, that the gentlemen came readily into it" (4:451–52). The most effective conversions bypass brutality and replace it with a gentle forbearance. English tolerance, it turns out, cures the excesses of foreign manners. The scene should be read not only for its display of English tolerance but also for its temporal value. By coding the Italians somatically and subjecting them to an English "cure," Richardson places them in a narrative of progress. The Italians are redefined as "primitive" rather than sophisticated and worldly, positioned in the historical past of bar-

baric and unenlightened practices and thus made suitable for incorporation in an English account of international relations. Englishness draws
on a progressive model of tolerance that casts Italy, and by extension all
of Catholic Europe, into the dark past of brutality and superstition.

Tide Waiters and Border Guards: Locating the Celtic Periphery

It is surprising then to realize how often the novel abandons gentle forbearance for violence. Reading the kidnapping scenes in the novel reveals
the limits of tolerance and the way violence regulates deviations from
Richardson's cultural agenda. That such violence often embeds references
to Celtic characters who work behind the scenes to drive the action seems
particularly telling. The novel begins with what has often been read as a
false start: the violent, bloody kidnapping and attempted rape of the virtuous but misread Harriet Byron by Sir Hargrave, one of the novel's lib-
ertines. Quickly supplanted by Grandison, Sir Hargrave fades into the
novel's background, resurfacing only at its end. The episode, despite its
structural prominence and saturation with international and colonial
signs, has generally been understood as a clumsy device meant only to introduce Grandison. But the scene should be read as a palpable manifestation of the subtler cultural kidnappings that inform the rest of the novel,
a guide to Richardson's concerns with international and internal colonial
relations. Rereading it as an exposure of Englishness to various forms of
dissemination and cultural diffusion suggests a major reinterpretation of
all the novel's kidnappings, including the Irish abduction of the novel itself.[27]

Untangling the layers of subordination in Harriet's kidnapping reveals
the embedding of the Celtic periphery in what seems to be a story about
English resistance to aristocratic decadence. Harriet personifies Englishness under the threat of dissolution from what Richardson would like
us to see as European corruption. Richardson is at pains to underscore
her Englishness in the early parts of the novel: Harriet comes from the
country, resists the influence of classical scholarship, and holds out for English entertainments, rejecting the Italian opera for "a good Play of our
favorite Shakespeare" (1:22–23). Such aggressive defenses of Englishness
are coded in the novel as masculine bravery, as behavior that borders on

27. I am indebted to William Warner's unpublished 1991 conference paper for this analogy. See also Warner's *Licensing Entertainment,* where he suggests that Richardson's anti-
piracy pamphlet "aligns an author's property in his text with the sentimental heroine's
property in her body" (283, note 3).

what is acceptable for women. At the moment she is taken, Harriet has abandoned her English principles and reluctantly donned the signs of cross-cultural exchange and imperial conquest which make her vulnerable to misreading.[28] Marked by a "Paris" cap, a "venetian" masque, a "persian" scarf, and an Indian fan (1:115–16), she is on her way to a masquerade, leading Grandison to remark after her rescue that "masquerades . . . are diversions that fall not in with the genius of the English commonalty" (1:143). Feminist psychoanalytic theory argues that all women assume masks: masquerade stands in for the mask of femininity, a mask assumed to hide the appropriation of masculine power. Here then it is doubly significant, as it is the very masking of her masculinized Englishness that leads to Harriet's downfall as symbol of national power.

The foreignness of Harriet's masquerade dress creates a momentary link to her kidnapper Sir Hargrave and his excessive aristocratic investment in Europe. Sir Hargrave argues in favor of Handel, and by implication the Hanoverian monarchy, and is fashionably frenchified. That he co-conspires with Bagenhall, the brother of an international merchant with connections to the customs hall, and Merceda, "a Portuguese Jew," suggests the very diverse community prepared to incorporate the temporarily un-Englished Harriet (1:170–71). While under Sir Hargrave's control, Harriet displays a performative vulnerability to assimilation, her speechlessness, bleeding, and weeping representing dissolution and the blurring of boundaries. Despite her obvious violation, Grandison's reaction is carefully controlled. In the almost laughably allegorical rescue which first introduces Grandison to the novel, Richardson contrasts Hargrave's brutality with Grandison's more nuanced display of force: rather than attacking him, Grandison breaks Hargrave's sword, then blocks the fleeing coach with Hargrave's body (1:140). Because aristocratic progress is thus self-checked, blocked by the very body responsible for brutal repression, Grandison avoids complicity in violence. When he exits the scene without avenging Sir Hargrave's insults, he displays a tolerance that leaves open the possibility of Sir Hargrave's later reform and even incorporation in Grandison's ever-expanding system.

In a demonstration of the relationship between English tolerance, European excess, and internal colonialism, Richardson complicates the story

28. My reading is obviously influenced by Terry Castle as well as by more recent discussions. In an introduction to a 1999 collection on eighteenth-century masquerade, Jessica Munns nicely lays out the various possibilities. Masquerade dress could offer "one of the many routes into self-orientalization, a kind of colonial cross-cultural cross-dressing that triumphantly transgresses national boundaries." It could also reestablish national boundaries, as "the very materials from which clothing was manufactured . . . were the 'stuff' of national assertion and economic rivalry" (18–21).

at its margins. Sir Hargrave does not act alone, nor does he turn solely to fellow aristocrats for aid. His servant Wilson has hired two Scots to kidnap Harriet. That Wilson operates as a crucial hinge between aristocratic force and the Celtic periphery is supported by the novel's exaggerated concern with his reform (1:123). Long after Harriet has been rescued and returned to her family, Wilson is restored to the world of order. He plans to take a job as a "tide waiter," a border guard whose responsibility it is to board foreign ships for inspection (1:176).[29] While Grandison's successful recovery of Harriet replaces brutality with tolerance (he "adopts" her, a word the novel uses repeatedly to signify tolerant acceptance of difference), it also demonstrates the complexity of revisionary threats against Englishness, always internal and external simultaneously, and complicated by the workings of the Celtic periphery.

In a second kidnapping scene embedded more deeply within the novel, Richardson offers us a troublingly less tolerant Grandison, one who resonates with Richardson's own behavior in the eventual interaction with the Irish printers. Here Grandison protects his ward, Emily Jervois, from her drunken mother's plans to marry her off to an Irishman. Emily's kidnappers, like Harriet's, are a mixture of the Celtic and the European. Described variously as "a man of one of the best families of Ireland" and "a low man," her stepfather, Major O'Hara, comes to abduct her accompanied by Salmonet, "middle way between a French beau and a Dutch boor" (3:20–27). Perhaps most significant here is Grandison's refusal to incorporate O'Hara into the family system of adoption and affiliation used so successfully to encompass other differences encountered in his travels. As in Harriet's kidnapping, a seemingly international threat is reduced to a comically Celtic one. The kidnappers' admiration of Grandison's international souvenirs and paraphernalia, signs of his cosmopolitan enlightenment, is quickly dismissed, and they are instead revealed to be "common men about the town," so clumsy that they bump heads. When the two interlopers attempt to carry Emily away with them, Grandison disarms them and—in one of the famous scenes meant to display his "flaw," a bad temper—turns them out of the house (3:65–66). Ironically, the novel "forgets" this triumphant display of rage as it sums up Grandison's achievements a few pages later. There Harriet characterizes Grandison as all the greater for being the "Friend of Mankind" rather than the "Conqueror of Nations" (3:70).

The novel's few direct references to Ireland similarly distance or trivi-

29. In her edition of *Grandison*, Jocelyn Harris defines "tide waiter" as "a customs officer who awaited the arrival of ships coming in with the tide and boarded them to prevent the evasion of the custom-house regulations" (7:483, note 176).

alize Irish and Catholic threats to Englishness. Before the novel begins, Grandison has already not only visited but also reformed Ireland. From volume 5 on he is poised to return and observe the effects of his interventions, delayed only by the importance of his Italian negotiations. References to Ireland emphasize its poverty and dependence. In one scene Grandison imagines Ireland as too impoverished to take on the responsibilities of a royal visit; in another Harriet subsumes a visit to Ireland into a longer list of Grandison's domestic duties (7:268, 4:260). As Harriet's friend and "cousin" Lucy Selby suggests, in a passage that was later amended to include some of Richardson's most "patriotic" remarks, "He will find no difficulty, I believe, to prevail upon [Harriet] to accompany him thither; nor even, were he disposed to it, to the world's end" (7:263).[30] Always distant, always already "settled," Grandison's Ireland seems a mere peripheral adjunct to Grandison Hall, its environs, and its international mission.

The subsuming of Celtic to larger concerns in these scenes echoes a similar dynamic at work in Richardson's representations of Italy and Ireland. The novel's very focus on Italy subordinates the Celtic periphery, containing the Protestant-Catholic conflict so important to English-Irish relations within a narrative of internationalism. Italy, of course, does not operate *only* as a site for displaced anxieties about internal colonialism. But it was peculiarly well chosen for such a role. Italy's reputation for violence rivaled only that of the Irish, known for their "ire." Yet because of its loosely allied city-states, it conveniently offered only the mildest political threat (Ingamells 21). In the English imagination, Italy's Papism was identified with a number of negatives: as Raymond Tumbleson puts it, it tended to offer a conflation of "alien Irish barbarism, French despotism, and corrupt Roman luxury" (13). Thus, *Grandison* contains a distanced, muted reference to the more immediate problem Catholicism presented to England. Could *Grandison* also have contained a veiled reference to Italy's link to the Stuart court, housed in Rome since 1745? The Pretender was regarded by the pope as Britain's legitimate monarch until 1763 (Ingamells 23–33). Grandison's aptly named Clementina evoked both Charles Edward Stuart's mother (Clementina Sobieska) and his lover (Clementina Walkinshaw). Such connections would have been immedi-

---

30. Later Richardson added, "But, see we not, that his long residence abroad, has only the more endeared to him the Religion, the Government, the Manners of England? You know, that on a double Principle of Religion and Policy, he encourages the Trades-people, the Manufacturers, the Servants, of his own Country?" (7:263). See Harris's edition of *Sir Charles Grandison* for a discussion of the complex history of Richardson's inclusion and exclusion of these remarks (508, note to 7:263).

ately apparent to Richardson's readers, suggesting that Grandison's En-
gishness was permeable to a specific and historically grounded Jacobite
invasion from England's own past.[31] In more specific references to the Jacobite threat of 1745, Richardson links Italy to the Celtic periphery. He
inserted the issue of the Jacobite Rebellion of 1745—during which Irish
recruits had accompanied the Pretender into Britain—into his Italian
episodes (Landon 169). Tellingly, in the novel, Italian support for the
Pretender temporarily ousts Grandison from his Italian circle. He flees
Clementina's family to avoid their gloating over the possibility of the
restoration of Catholicism in England (3:124). Despite all Grandison is
exposed to in Italy, he eventually returns to England unaltered by his Italian connections. To have Grandison survive Italy, not only "the Havock
of Despotick Power," as Lord John Hervey had put it in 1729 (quoted in
Black, *British* 174), but also the displaced sign of a more present threat,
must have been deeply reassuring to readers. He had been made "strange,"
having been exiled not just into the country but to one of England's binary "others," yet returned unaltered—in every sense of "alterity"—not
just unmarried to an appealing and sympathetically represented Italian,
but prepared to marry the exemplary English woman, Harriet Byron.

After more than two hundred pages of agonizing over Grandison's "divided love" for the English Protestant Harriet and the Italian Catholic
Clementina, Richardson ends volume 6 with redoubled resolution in the
form of a double ceremony: Grandison's church wedding, which Harriet
had wished to be private, becomes a hugely public celebration, followed
a few days later by the new couple's triumphant "parading time" at an
equally public church service. All of Harriet's suitors, not least the Welsh
representatives of the Celtic fringe, have been incorporated into the Grandison "family." Harriet's nightmares ("from England to Italy, from Italy
to England . . . these horrid, horrid incongruities" [6:149]) are supposedly laid to rest, replaced by the multiple images of first the wedding and
then the couple's communion "according to the order of the church, at
the Altar" (6:254). Overanxious about Clementina's unresolved status
(she languishes in Italy, herself daydreaming about a visit to England),
Richardson doubly underscores every reference to national integration:
the couple is described as the "loveliest couple in England," Harriet as the
"flower of the British world" (6:251). The jagged historical tear represented by Grandison's falling-out with his libertine father is made whole
through the maternal line. Within weeks of the marriage, Grandison will

31. See Doody, *Natural Passion* 123–25, for a reading of Grandison as an idealized version of Charles Stuart. See McLynn for a discussion of Charles Stuart's relationships with
Clementina Sobieska and Clementina Walkinshaw (3 and 204).

connect Harriet to his mother, announcing that "the last Lady Grandison, and the present, might challenge the whole British nation to produce their equals" (7:269). But the novel squirms under this heavy burden of national harmony. The volume ends by noting an epistolary critique of a "multitude of faults" and a request for a further richness of detail, a dangling postscript that recalls Clementina's dangling fate (6:254–55).

Econo-cultural Nationalism and Irish Identity

The Irish book pirates chose this moment in *Grandison*'s publication history to strike. Before Richardson could provide the requested "particulars" in volume 7, his own workmen stole the first six and part of the seventh volumes and shipped them to Ireland, where they were quickly printed and put on the market. The piracy seemed an uncanny reenactment of Harriet's kidnapping. Just as Harriet's extended family take care to protect her, Richardson had taken special precautions with the sheets of *Grandison,* printing the work at different locations and locking the finished pages in a warehouse.[32] And like Harriet, the novel was taken by a trusted servant: Irish printers bribed Richardson's workmen to pass the sheets on to Ireland. Richardson's revenge—a public attack on the Irish—tainted the agreement he had made with the Irish printer George Faulkner to print the work in Dublin. Realizing that he could not compete with the errant Dublin printers, Faulkner joined those who had received the stolen sheets. Faulkner proved to be a highly charged representative of Irish piracy since he was not only the most successful Dublin printer of the period but also an acknowledged Irish nationalist. Although one would not have known this from reading Richardson's tracts, Faulkner was far from a common hack printer. He was renowned for his gentleman's demeanor and dress and was friendly with Lord Chesterfield, who felt that he should be knighted (Ward, *Faulkner* 16). The publisher of Swift among others, he produced the *Dublin Journal,* the *Dublin Post-Boy,* and the *Dublin Spy.* Moreover, though a Protestant, he supported the Irish Catholic cause, calling for an end to repression of the Irish by the English minority.[33]

Thus the argument pitted the chief representative of the London print business against Dublin's leading printer. Revealing the civility and toler-

32. For accounts of the piracy, see Eaves and Kimpel 377–85 and Sale, *Bibliographical Record* 65–70. As Richardson wrote to Sophia Westcomb, he had made only three sets of proofs "that I may be sure that my Workmen may not give them out to Pyrates, in Ireland, &c., as has been frequently done" (Carroll 240).

33. See Tierney, Robert E. Ward, and Munter (96–98) for Faulkner's life and influence.

ance that *Grandison* represented as a thin veneer, Richardson reacted much more aggressively than he had to the piracy of the second part of *Pamela*. He produced first "The Case of Samuel Richardson, of London, Printer; with regard to the Invasion of his Property in The History of Sir Charles Grandison" and later "An Address to the Public, on the Treatment which the Editor of the History of Sir Charles Grandison has met with from certain Booksellers and Printers in Dublin." In "The Case," he conflated domestic and bodily metaphors, complaining that the Irish had made "an innocent man unsafe in his own house" and revealed themselves to be "intestine traitors" (3). Meanwhile he engaged in a vitriolic correspondence attacking the "worse than Pyrates, the Corrupters of the morals of people's Servants" (Carroll 243). The controversy played out in the *Gray's Inn Journal, Gentleman's Magazine,* and the *Public Advertiser,* with the Irish taking it up in the *Dublin Journal* and *Dublin Spy* (McKillop, *Samuel Richardson* 214, note 130). In London, Samuel Johnson entered the fray, while in Dublin, Richardson's friends tried to interest "a worthy lady . . . who is a great friend at the court of Dublin" (Barbauld 5:115). *Gray's Inn Journal* coyly claimed that it was "not inclined to cast national reflections," but suggested that the Irish were "literary Goths and Vandals" who had invaded "the Republic of Literature" and should be expelled (16). Richardson does not seem to have suffered any financial hardship as a result.[34] On the contrary, friends told him "that the excellent Performance will be more universally read, for the bustle that hath been made about it," a remark that Richardson included in his second attack on the pirates ("Address" 21). Richardson's outrage over the piracy and the uproar he incited seems to have distorted our historical understanding of both Richardson and book publishing: recent scholarship has pointed out that Richardson's attack shaped subsequent appraisals of the Dublin print industry, blinding historians to the broad collaboration between London and Dublin that actually characterized the industry (Tierney 133–34).

The Irish had no doubt that this was a political matter. The *Dublin Spy* advised readers to "discourage with hand and heart all editions printed in England . . . if ye let in so pernicious a custom, ye will be instrumental in ruining Ireland" (quoted in Cole 63). But Richardson's two widely read tracts trivialized Irish national concerns while conflating economic, moral, and aesthetic claims. By arguing that "this Cause is the Cause of Literature, in general" ("Address" 23), Richardson sanitized the debate's poli-

---

34. As a letter from Lady Echlin reported, "The wicked booksellers are disappointed, for they have not made any profit by their stolen books" (Barbauld 5:17).

[43]

ticized nature and participated in a larger, largely successful effort to divorce issues of literary property and authorship from their political and economic context and reframe them in aesthetic and moral terms. Both literary and bibliographic historians have dismissed the tracts' political context and seized on Richardson's remarks as evidence for a pre-romantic version of the romantic construction of authorship. Richardson's biographers took his side, and most critics have followed their lead, though not necessarily their tone. In their authoritative biography, Eaves and Kimpel offer one of the most dismissive remarks regarding the Irish, noting that the assertion of an Irish national cause was bewildering to Richardson "though perhaps not to . . . those better acquainted with that nation" (380). Others have adopted this disregard for the national rhetoric in the Irish tracts primarily by emphasizing the aesthetic rather than the political nature of Richardson's argument.[35] Reinserting Richardson's aesthetics into their political context reveals that originary authorship was constructed in the midst of heated political and economic debates. It is a tribute to the power of original authorship over our imaginations that it ever escaped that context.

The 1750s saw the convergence of economic improvement and cultural nationalism in Ireland, a development deeply unsettling to coherent constructions of English identity that had relied on Ireland's subordinate status.[36] The mere existence of the Irish destabilized such constructions of identity. Unlike the American colonies, Ireland vexed the very terms "same" and "different." The distance between the English and Irish borders was slight and the indigenous Irish inconveniently Caucasian.[37]

35. Rose refers to Richardson's argument as "an abstract claim to an author's right" (*Authors and Owners* 117), while Warner notes—without buying into Richardson's argument—that the tracts characterize the author as "one possessed of mysterious powers of originality that make him the controlling and presiding creator of the text" ("Institutionalization" 7).

36. Contemporary Irish politics as well as the difficulty of obtaining primary sources and the tendency to underplay the importance of Ireland have complicated current understandings of Irish history. See Bradshaw and Connolly for discussions of "revisionist historiography" and its opponents. While D. George Boyce and Brendan Bradshaw make strong arguments for a national consciousness manifested hundreds of years before Richardson wrote *Grandison*, others define national consciousness more narrowly, and find it evolving only in the 1790s. Bradshaw takes a measured position on this issue, arguing that "the revisionists have responded to the anachronistic projection of a nationalist ideology into the immemorial past by extruding the play of national consciousness from all but the modern period. In doing so, they have simply inverted the anachronism" ("Nationalism" 345).

37. As S. J. Connolly has suggested, "It could be argued that the key feature of eighteenth-century Ireland was in fact its ambiguous status: too physically close and too similar to Great Britain to be treated as a colony, but too separate and too different to be a region of the metropolitan centre; inheriting an undoubted division between settler and native, yet without the racial distinctions that could make these absolute" (26). Any number of historians and

Difficulties arose then as today whenever one attempted to make claims about a unified Irish population. "The Irish" were Catholic *and* Protestant, Jacobite *and* Royalist, descended from original Gaelic inhabitants *and* from various groups of English "settlers," inhabitants of a colony *and* of a more independent "kingdom."[38] More concretely and specifically, though, the Irish began to threaten the English domination of trade and politics in the 1740s and 1750s, demonstrating parallel developments in these areas. By the time Richardson wrote *Grandison,* Ireland could no longer be considered a dependent backwater. It had achieved a period of "heady prosperity" in the early 1750s after a decade of economic improvement (Connolly 20; Cullen, "Economic Development" 157–59). The print industry—more a threat to English writers like Richardson now than it had been when he published *Pamela* in 1741—offered only one microcosmic example of the rapid pace of development.

As John Hutchinson has argued, the 1740s can be seen as the "preparation" period for an Irish movement that began to crystallize in the 1750s, a movement evinced economically in the Money Bill dispute and culturally in the publication of Catholic organizer and historian Charles O'Conor's first major work, both of which coincided with the piracy. In Dublin the resistance to English rule that had been growing over the previous fifty years was figured through public debates that led to a night of rioting over the Money Bill of 1753—the same year *Grandison* was pirated (Walker 111). The crisis challenged English power over Irish affairs directly, and in a way that counted, by focusing on who was to control the spending of surplus funds, the Irish or the English. Four years in the making, discussions regarding the Money Bill encompassed most of the commercial issues that plagued the English-Irish relationship, including the Irish charge that the English had undermined the Irish linen industry in 1752 and more general complaints about England's restrictions on Irish trade reverberating even into the print industry. Moreover, the crisis played on the popular fears that England was expanding its power, partly by diverting funds from Ireland to England. Perhaps most interesting in regard to Richard-

---

literary critics have discussed the ambiguities surrounding Irish identity. See Bradshaw, Haydon, Hadfield, Beckett, Bartlett, and Boyce.

38. The difficulty of distinguishing between "natives" and "settlers" has been well treated by Thomas Bartlett and J. C. Beckett. Bartlett notes that "within a short time the English in Ireland found themselves endowed with those very characteristics and traits—excessive drinking, ruinous hospitality, rapacity for patronage, a propensity for violence and a way with words (and with horses)—that had long been inseparable from the 'natives' of Ireland" (*Fall and Rise* 37). The evidence suggests that this was a long-standing problem. Spenser had complained in the 1590s that the Anglo-Irish had become more "barbarous and licentious than the very wild Irish" (quoted in Boyce 55).

son's project in *Grandison* was that the Money Bill dispute led to an alliance between Irish Protestants and elite Irish Catholics like Charles O'Conor,[39] one similar to but more threatening than that between Grandison and the elite Italian Catholics in Richardson's novel. The English in Ireland were well aware that the controversy represented a sea change in English-Irish relations; those more loyal to England than Ireland described it as a "dangerous event" leading to "fatal consequences" (O'Donovan 84). Such consequences reached a cultural sphere seemingly far removed from the Money Bill's immediate concerns. During the crisis, when Thomas Sheridan's play *Mahomet* was performed, the audience insisted on hearing a speech against tyranny twice. When the actor refused to give a second reading, the audience vandalized the theater (Beckett 444–45).

The Money Bill dispute intersected with emerging Irish scholarly efforts to "invent" a historical tradition that could compete both with English history and, more important, with long-held English understandings of what it meant to be Irish.[40] As Hutchinson has put it, "In the hands of these scholars the polar images of Ireland and England came to be reversed" (54). Irish revivalism emanated from Catholics like O'Conor and laid claim to what the English liked to think of as the high English values of liberty and the more prosaic but still English values of good estate management.[41] Beginning in the 1740s with the collecting of Gaelic remnants, the Irish began to represent themselves as insular, as an "original, integrated and self-governing culture," a protected island (like England) with its own unique culture validated by historical artifacts (Hutchinson 55). The new Irish history emerging during the decade—primarily initiated by O'Conor—intersected with a movement to legitimate Irish Catholicism. O'Conor operated at the crux of Irish-English relations, corresponding on the one hand with Richardson's "pirate" Faulkner and on the other with Samuel Johnson.[42] Pretending at times to be a Protestant rather than the Catholic he was, he wrote a number of pro-Catholic and pro-agrarian tracts; by the end of his career, he was held to be Ireland's most prominent historian. He set out to compete with England's claims of a literate history, declaring that without the evidence of literate practices "as early, or near, as in any other European Country . . . our pretensions must ap-

39. See Bartlett, *Fall and Rise,* for the proposition that the Money Bill dispute was one of the issues that "gave Irish Catholics their opportunity to raise the Catholic question" (50). See Landon, Beckett, and Boyce for further accounts of the Money Bill crisis. Declan O'Donovan offers the fullest treatment of this affair.

40. I am indebted to John Hutchinson for this part of my discussion.

41. For fully elaborated discussions of O'Conor's contributions see Hutchinson, Leighton, and Bartlett.

42. See O'Conor's collected letters for this correspondence and for an account of his life.

pear as groundless as those of our neighboring Island of Britain, of which little is known before the entrance of Julius Caesar" (*Dissertations* 11). Given the relationship between claims of piracy and plagiarism to issues of cultural and national control, it is not surprising that his first major work emerged from what seems to have been a vicious battle over originality.[43] Charges of plagiarism aside, in the *Dissertations* he developed an understanding of pre-Norman Ireland as "the Throne of *Liberty*, the Emporium of *Literature*, and the Sanctuary of *Christianity*," a tripartite ideology that Richardson (and of course many others) had also claimed for England (quoted in Leighton 115–17). O'Conor suggested that the ethos informing Grandison Hall had been developed not in England but in ancient Ireland, where "grandeur was sustained, without pageantry; dignity without pomp; and power without terror" and the "discourse generally ran upon the topics of liberty and patriotism" (*Dissertations* 122–26). On a more prosaic level, he advocated a form of Grandisonian estate management, recommending tilling the land rather than pasturing it as a way of avoiding the displacement of the population.

O'Conor turned the tables on English accounts of Irish brutality, relocating brutal intolerance in England and blaming English paranoia for the destruction of Irish historical records. Focusing on textual rather than physical violence, he argued:

> We cannot . . . but lament the fatal policy of the English, who, until the time of King James the first, took all possible care to destroy our old writings. . . . But I must however observe . . . that had [the Irish] . . . received from England the benefit of equitable government, it would go infinitely farther towards securing their obedience, than the burning of all the books and laws which this kingdom ever produced. (*Dissertations* 160–61)

Claiming religious tolerance for his own culture, O'Conor attempted to sever religion from politics and took a conciliatory rather than a violent tone toward Ireland's Protestant majority. The tactic was a successful one. With John Curry, he was responsible for the renewed rise of public Catholicism which resulted in the establishment of the Catholic Committee in 1756. Whether Richardson knew it or not, O'Conor's projects made claims very similar to his own, but situated them not in the Grandison Halls of mid-eighteenth-century England but in Ireland. Richardson would

43. In 1753, O'Conor introduced his first historical work with a brief and cryptic discussion of plagiarism charges that had been leveled against him. As he said in his own defense, "No civilities, no acknowledgments of former obligations . . . can be a reason why, [a] Gentleman Should possess himself of another's property or invention" (*Dissertations*, advertisement).

not have been amused to find that O'Conor had trumped his positioning of England as dominant by imagining Ireland as performing much the same role hundreds of years earlier. Not only had Ireland "once been the prime seat of learning to all Christendom," but also it was "hardly more useful and beneficent to the Western world at home, then they were formidable to it abroad, when they daringly and justly made head against the Roman legions in Britain" (*Dissertations* 89).

The rise of Irish Catholicism helps us make sense of Richardson's efforts to domesticate Catholicism in *Grandison*. Raymond Tumbleson has demonstrated that in the first half of the century, "Catholicism became doubly stigmatized as both alien, what the vain French and the wicked Italians practiced, and frighteningly familiar as the accompaniment of absolutism" (1). But by the middle of the century, there were advantages to a tolerant Protestantism which could be effectively poised against intolerant Catholicism (Hunt, *Middling Sort* 210–11). Richardson seems to have been operating at a crucial moment of transition in England's management of the "Catholic threat"—the moment when the rise of the Catholic cause in Dublin virtually required the English to reassess their attitude toward Catholicism (Haydon 169). In 1754, Robert Nugent, an Irish convert to Protestantism, was kept out of office by anti-Catholic sentiment; a 1756 Hogarth etching showed the English being forced to convert. But the larger picture seems to be one of growing tolerance. Perhaps, the institution of the Grand Tour and increasing international awareness in general were reducing anti-Catholic sentiment in London. By the 1760s and 1770s, the courts were overturning convictions in London under the penal acts: the persecution of Catholics had begun to be seen as something associated with a lower class of people (Haydon 172–77). In this context, tolerance served to elevate Grandison as well as to diffuse the value of Catholicism as a unifying sign for Irishness.

This complicated cultural picture played itself out in relations between the English and Irish print industries, with Richardson striking his most effective blow by characterizing the Dublin printers as pirates in the post-piracy tracts. As Richardson well knew, his hyperbolic claims to the ownership of *Grandison* were legally unenforceable, at least against the Dublin printers. The copyright act of 1710 did not extend to Ireland. Under the Import Act of 1739, what John Feather has called the "perfectly legal" reprint business in Dublin became illegal only if the books were imported back into Great Britain (*Publishing* 78). Once Dublin printers received the pirated material, no law prohibited them from printing it. One might argue that the real "pirates" here were Richardson's own employees, not the Irish printers. But reading accusations of piracy uncritically

has a long tradition. As Mary Pollard notes in her study of the Irish printing industry, the complaints made by London booksellers against the
Dublin printers so consistently maligned them—and were so seldom
countered by English writers—that they "have passed unchallenged into
folk memory" (66).

The copyright law "vacuum" that made Dublin's reprint business legal
had a complex impact on both cultures which went beyond the issue of
the morality of copying. Although it is hard to know whether there might
have been an Irish market for full-priced English editions, the lack of protection contributed to a minor boom in an Irish printing industry largely
dependent on English reprints. While the Irish marketing of reprints to
the colonies was forbidden by law, those Irish printers who were willing
to smuggle could offer cheaper copies to international markets, and even
to England itself, thus competing directly with English printers for an English market.[44] Of less economic but more symbolic value was the fact
that the vacuum allowed Irish printers to appropriate English works, revising them at times to suit Irish purposes. As A. S. Collins reports anec-
dotally, "Such was the gap between England and Ireland in the middle of
the eighteenth century that there is a story of a certain Rolt having gone
to Dublin in 1745, and there reprinted as his own work Akenside's *Plea-
sures of the Imagination* which had been recently published anonymously
in London" (62). Piracy was at times accompanied by textual corruption,
by editorial changes that in colonial contexts tended to be politically sub-
versive. John Chambers provides a quintessential example. Reprinting
William Guthrie's *Modern Geography* in 1789, and adding substantially
to the sections on Ireland, he remarked that he had reprinted the work
"not more with a view to profit than to prove that this country has spirit,
when encouraged, not only to undertake literary publications on an English scale of liberality, but even to attempt improvement thereon" (quoted
in Cole 21). John Baxter's *New and Impartial History of England,* a
highly revised version of David Hume's *History of England,* provides an
example from the American colonies. As Thomas Jefferson wrote praising Baxter's "republicanized" history: "He gives you the text of Hume,
purely and verbally, till he comes to some misrepresentation or omission
. . . then he alters the text silently, makes it what truth and candor says it
should be, and resumes the original text again, as soon as it becomes innocent, without having warned you of your rescue from misguidance"
(McLaughlin 89–90, note). Given the lax international copyright protection, Baxter's edition, never very popular in England, could circulate

44. See Cole and Pollard for detailed studies of the Irish printing industry.

freely in America, its origins in the more traditional British establishment forgotten.

The copyright vacuum undermined English claims to authorship. Robert Griffin has demonstrated that the practice of affixing authors' names to their texts was relatively unusual. When authorial identity was revealed then, its significance was amplified. The author's name (or a general public understanding of the author's identity if the work was published with a reference to other publications by the same author) tethered not only the author to the work but also the work to the nation. But when "unauthorized" reprints were smuggled to the colonies, an author's identity and even national origin might be forgotten. Many authors—even Irish ones—seemed quite concerned about the problem. By 1778, the Irish writer Joseph Middleton, for example, was signing every legitimate copy of his edition of the *Correct Book of Interest* as a way of proving its genealogy (Cole 12). The literal erasure of the authorial name provided a site for larger anxieties about originality. As Boswell complained, "The *Filiation* of a literary performance is difficult of proof; seldom is there any witness present at its birth. . . . The true authour, in many cases, may not be able to make his title clear" (*Life* 255). This was particularly true when the link between author and text was attenuated by multiple piracies. As Richardson complained to a friend shortly after the piracy: "And these Irishmen! They do vex me: for I am informed from thence, that they are driving on with five volumes at different presses; and are agreeing with some Scottish booksellers to print them in Scotland, and intend to make the most of their wickedness by sending copies to France before publication.—What have I done, my dear friend, to be thus treated!" (Barbauld 3:69–70). In the face of potential cultural blurring, Richardson's outraged claims to individualized authorship—expressed most powerfully when he argued, "I borrow not from any author"—reasserted what Foucault has called the "fundamental unit of the author and the work" and supported the connection linking nation to author to idea. Only by asserting an individualized form of authorship could Richardson protect the English tradition which he and a host of other English authors were in the process of inventing.

While the copyright vacuum allowed for various forms of Irish subversion, it was a mixed blessing that offered the English benefits as well. Cheap copies facilitated a wide distribution of English ideas and English writing to the periphery, a distribution that might not have taken place at all at London's higher prices.[45] Worse, because Irish writers could not sell

45. Cole provides some examples of the reduced prices encouraged by the copyright vac-

their work at competitive prices in Dublin, they tended to flee to London. The impoverished Irish writer became a stock comic figure on the stage; such humor tended to obscure the fact that no Irish canon could develop in this economic setting. Such benefits, though buried in England's cultural unconscious, may have offset English concerns about economic losses and the occasional interference with authorial identity. Certainly, England failed to legislate against Dublin book piracy, a failure not quite explained by the weak political pressure Dublin exerted to protect its printing industry.[46] Although Richardson could not have known that an advertisement to the 1779 edition of *Sir Charles Grandison* meant for distribution in the provinces would advocate that the Irish buy the book because it contained "a complete system of all the relative and social duties, and which for important events, just reflections, and beautiful diction, has never been excelled," the advertisement indicates that "Grandison," both novel and character, became a useful tool in the English project to anglicize Ireland (Cole 72–73). By 1782, Richardson was to be called the "Shakespeare of Romance" in the *Hibernian Magazine* (quoted in Cole 83). Richardson's contemporaries seemed fully aware of this acculturation effect. Even during the height of the 1753 dispute with the Irish printers, a friend of Richardson's had reassured him by arguing, "Who knows, dear Sir, but the glorious Sir CHARLES may teach some honesty and dignity of soul, even to him who buys it, as stolen goods, a few shillings lower from the pirates than he could from you" (Richardson, "Address" 21). As Richardson's friend realized, cheap, available editions, though they might decrease Richardson's measurable income, would ultimately increase his readership.

By and large, the cultural windfall effected by the easy dissemination of English ideas went unremarked. English claims of Irish immorality trumped the arguments of the Irish that their printing industry resisted both English economic and cultural dominance, providing work for Irish printers and cheap copies to those on the Irish margins who could not afford more expensive English editions. The copyright vacuum persisted until the Union of 1800, but the 1785 effort to regulate the book trade re-

uum. In America, Blackstone's *Commentaries* cost double the Irish price but still less than in London. Robertson's *History of Charles V* cost three pounds in London but only fifteen shillings in Ireland.

46. Mary Pollard posits that Dublin interests prevented regulation against the Irish, but given that legislation against the Irish would have taken place in London with the full support of the London booksellers, pressure from Dublin seems unlikely to have been successful. It seems more reasonable to suppose that the failure to regulate copyright resulted from the complex balance of regulations and concessions that typified English-Irish relations during the period. See Pollard 71.

veals something of the power dynamics involved. The *Dublin Evening Post* summed up one version of the Irish position on April 5, 1785: "If the London booksellers won, reading in Ireland would become too great a luxury and would as in the days of barbarous ignorance be confined solely to the cloister—or the castle of the insolent and haughty Baron" (Cole 6). Other remarks about Irish-English print relations revealed the violence behind such cultural issues. Richardson's Anglo-Irish friend Philip Skelton had brought a fearful imperial consciousness to bear on the issue when he suggested an advertisement advocating the purchase of the English edition of *Grandison* because "English and Irish interests were one, that Ireland had a great debt to England, and that, besides, the latter country was more powerful and should not be irritated" (Eaves and Kimpel 382).

The Case against the Irish: The (R)use of Tropic Piracy

In this atmosphere of cultural contestation, reframing the Irish print industry's resistance to Richardson's control as "piracy" was a brilliant tactic. The juridical associations of piracy counteracted the prosaic public perceptions that associated Grub Street with petty disputes over earnings. Readers intrigued by discussions of crime, particularly crimes involving piracy, could enjoy the exploits of the Irish while identifying with Richardson's self-righteously heroic stance. Resituating the accusation of piracy in the internal colonial context of Irish-English relations allowed Richardson to invoke all of its discursive possibilities. He conjoined piracy and the international book trade, drawing on the lexicon of international maritime relations in order to criminalize the nonregulated and thus noncriminal acts of the Irish book pirates. In doing so, he marked the Irish as a threat to the normative channels of production and dissemination.

Richardson had much material to draw from. Although practices that we now refer to as piracy had existed since the spread of manuscript culture, references to literary piracy became more common after 1700. It is not surprising that Defoe, who may have written piracy into the public imagination in *The History of the Pirates,* is credited with the first use of the word to describe "some dishonest Booksellers, called Land pirats" (*OED*). Addison and Steele complained of London "pirates" in 1709 in an obvious attempt to gain support for the Act of Anne (*Tatler* 2:120). Richardson must have been familiar as well with the earlier London print wars that had polarized the print industry along class lines in the 1730s and 1740s. The use of print piracy talk during that period had done much of the work for him, setting up a dichotomy between mainstream "legit-imate" printers and marginal "illegitimate" printers which assigned re-spectability to the first group and criminality to the second (Harris, "Paper Pirates" 47). Non-mainstream printers had long been associated with prisons, quackery, Jacobite plots, and religious enthusiasm and ac-cused of illegal "confederacies" and criminality. Such a history offered a rich referential context for the tracts.[47] In lifting these categories from their class context and mapping them onto England and Ireland, Rich-ardson drew effectively on Irish stereotypes. The "wild" Irish were well established as rebels, abductors, and especially pirates in the popular imagination.[48] Henry Mainwaring had remarked in 1617 that Ireland "may be well called the Nursery and Storehouse of Pirates" (Appleby 1), and Richardson's lament of 1755 ("Are not the inhabitants on the coasts throughout Great Britain and Ireland the worst of plunderers?") suggests that the stereotype was still alive (Barbauld 5:61). When Richardson com-bined London's print piracy talk with common stereotypes about Irish sea pirates and the criminality of the less controlled Celtic fringe, he doubly marginalized the Dublin printers while legitimizing his own work.

In the first pamphlet, Richardson relied on the popular genre of "the case" both to reach an already available audience eager for details of scan-dalous lawsuits and to designate the issue as a national, juridical one. But for their popularity and readability the tracts depended on the ludic value of piracy discourse, the intense interest, even vicarious delight, Richard-son and his readers took in the transgressions of errant characters. Read-ers already titillated by the numerous tracts, cases, and histories of piracy could enjoy their outrage at the exploits of the Irish while congratulating themselves on their identification with Richardson. The carnivalesque possibilities of piracy transcended class: popular chapbooks detailing the scaffold confessions of pirates (Rediker 285) coexisted alongside elaborate pirate costumes worn at upper-class masquerades (Garber 180–81). As John Richetti has demonstrated, by Defoe's time, piracy was the stuff of popular legend, and the pirate himself was seen as a demonic "cul-ture hero" (74). Contemplating piracy offered a straightforward release from the constraints of an increasingly confining national loyalty, while the interest in pirate executions suggested a fearful pleasure taken in dis-

47. I am indebted here to Michael Harris's interesting analysis of London print culture in the first third of the century.

48. The modern work on Irish stereotyping dates back to Edward D. Snyder's essay "The Wild Irish," published in 1920. Joep Leerssen offers an interesting overview of the Irish stock character on the stage (*Mere Irish*). The issue of whether or not the Irish were particularly given to abducting young women has been debated in the historical literature since the 1820s and is still current. See Kelly.

solution, in contemplations of attacks on the unitary self and unitary state.[49]

The piracy trope exerted a tremendous energy and introduced a much greater level of deviance into the debates than a mere print dispute might seem to deserve. In part, the tracts were so enormously successful in branding the Irish printers as pirates because they reenacted and relied on the currency of Richardson's novelistic themes. They made full use of Richardson's awareness of the relationship between typographical and rhetorical control while inviting comparisons to the novels and thus shedding light on his larger concerns. In the tracts, Richardson characterizes the Irish booksellers as savages and invaders, underscoring his own writing as normative, that of a "lawful Proprietor of a new and Moral work" ("Case" 3). He places such "lawful" practices in opposition to Irish "piracy," setting in motion a discourse peculiarly suited to issues involving colonization, assimilation, and cultural hegemony. Calling Faulkner a "strange man" and a "savage," Richardson imagines him in much the same way as Harriet and her family imagine Sir Hargrave. Just as Harriet's family concerns itself with Sir Hargrave's efforts to ruin her good name, Richardson, noting the Irish printers' unauthorized use of his name in an advertisement, terms it "vile artifice!" ("Case" 2). By bribing his employees, the Irish have made "an innocent man unsafe in his own house" ("Case" 3); they have obtained the sheets of his novel through "the villainy of corrupted servants" ("Address" 15). Like Sir Hargrave, who abducts Harriet by corrupting a servant, the Irish intruded into and corrupted members of Richardson's household, penetrating the domestic boundaries that Richardson had attempted to protect. Noting that he had given not merely "a strict charge, before he put the piece to press, to all his workmen and servants" but a charge "in PRINT (that it might the stronger impress them)," he details instructions that dwell on the danger of "out-door attacks" from strangers. Like Harriet and her family, he had "no reason to distrust" his employees, no reason to know that they might be "capable of being corrupted to attempt so vile a robbery" ("Case" 2).

49. The debate over the romanticization of the pirates has such currency that it was picked up by *Lingua Franca* in a feature article in March 1998. Questions revolve around the historical accuracy of Christopher Hill's and Marcus Rediker's representation of pirates as rebels against the state rather than common thugs. Historical truth aside, that pirates were imagined as anti-authoritarian figures who offered an alternative to the dominant order seems obvious given the various legislative efforts against them as well as Defoe's *History*. See Turley, "Piracy," for the many accounts of piracy from 1695 to 1725 that "testify to the popularity and importance of the pirate figure to early eighteenth-century British culture and trade policy" (213, note 8).

The tracts draw on typographical devices—underlining and italics, but also the manipulation of blocks of text—made familiar in the novels. In the first tract, Richardson interjects his own comments into reprinted Irish advertisements for the novel, using the advertisements as evidence of Irish guilt. In the second, he manipulates epistolarity, himself pirating a number of Faulkner's letters in order to subject them to his own inserted comments and analysis. Richardson starts with two columns, one titled "Mr. Faulkner's Defence" and the other "Genuine History of the Transaction." Although on the first page the two are given equal space, by the beginning of the second the "genuine history" has completely overwhelmed "Mr. Faulkner's Defence." Like the intensely analytical Clarissa but with less delicacy, Richardson quotes Faulkner, placing significant words in italics and interspersing Faulkner's text with comments of his own: "'I am sorry to tell you,' *proceeds he, in this Letter,* 'that when *these people* produced their sheets, and *obliged* me' *[Mean Man!]* 'to shew mine, that I was *compelled* to give them up, in order to obtain a share with them.' *His very words!*—." ("Address") Dissecting one after the other of Faulkner's statements, Richardson demonstrates their internal inconsistencies and disproves them with references to other letters he has about him. In a particularly telling example, he reprints a paragraph from one of Faulkner's letters in which the hapless Faulkner offhandedly mentions "two or three letters" without describing them. Richardson responds: *In two or three letters following,* says he? How slightly is this mentioned by Mr. Faulkner! He had been parading to Mr. Richardson, from his Letter dated Aug. 4 to the 15th of September; sometimes pretending to detest the part his new partners acted, sometimes seeming to have it in view" (10–11). Demonstrating the same skills at close reading that he grants his novelistic characters, Richardson uses his own dated letters as evidence against Faulkner's claims: "You see, Sir, by the dates (for your notice of the theft is dated Aug. 4), that, from July 12, when your acceptance is dated, no time was lost in sending you the sheets" (18). After enmeshing Faulkner in a complex web of dated letters, statements, counterstatements, and accusations of misleading remarks, Richardson finally threatens him in metaphoric language drawn from his novels: "O Mr. Faulkner, take care of truth in any thing you shall publish or write, in an affair in which you have acted so strange a part! You are in the condition of a limed bird; the more you struggle, the more you will entangle yourself" ("Address" 18). Faulkner's text itself took on the characteristics of the limed bird: on some pages, Faulkner's letters defending the "theft" are confined to the top left of the page, while above, below, and to the right, Richardson places much longer comments and rebuttals. These pages suggest an English fantasy map of Britain—one in which England has encroached from the north, east, and south, enclosing Ireland on all but the west side.

Richardson's novels, with their disruptive kidnappings and subsequent reaffirmation of heterosexual hierarchy and normative familial relations, offered a context that lent pirates and their mythology a special force. Piracy metaphors relied on a peculiar logic in which almost any pirate behavior seemed to threaten regular channels of production and distribution, channels that Richardson had long reaffirmed through representations of normative family life with its reproductive rhythms and carefully regulated genetic exchanges. The very word "pirate" raised a host of reproductive associations, suggesting everything from the homosexual behavior of English pirates in the seventeenth-century Caribbean (Burg 1–41) to female rebellion. Piracy also evoked Ireland's Catholicism through what Cameron McFarlane has called the "cultural incoherence" of sodomitical groupings, an incoherence that condensed all sorts of transgressive figures—foreigners, Catholics (associated with homosexuality), plotters, and non-procreators—under one sign.[50] Not surprisingly, popular texts about the pirate community emphasized sexual deviance, either through stressing the role of the rare pirate women who rejected heterosexual marriage and "normal" family life in favor of the sea and sexual profligacy, or through representing pirates as forming a homosocial, potentially homosexual community. Sometimes these representations were deployed simultaneously, the illogical juxtaposition ignored in favor of its power both to eroticize and marginalize pirates—most of whom had been recruited from the legitimate, but extremely repressive, merchant and naval ships.

We find the interruptive nature of piracy recurrently appearing in all sorts of symbolic fields, from the historically "real" venue of the shipping lanes to the more symbolic areas of genetic reproduction and the reproduction of copies. The title of Defoe's 1724 history of piracy, *A General* HISTORY *of the Robberies and Murders of the most notorious* PYRATES, *and also Their Politics, Discipline and Government, From their first Rise and Settlement in the Island of Providence, in 1717, to the present Year 1724. With The remarkable Actions and Adventures of the two Female Pyrates, Mary Read and Anne Bonny,* conflates politics, sadism, and gender. The lengthy work contained a number of woodprints implying sex-

50. See Murry, Burg, and Sherry for assumptions about and recorded instances of sodomy among pirates. Hans Turley argues that the homosocial world of the pirates, eroticized precisely because of its transgressive nature, interrupts and threatens eighteenth-century constructions of gendered sexuality. His work and comments have helpfully complicated my argument here.

ual aggression and deviancy. In the cartoonish print meant to represent Blackbeard, a second sword hangs suggestively from between his legs, while behind him pirates board a burning ship. Woodcuts of the female pirates Mary Read and Anne Bonny show them fully armed and in masculine dress, the only sign of their gender their long flowing hair. Such woodcuts of sexualized but childless pirates can be compared to Hogarth's representation of legitimate authority in the person of Captain Woodes Rogers, who was commissioned as governor of the Bahamas to wipe out pirate activity. In Hogarth's painting, Rogers sits across from his wife and her lapdog. Rather than a sword, he holds a sextant, used for taking measurements of longitude and latitude. Rogers is shown not in action but with his obviously English family and servants in a maritime version of domestic harmony. Richardson and his family had been similarly portrayed in the often reproduced Francis Hayman painting of 1741.[51] The implications were clear. Pirate sexuality, if it produced anything, did not produce orderly families or reinforce orderly chains of reproduction and replication. Richardson's application of piracy discourse to the Irish thus suggested a relationship between deviance and the subversion of the "normal" publishing channels represented by Richardson and other London printers. Whereas his own practices were based on the model provided by the legalized heterosexual family, one in which female participation is essential but males control an ultimate product typified by its "newness" and originality, pirate practices were represented either as aggressively dominated by women who refused to submit to legalized marriage or as primarily homosocial.[52]

From reading Richardson's tracts, one would not know that by the 1750s, international sea piracy against Britain had largely been controlled. Conversations about piracy were no longer focused on an actual threat but on fantasies and reconstituted memories that traversed a number of different cultural fields but centered on what it meant to be national in the international context. As Janice E. Thomson has shown, the control of piracy signified the shift to the nation-state as a dominant form of government. But this was a lengthy process involving mass executions, not something to be accomplished overnight or even over the first decade of the century. "Piracy," and its more legitimate relative "privateering,"

51. The Hogarth painting of Woodes Rogers is reproduced in Manuel Schonhorn's edition of Defoe's *General History*. The Francis Hayman painting of Richardson's family appears in Eaves and Kimpel's biography of Richardson.

52. Richardson draws here on a connection that Cameron McFarlane lays out nicely when he suggests the linkage between "the 'proper' circulation of reproductive desire and the 'proper' circulation of money and productive labor" earlier in the century (53).

remained terms weighted with national import well into the 1750s.[53] The very idea of piracy, with its suggestion that dissident individuals could resist state primacy, represented a threat to the control that developing nations wished to exert, both internally and internationally. Moreover, controlling piracy was not simply a matter of policing the seas. It required as well an internal policing, a refusal to sanction privateering during wartime, and an effort to criminalize those who cooperated with pirates. Placing piracy and privateering in the context of state development, Thomson suggests that "in order to permanently resolve the piracy problem, Britain had to put its own house in order" (109). Crucial to this effort was piracy's abjection, its cultural transformation from an honorable effort at independent enterprise to a crime against civilization.[54]

Sea piracy offered a number of parallels to international print piracy. Like print piracy, sea piracy "displaces laterally what would otherwise turn into a chain of colonial command" (Aravamudan 93). By re-categorizing the Irish printers as pirates, Richardson displaced them geographically and located them symbolically with the dispossessed. As Srinivas Aravamudan has noted, "Merchants are pirates in disguise and pirates are aspiring merchants" (99). Attempts to enforce laws against both forms of piracy were plagued with legislative uncertainty; the state authorized sea piracy as privateering when convenient, providing, as Thomson argues, "the economic and legal infrastructure" that supported it (54). The line between piracy and legitimate activity was vague: privateers who held a letter of marque could find that the moment war ended, their authorization ceased and their activities were redefined as illegal. The piracy/privateering dichotomy was so unstable that delays in transmitting information could have a significant impact on the legitimacy of privateering activities (Turley, *Rum* 37). Richardson's correspondence with Faulkner—continually marked by criss-crossing letters and missed connections—suggests a similar instability, a slippage in which Faulkner, temporarily unaware of Richardson's instructions, shifted from legitimate privateer to pirate. Just as the Dublin printers were tolerated so long as they did not threaten London's monopoly, sea piracy was tolerated so long as it offered no threat to British trade (Turley, *Rum* 30–31). Faulkner's success, like

---

53. In 1744 all criminals who were willing to serve as privateers were pardoned in England, and by 1757 privateering had become a national object of interest (Thomson, *Mercenaries* 23–24).

54. That putting England's own house in order was a difficult proposition is evidenced by the discussion during the first third of the century about legitimate merchants who trafficked with pirates, which included a tract, possibly by Defoe, concerning what was then the common practice of trade with pirates (Turley, "Piracy" 205, 213, note 13).

that of Captain Kidd earlier in the century, collided with London's business interests and was thus inconsistent with English goals.[55]

Piracy had complex national implications. Joel Baer accurately delineates only one form its "symbolic force" took when he argues that "the pirate appeared to the eighteenth century as the complete criminal whose existence was a standing reproach to human nature and European civilization" (14–15). As Baer suggests, at times pirates were imagined as peculiarly detached from any national loyalties. In a much-reported piracy trial of 1717, the judge advocate declared that a pirate "can claim the Protection of no Prince, the privilege of no Country, the benefit of no Law; He is denied common humanity and the very rights of Nature, with whom no Faith, Promise nor Oath is to be observed, nor is he to be otherwise dealt with, than as a wild & savage beast, which every Man may lawfully destroy" (quoted in Baer 8). Such images of the pirate as deviant social outcast reflected piracy's interruption of the regular channels of British commerce but were also related to the threat piracy posed to all forms of state power. They suggested that pirates were lone figures, of great symbolic value but ultimately subordinate to the orders that they threatened. Like "a wild & savage beast," they could eventually be hunted down and eliminated.

Far more symbolically threatening than the individualized and disenfranchised pirate was the development of pirate groups into recognized sovereign powers, a development encouraged by the close associations among almost all the major pirate vessels operating in the first third of the century (Baer 20).[56] Marcus Rediker documents the establishment of various pirate communities in Madagascar, Sierra Leone, and the Bahamas. Whether or not pirate communities were led by radicals with articulated antigovernment agendas, such communities had many of the trappings of "nation."[57] They were, for instance, designing and adopting their own flags by the late 1690s (Casey 498). More important, at least some pirate groups imagined themselves as commonwealths, run by majority rule and subordinated to a social contract (Casey 536). As Matthew Tindal had recognized in his 1694 *Essay on the Law of Nations*, collectivized pirates "might have a Publick Cause, upon the account of that Nation, of making War." Tindal noted as well that "the beginning of most

55. See Ritchie for Kidd's trial and its illumination of issues involving piracy and privateering (206–27). See Aravamudan's discussion of the "complex moment-by-moment shifts in legal status" suffered by privateers (82).

56. See Rediker for a chart detailing relationships among the pirate ships and a discussion of the ways those relationships were manifested (268, 275–81).

57. See Casey (518) for a discussion of the debates over this point.

of the great empires were not much better: whatever any were at first, yet when they had formed themselves into Civil Societies, where foreigners as well as subjects might have Justice administered, then they were looked on as Nations and Civil Societies" (quoted in Baer 21). Richardson drew on the fears of a possible pirate "nation" in the second pamphlet, which he later inserted in the last volume of the novel. Whereas the first pamphlet categorized the printers as criminals and outcasts, in the second Richardson's greatest concern lay with the possibility that pirates represented *organized* opposition to English values. He evinces this concern primarily in an attack on Faulkner, whom he finally blamed for the Irish appropriation of *Grandison*.

The immediate occasion of Richardson's second tract was Faulkner's "Defence of Himself," published in the *Dublin Spy*. In response, Richardson, though focusing on Faulkner's behavior, attacks the very notion of Irish solidarity, with its underlying assumptions of Irish rights in law. Within a typographical frame that emphasizes borders and boundaries, Richardson assaults Faulkner's claim that his union with other Dublin printers was "in pursuance of an established, invariable, constant custom among the Booksellers of Dublin." As John Barrell has argued so convincingly, custom was seen as "the *direct* manifestation of the will of the people, voter and non-voter alike, and so of the political liberty of *all* Englishmen" (*English Literature* 121). Inscribed in Blackstone's *Commentaries* as a fundamental premise of English law, a claim to custom came dangerously close to a claim to law. According to *Lex Custumaria,* published in 1696: "When a reasonable Act once done is found to be good, and beneficial to the People, and agreeable to their nature and disposition, then do they use it and practise it again and again, and so by often iteration and multiplication of the Act, it becomes a Custom; and being continued without interruption time out of mind, it obtaineth the force of a Law" (quoted in Thompson, *Customs* 97).

Given the association between custom and law, a successful Irish claim to practices sanctioned as "custom" not only flew in the face of Richardson's argument that the pirates acted outside the law, but also suggested an equality between Ireland and England that called Richardson's project into question.[58] To counter this, Richardson reprints Faulkner's description of the "constant custom" and then revises it with his own insertions:

58. The association is, of course, a commonplace in legal history. See chap. 3 of Thompson's *Customs in Common;* Barrell, *English Literature* 119–21; and Baker, *Introduction* 1–13.

Will Mr. Faulkner say, that it is an *established, invariable, constant* custom among the booksellers of Dublin, to renounce their agreements with men they had contracted with, on their being notoriously robbed, and to join with the Corruptors, to supplicate a share with them in the plunder? How wickedly does he blubber over this part of his conduct, to the justification, as may be said, of that of his new Confederates!—Can such a man as this be too severely (if justly) dealt with?—Surely no! ("Address" 8)

The diatribe reflected English fears of "going native" and thus reenacted concerns more mildly expressed in *Grandison*. Unlike Grandison, who was ultimately able to hold out against the Italians, Faulkner had gone over to the other side and joined the enemy forces. Throughout the pamphlet Richardson dwells on Faulkner's disloyalty, which displaces the disloyalty of Richardson's staff, bribed, as he thought, by either Faulkner or his compatriots. Like the English drafters of fourteenth-century statutes forbidding the English from taking up Irish customs, Richardson attacks the Anglo-Irish Faulkner for his alignment with Irish interests, repeatedly expressing his shock that "so wholly was he, in an instant, detached from Mr. R. and attached to them, and his and their common interest," his dismay that Faulkner was in such "haste to join with the corruptors," and his distaste for Faulkner's "perseverance in so wicked a partnership," which Faulkner "was so little, as to creep to them for, on their own infamous terms" ("Address" 7–10). In focusing on Faulkner's disloyalty, Richardson reenacted four hundred years of English-Irish relations troubled by "the dangerous consequence of Hibernicisation" of the English in Ireland (Boyce 30).

Hanging Out the Lights: Richardson, Authorship, and Collaboration

Having put this complicated tropic machinery to work, in the last paragraph of the last copyright tract Richardson imagines himself as a one-man anti-pirate squad: "We will take upon us to add, that *every* man in Mr. R's station has not the spirit, the will, the independence, to hang out the lights to his Cotemporaries, to enable them to avoid Savages, who hold themselves in readiness to plunder a vessel even before it becomes a wreck" ("Address" 23). Calling on the "spirit, the will, the independence" of a Grandison, Richardson here associates himself with a maritime image suitable for describing enlightened English efforts to fend off the "savagery" of the Irish book pirates. But "hanging out the lights," a popular image in pirate mythology still current in contemporary romances, had multiple meanings.[59] At times, good citizens would light up the coast to warn ships away from rocky shores. But such lights were just as likely to lead ships to destruction as to warn them away from danger. Everyone knew that coastal pirates raised lights as a way of luring ships into dangerous waters, where they would be wrecked and looted. The tangled metaphor points to the ambiguities that plagued Richardson's claims to originality and sole possession of his work, linking Richardson himself to the very piratical practices he seems to reject. For the claims Richardson made to original production, whether in the prefaces to the novels or in the copyright tracts, were patently untrue. Instead, his assertion of original and solitary production flew in the face of both a highly imitative transhistorical and transnational reliance on romance and an intensely collaborative production process. Both were inconsistent with the claims of the originary right to ownership which he made for his work.

Of course, I do not mean to suggest that the notoriously honest Richardson was a cheat or a plagiarist. But investigating the ideology driving the apparent conflict between his theory and practice by relocating that conflict in its politicized context allows us to see the origins of originary authorship. By "forgetting" or suppressing his awareness of his collaborative practices at key moments, Richardson cemented his relationship to the work, and simultaneously reduced the possibility that its usefulness to promoting English hegemony would be compromised. Reclaiming Richardson's processes for the history of authorship but rejecting the temptation to moralize both rescues him from charges of duplicity and shifts the emphasis from ethics to issues of cultural hegemony. When he collected and packaged a range of different, even contradictory contributions, Richardson created a fantasy of national integration, the Richardson persona serving as an umbrella for a whole spectrum of views. Within English borders, Richardson's ability to incorporate almost any viewpoint into his works, or at least into their paraphernalia, implied that English diversity could be contained and that Englishness could be imagined as collective. Meanwhile, the recapitulation of diverse views in a simplified symbolic form called "Richardson" reaffirmed the connection between English views and an English-dominated British "nation" to colonial and foreign readers. On an international level, the Richardson name marked the novels as English. Thus, "originality" and a coinciding elevation of

59. As a student in a seminar on early romances pointed out to me, "hanging out the lights" still appears in contemporary romances as a sign for pirate brutality. See, for instance, Feather, *Bride* 1–4.

the author became discursive tools for consolidating English identity in an international marketplace.

The very pirate motif that Richardson repeatedly deployed in both the tracts and the novels had been borrowed from the romance and inflected through Defoe's history of piracy.[60] Such transhistorical, transcultural borrowing, as Clifford Siskin has argued, served to "tame" the technology of writing: by domesticating romance and making it familiar, Richardson "Englished it" and thus made the whole of literate culture feel less foreign and strange to newly literate English populations (431). Making Englishness comfortable was not a comfortable process, however. Richardson's representation of the novel as a form that had already subsumed romance cloaked the anxiety with which he alternately rejected and drew on romance conventions. His numerous disavowals coexist with comments about romances that he admitted to having read. As he wrote to Elizabeth Carter, he had once read Ariosto and longed for Angelica's "Invisible Ring," which as a shy boy he would have used to shield himself from prying eyes (quoted in McKillop, *Samuel Richardson* 287). Such a ring might have been more useful for hiding the influence of romance, still quite evident despite all of Richardson's disavowals.[61] His borrowing was not innocent of national implications, for in reinscribing both the ancient romance and French romances in his most English of fictions, he drew on forms that were equally interested in cultural assimilation and appropriation.[62] That he felt compelled to deny his dependence on romance conventions, including the romance's repetitive unoriginality, its recirculation of stock stories and characters, speaks to a telling anxiety about originary authorship.

To assert that originality and collaboration are inherently oppositional would be to adopt the very definition of "original" that tends to erase the political origins of aesthetic theory. As Jack Stillinger has argued, without collaboration, literary production could not take place. Wordsworth's appropriation of Dorothy's remarks on daffodils takes nothing away from the "originality" of "I Wandered Lonely as a Cloud," though it may well call into question the myth of solitary genius.[63] But despite their interde-

---

60. Examples are legion: Heliodorus' *Ethiopian Romance* opens with two consecutive pirate attacks. Xenophon's *Ephesian Tale* features a pirate captain who makes homosexual advances. See Williamson 28. Eighteenth-century works after 1720 tended to rewrite piracy as abduction, as Richardson did. Still, Penelope Aubin's novel *The Noble Slaves* was one of many accounts in which piracy played a part.

61. See Zach for a list of letters in which Richardson disavows romance and for Richardson's probable authorship of the preface to Penelope Aubin's collected novels.

62. See Moses Hadas's introduction to *The Ethiopian Romance*.

63. Compare Dorothy Wordsworth's April 15, 1802, entry from the Grasmere journals

pendence, an author's claims to originality and collaboration, when made overtly and simultaneously, suggest an unmarked underlying agenda just as any logical fissure in a text does. In Richardson's case, the celebration of collaboration worked with the simultaneous claim of originality to provide a methodological model for the formation of national identity.

Richardson's claims to sole authorship seem particularly strange in light of the overanxious solicitation of commentary that lurked beneath the surface of *Grandison*. An example of the truism that attacks on unauthorized copying are most intense when originality is most at issue, Richardson's career offers little doubt that he "pirated" the language of others, usually women, commodified it, and put it into circulation.[64] Tools in his own cultural kidnapping projects, his letters reveal numerous instances of collaborative efforts which, though they begin as early as *Pamela,* are perfected in the production of *Sir Charles Grandison*. Collaboration had often been blamed for the novel's fissures and for Richardson's difficulties in completing it. As Jocelyn Harris tells us, "The *Grandison* correspondence contains Richardson's most elaborate consultations. . . . [His friends] seized so eagerly at the chance of sharing in the new creation that they prolonged the new book's composition for years" (*Samuel Richardson* 132).

But such delays allowed Richardson to develop an extended community of advisers—mostly women—all of whom he drew on as he wrote his most community-oriented novel. That his community outreach extended mostly to women suggests its function in incorporating gendered hierarchies into the writing of the nation. In subordinating women to his efforts, Richardson tried to institute the common model for nation also offered in *Grandison,* one in which men naturally gather about them an affectionate, affiliative, and feminized circle of admirers. But Richardson's community was far from "natural." Instead, he made strenuous efforts to engage women readers in his project, efforts that suggest how carefully and laboriously constructed all such "natural" national communities may be. In one of the better-known examples, he asked Hester Mulso, later the well-known author Hester Chapone, to "set your charming imagination at work and give me a few scenes . . . that I may try to work them into the story" (Eaves and Kimpel 372).[65] Although such requests were com-

---

to Wordsworth's poem, written two years later. For a more sweeping statement about Dorothy's influence, see Stillinger 72.

64. Mary Jean Corbett quotes Catherine Gallagher on the same dynamic in Maria Edgeworth's use of Irish idiom: Edgeworth's aim is "to possess the non-identity of the other and then put it into circulation" (390).

65. Hester Chapone, born Hester Mulso in 1727, wrote poetry and entries for the *Ram-

plied with only erratically (Mulso never allowed herself to be "worked into the story"), they typified the novel's production process. Women had supposedly prompted the novel, "teezing" Richardson "to give them a good man." In turn, Richardson recruited them to the work of the novel, asking them to write sections, advise on behavior, respond to the characterizations of Harriet, Clementina, and Grandison, and even edit the work (Eaves and Kimpel 371).[66] He borrowed Lady Bradshaigh's epistolary remarks about the flippancies of old maids and inserted them into the mouth of *Grandison's* Lady G. (Carroll 268, note 92), and filled in the gaps in his knowledge of the upper classes by persuading various ladies to "describe a scene or two in upper life" (Eaves and Kimpel 353). At his urging, Lady Bradshaigh marked up her copy of the novel and sent it to him. That he took such suggestions seriously is supported by the fact that he responded with "a thousand thanks" (Pierson 176). Like Bradshaigh, Catherine Talbot "fell in love" with Sir Charles. In response, Richardson put her to work correcting the manuscript. Talbot spent long days and evenings editing the novel, making any number of corrections aimed at improving its style and accurately reflecting the "conversation and manners" of the upper classes. As Eaves and Kimpel assert, "There is no reason to doubt that a good many of her painstaking corrections were accepted" (363). Even Richardson's production fantasies involved collaboration: planning a fantasy continuation of the novel, he remarked that he would like to ask "every one of my Correspondents, at his or her own Choice, assume one of the surviving characters in the Story, and write in it: and that out of more than Half an hundred. . . . I shall pick and choose, alter, connect, and accommodate, till I have completed from them, the requested volume."[67] Ironically, the "piracy" of the early parts of the work allowed Richardson to intensify these efforts, giving him time to circulate the proofs and request further suggestions for revision from his readers (Harris, *Samuel Richardson* 135)—all the while claiming to his European editor Stinstra that Grandison was "entirely new and unborrowed, even of my self" (quoted in Eaves and Kimpel 376).

---

bler and *Adventurer.* Her most influential publications, *Letters on the Improvement of the Mind* (1773), *Miscellanies in Verse* (1775), and *A Letter to a New-Married Lady* (1777), appeared after Richardson's death.

66. Although the bulk of his collaborative efforts engaged women, he did occasionally contact men, enlarging his community of readers far beyond his immediate circle. He requested William Lobb, for instance, to ask his father for "a sketch [of Sir Charles Grandison] from his own heart" (Eaves and Kimpel 368).

67. Richardson claimed that an unnamed correspondent made this suggestion, but it seems more likely that he made it himself to test the idea on Lady Bradshaigh. See Eaves and Kimpel 412.

Grandison thus represented a public consolidation of Richardson's life-long collective urge to engage women readers and writers.[68] Richardson had been instrumental in finding a publisher for Charlotte Lennox, had printed Elizabeth Carter's edition of Epictetus (making her £1000), had printed Sarah Fielding's novel *The Governess* and even Jane Collier's "Essay on the Art of Ingeniously Tormenting" (Eaves and Kimpel 357, 202–3), and had made strenuous efforts to engage in intellectual correspondences with Mulso, Talbot, and Carter. He even helped Letitia Pilkington with gifts of money and clothes, although he never published her notoriously low memoirs. In Anna Meades's view he was a "guardian to ye female sex" (Eaves and Kimpel 565). More than a guardian, Richardson seems to have been an obsessive collector of women. In 1750 we are hardly surprised to find him composing the famous "list" of thirty-six examples of what he called "superior women" as part of a defense of women's learning and wit (Eaves and Kimpel 343).

Richardson's collaborative process, especially the long letters to young women giving advice on behavior as well as authorial development, makes modern readers uncomfortable. The lengthy intrigue with Lady Bradshaigh, organized around his desire to see as well as correspond with her, and his references, bordering on the illicit, to Sophia Westcomb's "hoops" undermine the construction of these relationships as purely paternal (Carroll 65). At the very least, his repetitive pleading with correspondents to continue what sometimes seem long and tedious exchanges suggests that the female communities he imagined were less consolidated around him than he may have wished. While many of the women enjoyed these lengthy correspondences, the contrast between his representation of these relationships as placid and mutually enjoyable and the resentment of at least some of those he wished to claim as female followers suggests a certain amount of coercion. For example, in 1747, Richardson appropriated Carter's "Ode to Wisdom" for *Clarissa.* Carter responded angrily; she was not in the habit of publicly circulating her work, which she quite possibly saw as above publication in what was, after all, a mere novel. Carter wrote, "To print any thing without the consent of the person who wrote it, is a proceeding so very ungenerous and unworthy of a man of reputation, that, from the character I have heard of you, I am utterly at a loss how to account for it" (Eaves and Kimpel 215). Although Carter forgave him, Richardson even more unaccountably reprinted the poem *again* in a later edition of *Clarissa,* again without permission, this time noting that it was set to music "in so masterly a manner as to do credit to

68. See McKillop, *Samuel Richardson* 159–225, for an extended discussion of Richardson's circle.

[Carter's] performance" (Eaves and Kimpel 216). Only for its third reprinting did he receive her permission.

Richardson's relationship with his friend Aaron Hill's daughter Urania, who after her father's death he called the "daughter of his mind," further suggests the double-edged nature of his relationships with women. She was left penniless by her father's death in 1750. In 1756 we find her expressing gratitude for Richardson's gifts of pens and paper and by 1758 begging him for a single frank. But when she sent him her novel *Almira,* no doubt hoping he could help her gain the same kind of success he had found for Elizabeth Carter, he responded with what sounds even now like damning criticism: "Need Brutus be made so very a brute? And withal so shockingly silly?" "Crudelia's false Letter not sufficiently clear'd up." "A Lady writer, should not, I think, be so particular in describing Florello's disposition to retire on the wedding night." Although the novel was apparently published almost immediately thereafter (the *English Short Title Catalogue* lists an anonymous novel called *Almira* published by Ann and Charles Corbett in 1758 and several subsequent reprints), Urania responded angrily and ended the decades-long friendship. Richardson later wrote to a friend, confessing rather defensively that "I might be mistaken. But surely, the unwelcome observations I made, show that it was not for want of pains and attention—at a time too—but I will only say, I truly meant service, not criticism. Who but the lady was to see what I wrote?" (Eaves and Kimpel 325–26)

Richardson's response to Urania Hill makes legible the stakes involved in managing the threat women writers represented. The criticisms of *Almira,* consistent with Richardson's lifelong project to distance English writing from the romance and other "foreign" influences and re-present it in a new but entirely naturalized form, focus on limiting female aggression and sexuality. But the collecting of women writers, their shaping and containment, should be read not so much as just another example of male domination but as one of the manifestations of Richardson's English project, his effort to cement into place a viable model of Englishness even as the old models were being dismantled. Although neither the compliant Catherine Talbot (her "considering drawer" full of unpublished writing) nor the derivative Sarah Fielding (in a letter to Richardson, Edward Young had said of her appreciatively, "I have read Miss Fielding with great pleasure. Your Clarissa is, I find, the Virgin mother of several pieces; which, like beautiful suckers, rise from her immortal root" [Eaves and Kimpel 202]) seems particularly threatening to a newly integrated model of Englishness, Richardson's writing is laced with concerns about disruptive women authors. To his Dutch friend Johannes Stinstra he wrote:

I think, Sir, we in England may glory in numbers of women of genius. I in particular may—I could introduce you, Sir, to such a circle of my own acquaintance!— . . . O that we had been able to keep our women of condition to ourselves; that we had not given way to their crossing the narrow seas into a neighboring kingdom! since we have very few instances of ladies returning from thence improved . . . they should not be allowed to go abroad, and to places of public entertainment so often as they do." (Barbauld 5:266)

Richardson's fear of women "of genius" who seek their entertainment abroad and in "public" suggests a conflation of women, the foreign, and romance, a powerful triad that threatened his efforts to consolidate the novel around Englishness. Amatory fiction, with its foreign influences, hidden codes, and its reduction of queens and princes to sexualized bodies, not only presented a direct threat to the government (prosecutions of authors had resulted in some cases) but also did so from a migratory perspective that tended to undermine any construction of Englishness as different or unique. If works critical of Englishness could be "translated from the French and then from the Italian," as Mary Manley's *New Atalantis* claimed to be, written by women drawing from the French romances, and filled with characters who exhibited "foreign" behaviors and had "foreign" names, then how could England maintain its moral superiority over Europe?

Richardson reiterated such concerns in Grandison's remarks on female writers where when Grandison argues that "the titles of wit and poetess, have been disgraced too often by Sappho's and Corinna's ancient and modern" he suggests the complex conglomerate threat that women presented to Richardson's orderly view of Englishness. In *Grandison* the simplistic model of power and resistance so often invoked in postcolonial studies appears in more complicated form in the tangled relationships Grandison forges with intelligent, ambitious, only intermittently compliant women—women who by virtue of the epistolary form compete with him as writers.[69] That in *Grandison* the foreign is represented in Clementina, a woman who could have been taken directly from the early-eighteenth-century romances Richardson so clearly rejects, seems hardly coincidental. Clementina's excessive writing, her madness, her rebellious and troubling invasion of England seem symptomatic of the disruptive potential women writers represented to Englishness. As one of Richardson's

69. Anne McClintock helpfully articulates the critical rejection of the postcolonial model of power and resistance. She favors a model focused on the "dense web of relations between coercion, negotiation, complicity, refusal, dissembling, mimicry, compromise, affilation, and revolt" (*Imperial Leather* 15).

female admirers remarked, Clementina "annihilated" *Grandison,* consuming reader interest and attention so comprehensively that she turned the other characters into mere shadow figures (Eaves and Kimpel 353–54). Clementina's refusal to be woven into the story of Englishness gets to the heart of Richardson's ambivalent relations with women, operating at the intersection of the romance with the foreign, the female, and the ungovernable and thus revealing an anxiety about difference that Richardson never successfully resolved. That he worked so hard and yet was so clearly unable to integrate female authority into his vision of a coherent community marks her as the limit case, the outer edge of English authorial tolerance for difference. Faced with a similar resistance in his real world mentoring of Hester Mulso, who argued in favor of women's economic independence, Richardson offered up a vivid metaphor for female containment. Dismissing her arguments he remarked airily, "We love our wives so well, that we could eat them and drink them" (Eaves and Kimpel 563).

Consumption or Abjection: Sending Them to America

The consumption of radical difference, its incorporation into the body politic, drives Richardson's efforts in *Grandison.* As I have suggested, the novel's biggest difficulty lay in digesting Clementina, that unresolved and dangling "particular" that vexed the end of volume 7.[70] By the end of Grandison's last visit to Italy, he has extricated himself from the prospect of a Catholic marriage and can announce that "the writer of this will be allowed to consider himself wholly as an Englishman." But while the rejection of Catholicism marks one as "wholly an Englishman," only the digestive, assimilative virtues of "tolerance" allow Englishness to dominate internationally. Clementina's movement from Italy to England demonstrates the dynamic. Tolerance reverses the poles of attraction: in the last volume, when Clementina flees her oppressive and brutal Italian relatives on the aptly named ship *Scandaloon* to seek a cure at the more liberal Grandison Hall, she sees England as a remedy for foreign absolutism. Her sudden appearance is remarkably destabilizing. She engages all of the suddenly feverish Harriet's attentions, distressing Grandison's bevy of adoring women, who begin to fret over the possibility that Harriet will miscarry Grandison's progeny. The reintroduction of the metaphor of the ever-growing family suggests a lateral disruption of what should be linear

70. See Harris, *Samuel Richardson* 135, and Chaber for other interpretations of the unsatisfying lack of closure in volume 7.

growth: Harriet's pregnancy and subsequent production of heirs. That Harriet agrees to correspond with Clementina's mother "to make myself, as the Marchinioness fondly says, an Italian woman, and her other daughter" does not seem reassuring (7:458).

In struggling to bring the Italian and Catholic threat that Clementina represents under English control, Richardson lights on a powerful device borrowed from the history of English-European relations: the erection of a "temple" to tolerance. Charles I's courtship of the Spanish infanta in 1623 had raised similar issues and resolved them with a similar device. During the complex negotiations that plagued that affair, Charles had been encouraged to feel "at home" at the Spanish court while his putative bride attempted to learn English. But like Grandison and Clementina, the royals had difficulty resolving whether the children would be raised Catholic or Protestant, and the engagement was broken off. King Philip signaled a friendly end to the encounter when he "erected a pillar, on the spot where they took leave of each other, as a monument of mutual friendship" (Hume, *History* 5:108). Richardson appropriates this device. On entering his English gardens with Harriet and Clementina immediately prior to Clementina's final departure for Italy, Grandison chooses a "blessed spot with my eye." All three "mark" the place as Grandison announces his plan to build "a little temple . . . on that very spot, to be consecrated to our triple friendship" (7:455). As Grandison proclaims in Richardson's most famous "cosmopolitan" passage: "Friendship, dearest creatures, will make at pleasure a safe bridge over the narrow seas; it will cut an easy passage thro' rocks and mountains, and make England and Italy one country" (7:454). English tolerance trumps Italian tyranny and unites the two despite their differences. As Richardson's final word on English tolerance, the passage offers an idealized response to difference, one that seems unconvincing given Richardson's real world response to the "vileness" and "wickedness" of what he called the Irish "invasion." In fact, the novel ends not with the "temple to friendship" but with what seems like an afterthought to an afterthought—the carefully observed and recorded death of Harriet's ill-fated kidnapper, Sir Hargrave, the last of those Europe-influenced aristocrats who had conspired against her. "It is a hard, hard thing to die," moans Harriet, who inherits a sizable chunk of his estate. The death of the kidnapper reinvests Grandison's tolerance with the authority of narrative closure, but it also points to the brutality that meets those who cannot be absorbed into the story.

Richardson could not do away with the Irish pirates quite so easily. His reaction to the piracy—because it revealed the brutality behind English tolerance—complicated *Grandison*'s construction of an English identity based in tolerance and memorialized in the temple to friendship. In the preface to *Grandison*, Richardson tried to "produce into public view a man of true honour" (4), to construct a "good man" capable of withstanding violence without engaging in it. Like the successful nation, the good man manages threats to his authority through recruitment and assimilation. Yet as the ending of the novel reveals, brutality undergirds this civil facade. Grandison's refusal to turn to violent solutions is a power play of sorts; the astute reader realizes that Grandison's efforts to control others without exercising violence over them works only because the plot holds violence in reserve. The Irish piracy "outed" English violence by testing the tolerance the novel promoted. Unlike Grandison, Richardson and his peers failed the test; in their tracts, newspaper articles, and letters, they abandoned the civil discourse of the novel to adopt a language of xenophobic accusation. Because the Irish printers refused English "reform," they were branded pirates and threatened with, if not a metaphorical execution, at least expulsion from the community of printers. The anti-piracy tracts thus revealed the lurking threats of violence behind claims to national integration. When "nation" fails discursively, the threat of punitive measures steps in. This potential violence shores up the nation and operates as its fail-safe mechanism, but it also points to the weakness and contingency of its cultural construction.

Unable to integrate the Irish "invasion" into the composition of the novel, Richardson eventually charged the Irish with cutting short both the novel and his career as a novelist. Ending the novel much more abruptly than he had intended, he blamed the "unprovoked treatment I met with in Dublin" for its unresolved conflicts (Barbauld 5:159). He seems to have been unaware that this understanding of his "treatment" by the Irish as "unprovoked" pointed to a central conflict plaguing his construction of Englishness—the desire to escape responsibility for violence while simultaneously enjoying the benefits of a history of colonization and imperialism. The "little temple" stood for the proposition that radical difference could coexist in harmony. If it had been Richardson's final comment on the Celtic periphery, it might have suggested that he had integrated the Irish "invasion" into his understanding of English tolerance by the time he finished the last pages of the novel. But Richardson's 1758 correspondence indicates otherwise. There he speaks directly to English-Irish affairs in the real world context of imperial violence:

> Why is it necessary, in Ireland, any more than in Prussian Silesia, a conquered province, that a Roman Catholic must be looked upon as an enemy to the government that protects him? I too well know from history what

may be said. But what an additional strength would unanimity bestow upon both islands, could both sides meet in love and trust? What wisdom in the measure of sending to America batallions of brave and hardy Highlanders! (Barbauld 5:187–88)[71]

Writing while still immersed in revisions of *Grandison,* Richardson argues here for a Grandisonian truce between England and Ireland in terms that barely conceal such an agreement's underlying aggression. This transformation of the Irish into imperial cannon fodder reveals the usefulness of English tolerance to the pursuit of empire and—because it delineates the nature of Grandisonian tolerance so clearly—calls into question the novel's construction of a disinterested cosmopolitan England.

71. Richardson was writing a supportive response to a treatise by Smyth Loftus, who had recommended that Irish Catholics be persuaded to support the English war effort (Eaves and Kimpel 549).

[2]

Ossian's Embrace: Johnson, Macpherson, and the Public Domain

> Are forgeries . . . and their exposure not
> almost essential to national movements?
> CHRISTOPHER HARVIE, "Anglo-Saxons into Celts"

We now leap from Samuel Richardson to a third-century Scottish bard called Ossian, a leap that others have made before us. Walter Scott compared Richardson's exemplary Sir Charles Grandison to Ossian's central male character, suggesting that Ossian's Fingal combined "all the strength and bravery of Achilles, with the courtesy, sentiment, and high-breeding of Sir Charles Grandison" (quoted in Moore 43). Overlooking the question of Ossian forgeries to place the phenomenon that was Ossian between the civility of Grandison and the brutal national epics of Homer, Scott prefigured contemporary critics who have focused on Ossian's role as a Scottish national symbol, a symbol that made Scotland whole as a result of its ability to straddle genres, worldviews, Highland and English culture, oral tradition and literate transmission. The discussion in this chapter sets Ossian—and his forger-translator James Macpherson—not against Grandison but against Samuel Johnson, Ossian's most influential and vocal detractor. Despite Johnson's best efforts to debunk the Ossian forgeries, the collected poems became a prominent national sign in international and intercolonial contexts, one that influenced not only European but also English constructions of orality and literacy, reaching even into the heart of England's national life by reinventing its copyright law.[1]

---

1. Dafydd Moore offers a nuanced understanding of Macpherson and his cultural milieu. In refining and sentimentalizing the Ossian epic, James Macpherson evinced a "mus-

The story of the Ossian poems is now well known. James Macpherson, alternately described as Ossian's popularizer and translator or as an outright forger, brought Ossian into the international limelight in the 1760s.[2] Born in Highland Scotland in 1738, Macpherson received his education in the Lowlands from men such as Thomas Blackwell, whose work on Homer was a major influence. In 1758 he wrote and published a long but unsuccessful poem, *The Highlander.* After the failure of this, his only "legitimate" poetry, he aligned himself with Scottish scholars to recover and repackage what he claimed were fragments of ancient Scottish verse. The support of this "Scottish cabal" led in 1760 to his first successful publication, *Fragments of Ancient Poetry Collected in the Highlands of Scotland and Translated from the Gaelic or Erse Language.*[3] Later Macpherson's Edinburgh supporters—Scottish nationalists who had also advocated for a Scottish militia against English opposition—raised a subscription to finance Macpherson's travels to rural Scotland so he could research additional Gaelic works. Between 1762 and 1765 he published a number of poems which he claimed were genuine ancient Scottish epics. The poems directly engaged the relation between authorship and competing definitions of British identity which were being played out in both aesthetic and legal arenas throughout the second half of the eighteenth century. In doing so, they provoked more than fifty years of controversy over their status.[4]

The poems became a best-selling sign of a romanticized version of

cular sensibility" that testified to the continued tension between the brutality of an earlier era and late-eighteenth-century efforts to civilize or "feminize" Britain (44). Sir Walter Scott's commentary on Macpherson's "translation" of the Ossian poems can be found in his review of the *Report of the Committee of the Highland Society* and of Malcolm Laing's edition of the poems. After studying the new evidence these two works presented, Scott concluded that the poems were more forgery than translation or even adaptation. For bibliographies of Macpherson and Ossian, see Weinbrot 526–27 and the on-line resource at *http://www.c18.rutgers.edu/biblio/macpherson.html.* The best and most widely available edition of the Ossian corpus is Gaskill's edition of Macpherson's *Poems of Ossian.* Stafford and deGategno offer full accounts. Trumpener's *Bardic Nationalism* offers a compelling reading of the Johnson-Macpherson controversy and of the battle for oral culture.

2. See Trevor-Roper for a diatribe against Macpherson. See Murphy for the argument that Macpherson was a translator in the largest sense of the word "translate" (*Poetry* 27–28). Matteo argues that because the Ossian poems were represented as "translations," they exercised a particularly destabilizing effect. In "Ossianic Liminality," Leerssen offers a nuanced view of the current state of the question of Ossian's authenticity and its impact on the critical conversation: "The question of *Ossian*'s authenticity is intractable. There is no clear-cut Boolean alternative between 'true' or 'false'. There is, instead, a blurred grey zone between the authentic and the counterfeit, a sliding scale from literal translation to free translation to adaptation to reconstitution to re-creation to manipulation to imitation to falsification" (2).

3. See Sher, "Those Scotch Imposters," for a sympathetic discussion of the political aims of Macpherson's supporters.

4. See Folkenflik for an early recognition of Ossian's importance as a threat to the construction of an English national literature.

the Scottish past. As Peter Murphy has remarked, "Macpherson was one of the greatest of Highland exporters" (*Poetry* 36), marketing the Highlands to the Scottish Lowlands, to England, and most successfully to Europe. Acclaimed by Europeans and Scots alike as great epic works, Ossian's poems were immensely popular. They served to transform the image of Highland Scotland in the minds of both Lowland Scotland and England, persuading those who believed in Ossian's authenticity that the Highlands were typified not by dreary, arid landscapes and an illiterate population, but by a primitive, sublime grandeur with almost universal appeal.[5] After Macpherson's first Ossianic publication in 1760, others began to appear in Italian and French. Ossian became "proverbial" in German circles.[6] The list of those influenced reads like an international hall of fame: Napoleon, Goethe, Madame de Staël, Schubert, Brahms, Oscar I of Sweden, and Jefferson (Pittock 154–55). Serving as the basis for at least two operas, *Les Bardes* by Lesueur and *Uthal* by Mehul, the poems also inspired a series of politically telling paintings (Rosenblum and Janson).

In 1802 the painter Anne-Louis Girodet-Trioson first exhibited one of these paintings, a work commissioned by Napoleon titled *Ossian and His Warriors Receiving the Dead Heroes of the French Army* (figure 1).[7] Although the work thrilled the French with its allegorical content and its mix of classical and romantic styles, its provocative subject would have been what most interested an English audience. Girodet's work captured the political concerns that transformed Macpherson's popularization of Ossian into an international literary scandal. In the painting, he foregrounds the famous bardic representative of Scottish Highland culture, splashing him with light and surrounding him on all sides with symbols of European national interests. Ossian and the Ossianic warriors welcome the French with outstretched hands, as a soldier meant to represent the English stabs at a young French officer (Okun 351). While granting Ossian status as an important Scottish national symbol, the painting marginalizes the English role: the Englishman is reduced to a mere annoyance, a metaphoric hornet in a scene dominated by Austria, France, and, most important, Scotland. Merging issues of authorship and international pol-

5. See Leneman. For the effects of Ossian on English literature in particular, see Stafford, "Dangerous Success."

6. Howard Weinbrot quotes John Colquhuon's remark of 1806: Ossian is "almost proverbial in Germany for everything that is wild, romantic, melancholy, pathetic, and sublime" (546). For Ossian's international influence, see Gaskill, "Ossian in Europe"; Tombo; Van Tiegham; deGategno, "Source of Daily and Exalted Pleasure"; Matteo; and Boker. For an analysis of Ossian imitations and adaptations, see Laughlin.

7. For detailed discussions of the painting, see *French Painting, 1774–1830: The Age of Revolution* 455–57, and Okun.

Fig. 1. Anne-Louis Girodet-Trioson, *Ossian and His Warriors Receiving the Dead Heroes of the French Army* (1802). Courtesy of Giraudon/Art Resource, New York.

itics, the painting makes Ossian a representative of Scottish culture in the battle for cultural hegemony, associating him with images of conquest and invasion. Yet it also suggests Ossian's embrace of European interests, an all-encompassing tendency toward expansion reminiscent of Grandison. By juxtaposing the larger-than-life bardic Ossian's embrace of the French military officers with the relatively insignificant English soldier and his pen-like sword, the painting trivializes English concerns and capitalizes on the bard's value as a threat to English cultural dominance.[8]

8. See Colley's *Britons* and Newman for discussions of England's relationship to France during this period.

The painting suggests Ossian's centrality to a swirl of conflicts, all of which were played out in the forgery accusations against Macpherson as well as in the copyright debates of the 1770s. As much as the painting, the forgery accusations, counteraccusations, threatened lawsuits and violence, and a flood of tracts and treatises attacking and defending Ossian provide insight into the Ossian poems' cultural value. The struggle involved a complex web of cultural and legal forces that not only elevated Ossian but also helped transform Samuel Johnson from London author into a traveling monument to English values. I began this book with the image of Johnson fending off Macpherson with a prototypically English oak staff. As that image suggests, Johnson played a key role in opposing Macpherson, stirring up English doubts about the Ossian poems' origins and even traveling to Scotland to contest their authenticity. In the process he consolidated his representative value by reinscribing a divisive dichotomy between English literate and Highland oral culture, between modern authorship and bardic orality.

Johnson was perhaps more than any other eighteenth-century author responsible for a persistent normalization of literacy, for associating literacy with a newly modernized England. But his effort to equate orality with the past and literacy with the present strategically misrepresented a relationship between the two characterized by interdependency and synchroneity. Most of the English as well as most Scots were still illiterate and if anything, the Lowland Scots had a higher literacy rate and a more developed educational system than the English did. England continued to cling to many habits typical of oral cultures until at least the nineteenth century. Even its legal system, which was beginning to resist orality as it became more and more dependent on written records and printed codifications, was, and still is, heavily dependent on oral declamations from judges. The print industry itself relied on orality, using sometimes illiterate criers to advertise its wares. No better example of the intertwining of oral and literate culture exists than that of the Johnson-Boswell relationship, an ironic reversal of the literate-oral split in which English orality was inscribed by a Scottish pen. In an environment in which both England and Scotland occupied similar positions on the oral-literate continuum, to claim literacy for England revealed an anxiety about the hierarchies of internal colonialism as much as any reality about stages of development.[9]

9. See Cressy and Vincent for discussions of literacy during this period. There is much scholarship on the oral-literate continuum, a concept that informs recent work in the "oral tradition" as well as literacy studies. See Edwards and Sienkewicz and Tannen. Comparative studies of literate and oral cultures commonly argue that literate cultures tend to devalue oral ones as part of a desire to establish cultural dominance (Goody 201).

In this context, and under pressure from his Lowland supporters, themselves caught up in the need to construct a version of Scottish history that could compete with Englishness, Macpherson attempted to straddle oral and literate culture, mixing the celebration of Ossian's preliterate status with claims to written proof of the poems' authenticity. The claims he made and categories he adopted in Ossian's defense were largely inapplicable to his authorless, mixed oral and written sources. Refusing to admit to anonymous, diffused authorship, he not only overemphasized the authorial role of the bard, attributing works to Ossian when such attribution was hard to prove, but also claimed written sources when much of his information was orally transmitted. By distorting his material, he competed successfully in a marketplace that elevated authorship and required a strong author-text connection, in part so that nations could promote themselves through their subject-authored works. At the same time, by adopting literate values, he unintentionally exposed his project to the authenticity challenges he was trying to avoid.[10]

The very popularity of Macpherson's project drew intense criticism from the English and from some Lowland Scots throughout the last third of the eighteenth century. They accused Macpherson of forging the poems, or at best of having created the stories from a few hints derived from Irish, not Scottish, songs and stories. In response, he equivocated; he never presented the original manuscripts for public inspection in England, and after the bitter feud with Johnson, refused to discuss the issue. As late as 1805, the Highland Society of Scotland formed a committee to produce a quasi-legal report on the work's authenticity. It concluded that the legends Macpherson claimed as real *were* real, but that he had edited, rewritten, and inserted much new material.[11] Other, less invested forums were harsher. Over the years volumes have been written in attempts to prove either that Macpherson was the translator he claimed to be or that he was a fraud.[12] But in the 1950s, Derick S. Thomson established that Macpherson had at least based his work on authentic Gaelic sources, including "some fourteen or fifteen Gaelic ballads" (*Sources* 10). More recently, Howard Gaskill proposed a reevaluation, one that sees Macpherson's work as based on an authentic oral tradition and views Macpherson himself as having been "under considerable pressure to produce something which could serve as a much-needed boost to national pride" ("'Ossian' Macpher-

10. For an interesting discussion of how Macpherson's claim to written sources undermined his cultural authority, see Groom.

11. See Mackenzie.

12. For two opposing views, see Graham and Laing.

son" 134).[13] Although scholars continue to be influenced by national politics, the most reasonable and useful position still seems to be that of the Highland Society's report, which viewed Macpherson's works as a mixture of bardic tradition, folk tradition, and Macpherson's ingenuity. This view is supported by Thomson's judgment that "Macpherson was neither as honest as he claimed nor as inventive as his opponents implied," an assessment based on the finding that "in *Fingal,* his most elaborate work, we can identify at least twelve passages, some of them fairly lengthy, in which he used genuine Gaelic ballad sources, sometimes specific versions" ("James Macpherson" 190). In short, although no one can argue for Macpherson's honesty when he claimed in the introduction to the *Fragments* that "the translation is extremely literal" (6), the charge that Macpherson created Ossian independently of source materials also seems too extreme.

Like other investigations of Ossian and Macpherson, mine reinserts the moral questions presented by Macpherson's literary career into their intercultural context. The cultural war over defining Britishness of course engaged questions of Scottishness and Englishness, but in a larger sense it pitted two views of nation—and of national authorship—against each other. On the one side stood Samuel Johnson's "little England," an insular, protected, and exclusionary imagined community that sought to protect itself from foreign incursion.[14] On the other stood a more diffuse understanding of community, not precisely Scottish but expansionist and assimilationist. As Howard Weinbrot has argued, Macpherson's *Ossian* may have been directed south, toward England, but it represented "the expansion of literature in English beyond specifically English borders and concerns," one which contributed to an "emerging definition of 'British' that includes far more than Anglo-Saxon mythology, history, and literature" (529). These conflicting conceptions of nation were played out in impossibly distorted constructions of authorship and text: Johnsonian authorship with its emphasis on individual production and obsession with the fixed, immutable text was set against Ossianic bardism, with its collaborative production process and mutable oral performances. Neither version of authorship "worked," of course, but what was especially ineffective was the dichotomy between literate and oral, authorial and bardic culture. In truth, Johnson's production of Englishness relied on the collectivist, collaborative, mutable processes of orality, while Macpherson's

13. See also the essays Gaskill has collected in *Ossian Revisited.*
14. See Brooks and Greene for descriptions of Johnson's anti-imperialistic, anti-expansionist tendencies. See Scherwatzky for a discussion of Johnson's "little England" ideal in *Rasselas.*

re-creation of bardic culture could not have been accomplished in the absence of his scholarly literary training in Edinburgh. The instability of this opposition suggests two systems in dialogue with each other rather than a rigid dichotomy.[15] Perhaps Macpherson evoked so much retributive anxiety because he teetered on the knife edge between literate and oral culture, making legible the continuing struggle of all eighteenth-century writing to negotiate concerns associated with oral traditions—concerns with authenticity, mutability, collaborative authorship, the status of the collection, in short, the status of the oral in a post-oral world. The emerging concept of the "oral tradition" would eventually offer one solution to the uncomfortable mixing of oral and literate tradition that Ossian represented. In suggesting a new way of managing the relationship between oral and literate cultures, it would domesticate orality and set it off from what eventually seemed a more stable and normative literacy.[16]

The juridical recirculation of Ossianic concerns in both Scottish and English case law and statute suggests that the Macpherson debates intersected with major cultural and national issues of the period. By examining such intersections, we can reevaluate both the debates and the law: both advanced the cultural categories relevant to the use of literary texts to promote cultural hegemony. On the one hand, English law claimed to be "natural" and politically disinterested, but its investment in literate culture and its growing rejection of its own oral origins implicated it in a pervasive rejection of oral culture, including that of the Scottish periphery. On the other hand, that these concerns so infected English legal culture suggests that the Macpherson controversy had as much to do with England's relationship to orality, with the management of an English oral residue, as with the control of the periphery. The copyright debates of the 1770s reveal that the denial of orality—which, with its uncertainty and mutability, haunted legal culture as much as the literary world—depended on a double displacement. English law still relied on oral practices as well as literate records, and it located its origins in orality so as to appear a local, national phenomenon rather than a foreign import. Locating orality on the periphery *and* in the historical past naturalized English literacy, but it also suggested a fundamental conflict in juridical attitudes toward the oral. In both English culture at large and in the law, literacy represented that which could be collected and kept within bounds while orality troped

15. I rely here on a central tenet of recent theory regarding literacy and orality. As Bruce Smith puts it, "Orality and literacy, far from being fixed entities, are systems of communication that exist in complicated, changing, culturally specific relationships to each other" (120).

16. See Hudson for a history of the term "oral tradition" and for the suggestion that Macpherson and Wood were prominent in developing the concept.

the uncontrollable fringe, that which could never be defined, bounded, or contained and thus had to be wished—or more forcibly thrust—away. But the opposition was unstable. While literacy was essential to large "imagined communities," increasing literacy rates suggested a world of writings spun out of control, disassociated from their origins and put to purposes unimagined at their inception. The reaction was twofold: such anxieties were displaced onto oral culture, which was imagined as *both* a hopelessly diffuse and debased collection of detritus *and* a potentially dangerous sign, as *both* a collection of old "low" songs *and* the gossipy rumor powerful enough to fuel the mob.[17] Those fears that could not be displaced onto orality drove the laws against forgery that might seem most applicable to Macpherson's work, but they were also written into England's first copyright statute, the 1710 Act of Anne, and were reflected in later literary property law developments.[18]

Copyright in England—and only in England, as the Scottish courts were quick to point out—attempted stability by attaching authors firmly to their works. Almost every other jurisdiction gave only limited ownership rights to authors: after a period of ownership, authors were required to cede control of their works to the "public domain" so that they would become accessible and replicable by anyone. The idea of "copyright in perpetuity," the right of authors to control the dissemination of their works even beyond the end of their lives, tended to limit the free and open exchange associated with the public domain—the domain of recirculated stories that had made the oral tradition possible. Thus the English rejection of the public domain in time proved too restrictive even for the English. As Johnson himself eventually realized, strict adherence to authors' rights limited a culture's ability to produce a rich literature capable of serving national unification. By 1774, English law, copying the Scots, had incorporated this realization, loosened the bond between authorship and text, and duplicated the open access to works in the public domain that oral culture had always depended on. We might expect (as I show later in the chapter) that English copyright—with its "fixation" requirement and its authors' rights approach—was constructed in opposition to the "other" of oral culture. Less obvious perhaps are the ways in which it patched literate practices together with a free and open public domain drawn from the oral fringe. The Scots helped invent English copyright law; Ossian was a party to that invention.[19]

17. See Donald for a discussion of London mob activity against the Scots in the 1760s.
18. Statute of Anne, 8 Anne, c.19. See Patterson; Rose, *Authors and Owners;* Feather, *Publishing;* and Ransom for the best discussions of the development of early copyright law.
19. See Tompson for a detailed discussion of the relationship between Scottish and English copyright cases.

"Tumbling in the Hogstye": National Ambition and Literary Fame

That a man of Johnson's stature would expend so much energy on Macpherson seems odder than anything else about the story. Yet Johnson's attentiveness to Macpherson speaks to the important and competing set of values Ossian asserted. Characterizing Macpherson as a man who "would tumble in a hogstye, as long as you looked at him and called to him to come out," Johnson did not hesitate to suggest that Macpherson was capable of stealing the spoons if invited to dinner (Boswell, *Life of Johnson* 306). Such comments provide coded references to Macpherson's career, to what Johnson saw as Macpherson's attention-getting, quasi-criminal forgeries, but also to a refusal to respect cultural boundaries that seemed to Johnson self-evident. Having invited Macpherson to eat at the table of a literary establishment controlled by London and Edinburgh, writers at the center soon found that Macpherson was turning the invitation to his own advantage, using it to promulgate an internationally appealing version of Highland cultural history. The nastiness of the debate, played out in newspapers, pamphlets, and the theater, suggests that the stakes were high. Johnson's account of his trip slammed Macpherson and the Scots in ways already familiar to English readers. Sarcastic English attacks on Macpherson as a low and opportunistic forger seem to appear in almost every genre, from the "ballet pantomime" to manuscript "discoveries" which on closer examination turn out to be parodic imitations poking fun not only at Ossian but also at the arguments of those who supported the works' authenticity.[20] In a typical move, for instance, "The Airs, Duets, Choruses, and Argument, of the New Ballet Pantomime, (Taken from Ossian) Called Oscar and Malvina; or, The Hall of Fingal" mixes the bard's heroic claims with silly songs, a comic reversal that demonstrated the "low" forms that some of the English believed represented real Scottish culture. "I romp'd to'other day with Peggy the brown, And swore I'd give Jenny the fair a new gown," goes one song. In another critique, Ossian is trivialized as a "hocus pocus trick" by a "common poet" (quoted in Metzdorf 49). Johnson could not read Gaelic and thus could not have read the Gaelic verses that transformed his imperial "Tour" through Scotland into an oozing "crawl along ditches" and Johnson himself into a "frog," "toad," "lizard," and "reptile."[21] The brutality

20. See *The Prophecy of Queen Emma: An Ancient Ballad lately Discovered*. For a jab at "Scotch lairds and Scotch professors" who "by mere dint of dissertation . . . proved [the poems'] authenticity," see the cameo appearance of Ossian in the short drama *Rowley and Chatterton in the Shades* (Hardinge 14).

21. Robert Metzdorf translates this sally from the Gaelic and provides a good summary

and crudity of the attack would only have lent support to Johnson's account of the deficiencies of Scottish culture. As a result of one three-month trip to Scotland, he claimed to have produced an authoritative, "extensive," and yet very unflattering overview of Scotland.[22]

Johnson's critique capitalized on Scotland's own anxieties: the country's internal division and cultural insecurity played into English hands. Roy Porter sums up much work on Scottish history when he argues that after the 1707 Act of Union abolished the Scottish parliament:

> Scotland lacerated itself becoming increasingly torn between the Jacobite-sympathizing, Gaelic-speaking Highland clans, which were proscribed after the quietus at Culloden of the Young Pretender's 1745 rebellion . . . , and the Edinburgh-Glasgow axis of capitalist landlords, merchants, graduate lawyers, and clergy, who believed that Scotsmen's economic, cultural and even religious future lay in throwing in their lot with England. (48–50)[23]

As Porter points out, the Scots sacrificed culture to economic security. While Highlanders were systematically and forcefully assimilated into mainstream culture after 1745, even Lowland Scots were encouraged to see their cultural differences as signs of inferiority.[24] Scottish authors adopted English habits. Writers such as Sheridan and Smollett trained themselves to avoid "Scotticisms," to speak like the English (Ferguson, *Scotland* 222). While Boswell at times made a point of "insist[ing] on scot-

---

of the attacks on Johnson, which included slightly more sophisticated but still crude volleys at his sexuality. He suggests as well that Macpherson had a hand in writing Donald M'Nicol's *Remarks on Dr. Samuel Johnson's Journey to the Hebrides.* Boswell generally kept Johnson up-to-date about Scottish attacks on his position (Metzdorf 48, note 13).

22. See Lynch, "Beating the Trail," for an argument that takes up both the brevity of Johnson's visit and his claims to an expansive "view." See Hickey for a discussion of the relationship between Johnson's "extensive view" of Scotland and his position on the relationship between the general and the specific.

23. See Sorensen for an excellent discussion complicating and historicizing Porter's overview.

24. For the methods used by the English to incorporate "this durably foreign culture in with the rest of Britain," methods that included replacing clan law with British law, outlawing Highland clothing, building military roads so that British troops could move more easily through the region, and teaching English, see Murphy, "Fool's Gold" 568–69. Iain Grigor's more personalized account details England's "colonial occupation" as consisting of "clearance and emigration; the exploitation of natural resources through sheep farming and deer afforestation; the exploitation of population resources through military recruitment, the smashing asunder of the traditional society and its established class relations; the divorce by force of the common people from the occupancy of a land they looked upon as their own" (24). He notes as well that during the second half of the century, the Lord Chamberlain's office licensed only plays "which portrayed Scots as quaint pastoralists or as comic characters, and which ridiculed Scottish manners, character and speech" (7).

tifying," such efforts denaturalized the Scots dialect even as they emphasized it.[25] In the end, he also worked carefully with Edmond Malone
(ironically an Irishman) to eliminate many of the Scotticisms from his account of the trip to the Hebrides (McGowan 133). Like Boswell, many
Scots signed on to English linguistic standards as well as other supposedly
"English" values. Typical is John Ramsay of Ochtertyre, who noted that
"the appearance of *Tatlers, Spectators,* and *Guardians* in the reign of
Queen Anne . . . prepared the minds of our countrymen for the study of
the best English authors, without a competent knowledge of which no
man was accounted a polite scholar" (quoted in Duncan 51).

But the relationship between the English and the Scots was more complex than a simple model of assimilation can accommodate. What some
saw as Scottish assimilation into English culture, others read as Scottish
appropriation not only of English ideas, but also of Dutch and other European ones.[26] Scottish adaptability led to a degree of success that carried
a threat of its own. Hume, a strong supporter of Macpherson in the early
days of the Ossian debates, recognized the unsettling nature of the relationship between Scotland and England when he complained in 1757: "Is
it not strange that, at a time when we have lost our Princes, our Parliaments, our independent government, even the presence of our chief no-
bility, are unhappy in our Accent and Pronunciation, speak a very corrupt
Dialect of the Tongue which we make use of; is it not strange, I say that,
in these circumstances, we shou'd really be the People most distinguished
for Literature in Europe?" (*Letters* 285). Although Hume may have over-
estimated the power of the Scottish Enlightenment, he recognized, even
personally embodied, the threat the Scots presented to the English. At
least some Scots offered the English an intellectual challenge that could
not be attributed to simple assimilation.[27] English anxiety in response to
the Scottish threat appears in a number of forms, most graphically perhaps in the many political cartoons representing the Scottish minister Bute
as sexually involved with the English Princess Dowager. As Linda Colley
explains, "The accusation that one Scottish Minister was penetrating the
mother of the King of England was symbolic shorthand for the real anxiety: namely, that large numbers of Scots were penetrating England itself,
compromising its identity" (*Britons* 122). Fears of the "creeping Scotti-
cization of national life" were particularly strong in the 1760s and 1770s,

25. For an interesting discussion of the English distaste for Scotticisms, see Basker.
26. For a discussion of this dynamic, see Phillipson.
27. For discussions of Hume's letter, see Nairn 139 and Mossner, *Life* 389. For a detailed
comparative study of Scottish and English literacy rates and educational systems, see Houston.

when Bute was in power and Scots seemed to be flooding into London (Rogers, *Johnson and Boswell* 193). Predictably, in such a setting national fervor increased.[28] The threat of an encroaching French empire led the English to paranoid imaginings of a French-Scottish alliance, later rein-scribed in Girodet's Ossian painting. Indeed, after Culloden the British prohibited the Scots from maintaining a militia: it is no coincidence that the same politically active Scots who complained of this tyrannical English prohibition helped organize and fund Macpherson's collecting journeys into the Highlands and the publication of the first Ossian poems (Sher, "Imposters" 56).

Although the Princess Dowager in one lewd print is made to remark of Bute, "A man of great parts is sure greatly to rise" (Colley, *Britons* 122),[29] the rise of a Scot before 1760 tended to be controlled by English institutions, whether political or literary. What the Scottish Enlightenment lacked was the populist connection to Scottish culture provided by the Ossian works.[30] In this environment, Macpherson's Ossian was brilliantly conceived to consolidate a competitive version of Scottish identity. The Ossian works geographically united Scotland by representing the Highlands in genteel terms acceptable to Lowland scholars. But they also suggested the possibility of a cultural shift in which Scots could combine the intellectual interests they were thought to have acquired from Europe and the English with a tradition of their own, one that could not be seen as derivative because it gave voice to an independent and ancient Scottish past. Such ancient origins could be demonstrated only through the discovery of an oral tradition, partly because a tradition that predated writing trumped both Irish and English literary histories with their reliance on written records, and partly because an oral tradition sustained across centuries attested to the integrity and unity of the Scottish national community.[31] As John Home wrote in 1761, he traveled with Macpherson "to visit those regions that nursed the genius of Ossian and to gather . . . some

28. Anthony Smith speaks of the English "rise of national sentiment" during the period, and John B. Owen mentions national instability and the resulting insecurity "aggravated by the post-war depression, the emergence of new radical forces, and the growing dispute between Britain and her American colonies." See Smith, "Neo-classicist and Romantic Elements" 86; and Owen 169, 277.

29. See Donald for a discussion of a number of anti-Scot and anti-Bute prints of the period. Some used the Scottish harp in unexpected ways; many reveal the English as under threat (50–56). For instance, in "The Jack-Boot Exalted" (1762), the boot (Bute) "subdues the British lion and scatters the nation's gold to his Scottish placemen, while the English ministers are expelled at sword point" (Donald 52).

30. For further discussion of Scotland's need for populist roots, see Nairn 143.

31. See Groom for the argument that only an Ossian drawn from oral tradition could compete with Irish claims to epic history.

of nature's gems" (quoted in Stafford, *Sublime Savage* 117). The High-lands had nursed Ossian; he had repaid this rocky mother with gems that were even then held in the bodies and minds of local people. Whether Os-sian had ever breathed or not, the idea of an oral tradition joined land and people together seamlessly and "naturally," making of them one body. No more stunning claim to national integrity could be imagined than this: a national community that knitted land, people, and voice together by con-tinuous oral transmission rather than by the later artificial device of print.

Macpherson's claims to a sophisticated (rather than rustic) oral tradi-tion challenged Johnson's lifelong construction of an English literary tradition. In comparison to Ossian's melancholy antiquity, Johnson's Shakespeare and Milton could seem mere boisterous adolescents, while the *Dictionary*'s efforts to "fix" the language through relying on printed quotations suggested all too readily the unnatural cobbling together of English culture. Not surprisingly, Johnson reacted to Macpherson with a powerful combination of Scotto-oral phobia. If the Scots insisted on ex-porting the Ossian poems and with them a hegemonic oral tradition that the English could not match, Johnson would go to the farthest reaches of Scotland in order to demonstrate that such a tradition was impos-sible. Johnson framed his anti-Macpherson campaign as a moral-ethical policing of Scotland. Attacking the "Scotch conspiracy in national false-hood" (Boswell, *Life* 578) and arguing that any Scot who would defend Macpherson proved merely that he "love[s] Scotland better than truth" (Johnson, *Journey* 119), Johnson offered his own character as an indict-ment of Scottish loyalty to Ossian.

But to the extent that Johnson's attack on Macpherson was founded in abstract moral claims based in literary property rights discourse, he was an odd one to make it. As Fredric Bogel has pointed out, much of John-son's own writing "enact[ed] a fraying or dissolving into the texts of oth-ers that precisely undoes the ability to assign property or authorship with certainty" ("Authority" 199). Bogel details various instances in which Johnson's relationship to writing simultaneously intersects with and par-ticipates—however innocently—in literary "crimes" involving writing. What makes these incidents so interesting is that they not only place John-son in close proximity with forgers, but also allow him to assume the voices of the forgers and tricksters he seemed drawn to. In 1749, for in-stance, Johnson ghostwrote a confession for William Lauder, who had in turn written a faked scholarly work "proving" Milton to be a plagiarist (Bogel, "Authority" 200–201). More significant in light of the Macpher-son controversy was Johnson's ventriloquism on behalf of William Dodd, who was accused of criminal forgery for faking Lord Chesterfield's signature on a £4,200 bond (Bogel, "Authority" 201). Taking part in what became a widespread campaign for Dodd's life (23,000 people signed a petition requesting his pardon), Johnson repeatedly begged forgiveness for a forgery he had not committed, writing Dodd's letters and even his *Last Solemn Declaration*. After ghosting this material, Johnson wrote to Dodd in his own, by now compromised voice, defending the act of forgery by saying, "Your crime, morally or religiously considered, has no very deep dye of turpitude. It corrupted no man's principles; it attacked no man's life" (Boswell, *Life* 834).

Johnson's biography reveals a fascination with literary transgression expressed not only in his pursuit of the ethnographic forger George Psalmanazar, whom he pointedly claimed to like better than Richardson, but also in his unveiled admiration for the young literary forger Thomas Chatterton (Bate 211).[32] As Boswell points out, Johnson investigated the Chatterton incident, "enquir[ing] upon the spot" through personal inspection of Chatterton's manuscripts and of the famous church "as I had seen him enquiring upon the spot into the authenticity of 'Ossian's Poetry'" (*Life* 751). Yet Johnson reacted quite mildly to the English Chatterton, despite the fact that, ironically enough, Chatterton was an Ossian forger in his own right (Kaplan 131). Remarking, "This is the most extraordinary young man that has encountered my knowledge. It is wonderful how the whelp has written such things," Johnson summed up Chatterton by reversing the issues of forgery and literary worth, making Chatterton's fraud indicative of precocity rather than mendacity (Boswell, *Life* 751–52). Later Johnson was to distinguish Macpherson from Chatterton. "In Ossian there is a national pride, which may be forgiven, though it cannot be applauded. In Chatterton there is nothing but the resolution to say again what has once been said," he argued in a 1782 letter to Edmond Malone.

The desire "to say again what has once been said"—and to say it in writing—typified Johnson's own relationship to the Macpherson controversy. Johnson's famous letter to Macpherson lent itself to authenticity problems. As it was reprinted in newspapers, copied, passed around, and placed on display, the letter's dissemination and transmission made its authenticity doubtful. Boswell easily persuaded Johnson to authenticate the letter in an after-the-fact reconstruction that suggests Johnson's insecurity about his own auto-forgery: "I give it as dictated to me by himself, written down in his presence, and authenticated by a note in his own hand-

32. George Psalmanazar claimed to be first Japanese and then Formosan, even translating the Anglican catechism into an invented Formosan. See Stewart, *Crimes of Writing*, for an analysis of Psalmanazar's career (31–65).

[87]

writing, '*This, I think, is a true copy*'" (*Life* 579).[33] A final effort to "say again" the Macpherson controversy combined the reiterative desire with what Bogel calls "textual fraying." In 1782, William Shaw, a Scottish disciple of Johnson's, published the last of his series of attacks on Macpherson's Ossian. In light of Johnson's history of ghostwriting, it is hardly surprising to discover that Johnson at least edited and may have ghostwritten much of Shaw's "Reply to Mr. Clark." A comparative examination of the "Reply" reveals a curious mixing of Johnson and Shaw, as if Shaw had plagiarized a summary of Johnson's concerns about authenticity, lexicography, Macpherson, and Scotland.[34] Allowing Johnson one last strike against Macpherson, the final product went to press under the presumably less interested name of a Lowland Scot rather than under Johnson's signature itself (Shaw 400).

When we compare Johnson's intense reaction to Macpherson with his genial reaction to Chatterton, and reconsider the Macpherson controversy in light of a larger contextual field in which ambiguous claims of ownership and authorship often went unchallenged, Johnson's reaction to Macpherson seems particularly illuminating. Johnson's unstable and underarticulated juggling of right and wrong, originality and collaboration, legitimate and illegitimate acts of writing disintegrated when he confronted the relationship Macpherson had constructed between bardic authorship and nation, between oral tradition and authenticity. Perhaps Macpherson provided a simplified, all-too-legible demonstration of what Johnson had attempted in his own career, the construction of a nation-bolstering version of authorship and a corpus of national texts. Macpherson's career provides a parodic and distorted mirror image of Johnson's concerns with collecting and reinscribing the best Englishness had to offer in the most authentic and permanent form, and offering it to the public in the hopes that a rapidly changing culture undergoing modernization could maintain its commitment to the past. Lawrence Lipking, who has said that "no author can teach us more about the literary canon than Samuel Johnson" (159), might as well have argued that no author was more responsible for creating the canon than Johnson.[35] Johnson's works

33. According to Bate, the original letter was eventually located after generations of literary historians had relied on Johnson's dictated version (521). See Johnson, *Letters* 168. See Baines for a discussion of the letter related to forgery.

34. For a discussion that claims the work to have been ghostwritten by Johnson, and for a reprint of the "Reply," see Curley. For an opposing view, see Sher, "Percy, Shaw, and the Ferguson 'Cheat.'" Sher argues that Johnson, though "closely allied with Shaw," should be thought of as a "stylistic editor rather than ghostwriter" (210).

35. Johnson himself engaged in the "invention of tradition" referred to in Eric Hobsbawm's "Introduction: Inventing Traditions," in *The Invention of Tradition*.

provided a collectivist foundation for Englishness, one that, like Macpherson's projects, relocated fragmented cultural ephemera in encyclopedically accessible texts. Thus Johnson's reaction to Macpherson may have involved abject horror rather than bad faith, as Katie Trumpener has argued—a horror arising from the realization that Macpherson had inverted a lifetime of concerns, highlighting what Johnson had understated and trivializing what Johnson had emphasized (Trumpener 81). Macpherson's forgery spoke to Johnson's own ways of concealing his national motives, hiding them even from himself, however obvious they may seem when reviewing the work of his whole literary career. To stop this larger fraying of career into career, textual production of nation into textual production of nation, and thus the diminishment of all that Johnson had accomplished required an exaggerated response that clearly marked the difference between Johnson's aims and methods and Macpherson's.

A "Natural Tendency to Degeneration": National Collections, Authorship, and the Authenticity Effect

In producing the periodicals, the *Dictionary,* the edition of Shakespeare, the *Lives of the Poets,* but also the *Vanity of Human Wishes* and even *Rasselas,* his "little storybook," Johnson served the nation as effectively as the British museum (quoted in Bate 337). He collected the language of the nation, but also its cultural material, its stories, philosophies, and quirks. In *On Longing* Susan Stewart offers Noah's Ark as an apt metaphor for the collection: its production implies the destruction of its origins and their replacement with a new order. Macpherson's own work provides a second example a bit closer to home. In the *Dissertation* he attached to the 1765 version of the *Poems* he argues that the German oral tradition was preserved for centuries through oral transmission and memory: "It probably would have remained to this day, had not learning, which thinks every thing, that is not committed to writing, fabulous, been introduced" (*Ossian* 50). Ironically, given his own project, Macpherson represents literate culture as destructive: it operates not to collect the oral and save it from obscurity but to destroy it. Like Macpherson, Johnson collected various cultural fragments, standing somewhere between the souvenir hunter and the collector. Like the souvenir hunter, he attempted to take items out of history and move them into what Stewart calls "private time," while like the collector, he appropriated the private and made it available for public view. Whereas the souvenir has value only because of the origins that it embodies, the collection destroys origins, removing items from

[89]

their original context and resituating them in a new location, one ordered and given meaning by the collector himself. While Johnson gathered material that referred to the past, he replaced origins with a new system of classification meant to re-authenticate the materials he had collected. Souvenir hunter and collector collapse into each other here, as Johnsonian classification always attempts a return to origins—a foregrounding of the very origins destroyed by the process of collection.

Johnson figures what turns out to be the unattainable origins of the national language through oral culture. What is unrecoverable in his system, almost unimaginable even when most desired, are the oral origins of the nation. Nevertheless, he continually tried to access those origins through collections large and small, of words for sentences and the *Dictionary*, of Shakespeare's plays, and of the English poets. Such gestures toward what can never be fully recovered are foundational to the nation (Wechselblatt 130–31). They suggest a moment of unified integration located in an irretrievable, immemorial past that must be continually supplemented in the present. Even Johnson's less monumental works are important here: the various periodicals—so helpful in constructing a national audience—formed, as W. Jackson Bate tells us, "a repository of some of the finest proverbial wisdom in the language" (335), collecting and unifying the disparate bits of intellectual history, philosophical ideas, stories, and ephemera that make up a nation's shared culture.[36] Bate's use of the word "proverbial" connects Johnson's material to oral culture and suggests that we reread all of Johnson's efforts in light of their position on the oral-literate continuum. The problems his constantly thwarted desire for orality created vexed all of Johnson's projects; it was as if Ossian's ghost hovered in the margins of his works.

Difficulties with orality so undermined the very idea of an English dictionary that Johnson bracketed them from the start; in his heightened claims for the importance of "authors in the language," he denied any role at all to oral expression. The *Dictionary* effected a huge collection—of words, but also of previous dictionaries and grammars, of authors, and of collaborators.[37] Far from the solitary effort that Johnson celebrated when he compared it to the French Academy project, the final product, significantly the first of his works to announce his authorship on the title page, rested not just on thousands of authors' quotations, but on the labor—which may or may not have been confined to transcription—of Robert Shiels, Alexander Macbean, Francis Stewart, and V. J. Peyton, of

36. See Wechselblatt and, of course, Benedict Anderson, for discussions of this process.
37. I am indebted to Allen Reddick and Janet Sorensen, and to Deidre Lynch's "Beating the Track," for my approach to the *Dictionary*.

whom only Peyton was English (Reddick 62). That Johnson relied on Scottish helpers in a work that famously rejected Scotticisms seems inconsistent, yet the use of Scottish assistants made perfect sense: they were non–native speakers, at least of the version of English promulgated in the *Dictionary,* and thus were particularly alert to English usage.[38] Johnson had always admired the Scots for their English. More important, perhaps, they served a symbolic collective function: as invisible translators of the scraps of paper Johnson had collected, they transformed fragments into the text of the *Dictionary,* yet they were also items in the collection, collaborators in a project that would carry Johnson's name. Their role replicated that of Scotticisms in the *Dictionary:* they were not so much incorporated into Britain as subsumed to Englishness. The education of Francis Barber, the young African boy Johnson rescued from slavery, offers a related image of Johnson's effort to align empire with nation. Johnson educated Barber and cared for him, teaching him to read and write. Barber apparently spent at least part of his childhood under the great table in the attic, tracing out, significantly enough, the word "England" on the back of slips used to produce the *Dictionary.* In Barber we see enacted the imperial didactic experience the *Dictionary* meant to effect, one that placed the literacy of the London center hierarchically above the oral cultures of the periphery. Overwritten by the great *Dictionary,* Barber's fragments, his own peripheral history, would not be reassessed until Allen Reddick encountered them in the archives in the late twentieth century.

Johnson relied heavily on previous lexicographers, including Nathan Bailey and Benjamin Martin, and borrowed as well from John Wallis and others for the "History of the Language" and the "Grammar," which he included with the first edition (Reddick 27, 51). The *Dictionary* was, as Johnson said, "bookish," new and interesting because it was the first to rely on word usage in *written* works for its meanings (Reddick 15). Johnson's method, his physical collecting of words and meanings from published works, attempted to formalize and codify a national culture defined by the use of written, not oral, sources, and yet it tried also to "fix" orality. At moments Johnson seemed to think the method equal to his purposes: "If the language of teleology were extracted from Hooker and the translation of the Bible; the terms of natural knowledge from Bacon; the phrases of policy, war, and navigation from Raleigh; the dialect of poetry and fiction from Spenser and Sidney; and the diction of common life from Shakespeare, few ideas would be lost to mankind for want of English words in which they might be expressed" (Preface to *Dictionary* 289). But

---

38. See Sorensen's *Grammar of Empire,* for this insight and for a discussion of the relationship between the Scots and the production of the English language.

Reddick offers some vivid portraits of Johnson's difficulties with books, which in their unmanageability, their dustiness and voluminousness, became a sign of his frustrated desire for a fixed language. As is well known, the great collector eventually had to face the limitations brought to the fore by this production method. The national collection was limited by its inability to deal with the mutability of language: Johnson devoted a good part of the Preface to a lament on language's escape from the *Dictionary*'s capacious hold, reserving some of its most dramatic diction for this problem. Mutability was not simply an oral problem, but he tended to represent it in terms that evoked the physicality of the oral. He wished that language "might be less apt to decay" (280) and regretted "the boundless chaos of a living speech" (282). He had wanted to "fix" the language, but "to enchain syllables and to lash the wind are equally the undertakings of pride" (294). Johnson links the "wind" of oral expression to anxieties about the nation, noting that "life may be lengthened by care, though death cannot be ultimately defeated: tongues, like governments, have a natural tendency to degeneration; we have long preserved our constitution, let us make some struggles for our language" (296). Although the comparison between "tongue," that sign for orality, and "constitution," the sign for government, suggests that he has some hopes for preserving the former, the earlier mention of death has already undone such hopes. Given his frustration and what at times sounds like outright grief, we need wonder less at Johnson's tendency to connect language's mutability to foreign influences, displacing it geographically in an attempt to distance it from the very problems in national identity that the *Dictionary* was supposed to address. Thus Johnson's brief rave against translators: if the English ever "went French" by establishing an academy, he hoped they would use the institution to ban translation rather than compile dictionaries and grammars.

At times, Johnson located this troublesome mutability in literate culture: one reason he offers for the ever-changing quality of language is modernity itself. In complex societies with hierarchically organized labor forces, whole classes have the "leisure to think" and in thinking they tend to enlarge the stock of words (294–95). But Johnson's praise of literate culture's inventiveness participates in a complex and contradictory effort to create a literate middle class against a more negatively portrayed mercantile segment of society. Johnson obviously considers "the leisure to think" and thus create new words a good thing; he contrasts it with what he finds objectionable about mercantile culture, with "the fugitive cant" of the commercial world "always in a state of increase or decay." Commercial words and phrases cannot thus form "the durable materials of a language" and "must be suffered to perish with other things unworthy of preservation" (293). Fair enough. Alastair Fowler makes the same argument in a review of twenty-first-century dictionaries which include words such as "cyberculture" ignoring how quickly they fall out of fashion (5). But Johnson's rationale for omitting the terms of commerce is more complicated than this. Many of the problems involved in capturing this "fugitive cant" he blames on its orality: "I could not visit caverns to learn the miner's language, nor take a voyage to perfect my skill in the dialect of navigation, nor visit the warehouses of merchants and shops of artificers to gain the names of commodities, utensils, tools, and operations, of which no mention is found in books" (292). Could not or would not? The task overwhelmed him in a way that books never could: "It had been a hopeless labor to glean up words by courting living information," he concludes with obvious regret (292).

Johnson's rejection of commercial culture reveals him slipping along the oral-literate continuum. Even the quickest read through Defoe would make one wonder whether words for "commodities, utensils, tools, and operations" were not already available in manuals and books of the period, but if they were not, it could not have been more difficult to visit mines, warehouses, and shops than to cull the famously gargantuan 240,000 quotations from books (Bate 395). Certainly Johnson seems to have had no difficulty sending William Shaw to the Highlands in the 1770s to compile a Gaelic dictionary.[39] But though Shaw overcame Johnson's reluctance to "visit caverns" or "take a voyage," he could not overcome a Johnsonian distaste for the oral. It was not the actual traveling that was at issue, the delving into Highland cottages and homes, but a perplexing failure of imagination. As a disappointed subscriber later testified, Shaw "was not solicitous to hold conversation or enter into correspondence with those who were deemed deeply conversant in the Gaelic language" but instead revealed himself fully invested in the literate practices of his day, more interested in collecting subscribers than lived language. He would not *talk* to people who knew Gaelic (Sher, "Percy" 217, 241, note 36).

With Shaw's example in mind, we might take Johnson's argument against travel metaphorically rather than literally. The physical difficulties of discovering oral usage trope the intellectual difficulties Johnson had in coming to terms with oral culture. Its immateriality and mutability represented an unthinkably exaggerated version of the problem "fixing" the language presented. While the labors of past lexicographers, the tran-

39. See Sorensen 172–96 for a full discussion of Shaw's work.

scriptions of the Scots, and the writings of the nation could be collected, what could not be collected was that "wild and barbarous jargon," which represented both the natural effusions of language and also oral expression with its connections to the land, the wind, chaos, and the very material of lived national life. But commercial culture was, in fact, essential to that national life; ironically, it was the very development that made Johnson's "leisure to think" possible. Johnson's failure to grasp its importance was not merely a matter of personal frustration but something more serious than that. The refusal to engage with issues so deeply integrated into what Englishness meant called any national project into question.

Thwarted by the gap between lived language and its representation, Johnson was to write in 1775 of the elusiveness of colloquial expression: "By reading great Authors it cannot be obtained, as books speak but the language of books" (quoted in Reddick 35).[40] The gaping chasm between writing and oral expression marked class differences and regional differences, but also his own limitations. *Irene,* for instance, his only attempt to stage dialogue, is most often criticized for a "woodenly self-conscious" style that struck listeners as stiff and distancing (Bate 157–58). The failure of style was not for lack of trying; Bate tells us that Johnson suffered over the script, tormenting himself line by line. Revisiting such concerns from a more mature perspective when he edited the edition of Shakespeare and wrote the famous Preface, Johnson celebrated Shakespeare's skill at dialogue. Could he have been comparing Shakespeare's successes to the failure of *Irene* when he said in the Preface to his edition of Shakespeare that most theater "is peopled by such characters as were never seen, conversing in a language which was never heard, upon topics which will never arise in the commerce of mankind"? In comparison, Shakespeare's dialogue "seems . . . to have been gleaned by diligent selection out of common conversation and common occurrences" (302). Johnson imagined that by staging "common conversation," but not low or mercantile conversation, Shakespeare had located and preserved the national treasure of language that had eluded Johnson: "If there be, what I believe there is, in every nation a style which never becomes obsolete . . . this style is probably to be sought in the common intercourse of life, among those who speak only to be understood without ambition of elegance" (306). This did not mean that Shakespeare replicated the vulgar language of the uneducated. Instead, Johnson praised Shakespeare's successful ne-

40. The comment is taken from Johnson's preface to Giuseppe Baretti's *Easy Phraseology, for the use of Young Ladies, who intend to learn the colloquial Part of the Italian Language,* published in 1775. See Reddick 203, note 28.

gotiation of oral expression—his replication of "conversation above grossness and below refinement where propriety resides" (306–7). Such praise resonates oddly with the critical reaction to Ossian, the praise directed at Ossian's ability to straddle the "grossness" of the barbarous past and the civility of the present. Like Macpherson, who in the preface to *Fingal* offered an ancient Scottish culture more concerned with "generous sentiments" (*Ossian,* ed. Gaskill, 36) than with brutal conquest and internecine warfare, Shakespeare had provided the "diction of common life," but in such a civilized package that one would never confuse it with a romp with "Peggy the brown" much less with a trip to London's docks or moneylenders.

Shakespeare's scripts were in disarray when Johnson began working with them. Relying both on handed-down scripts and on the many editors who had attempted the task before him, Johnson tried to bring them to order. The transformation he effected by publishing his edition tells us much about the relationship between the oral and the literate, authenticity, scholarship, and authorship. As Johnson remarked, what had happened to Shakespeare's plays represented a potentially tragic loss: "His works were transcribed for the players by those who may be supposed to have seldom understood them; they were transmitted by copiers equally unskillful, who still multiplied errors; they were perhaps sometimes mutilated by the actors, for the sake of shortening the speeches, and were at least printed without correction of the press" (Preface to Shakespeare 323). Transcription, the rendering of orality into literate form, introduces opportunities for multiplications, for errors, but also for "mutilation" to the natural body of the original. It represents in itself the multiple gaps between Shakespeare's original expression, its replication on stage, the copytexts made at the time, and whatever documents Johnson could obtain. Other potential gaps (just how did Shakespeare manage to capture the original speech of the people that Johnson so admired?) are not addressed, and are instead buried beneath Johnson's preoccupation with transcription. Eliding any examination of Shakespeare's own collection process, Johnson displaced his anxieties onto the collection of copytexts, a concern that reiterated the desire to fill in the gaping distance between oral expression and textual collection. He focused on one issue: Was the "Shakespeare" that Johnson was in the process of repackaging for the world the same as the one that had appeared on the original stage? In the Preface, Johnson sets himself off from previous editors by evincing his concern with the "genuine state" (322) of the plays and their "corruption" (323, 331). Indeed, a good portion of the preface consists of a summary of previous editorial efforts and a meditation on their effects.

Although he had promised in the "Proposals" that "the corruptions of the text will be corrected by a careful collation of the oldest copies" (quoted in Bate 396), he found this difficult to do without ready access to a range of copies. In the end, he "collated such copies as I could procure and wished for more, but have not found the collectors of these rarities very communicative" (331).

Bate suggests that Johnson's efforts to collect early copies of the plays were often unsuccessful: Garrick refused to let Johnson take them out of his house, keeping them locked up with a servant. Others may have been concerned by his cavalier treatment of books he had borrowed when working on the *Dictionary* (Bate 396). If Johnson saw mutilation everywhere in the past, he was not above reproducing it when he tore pages from books as he gathered materials for the *Dictionary*. As Stewart suggests, the "scandal" of collection is its removal of objects from their natural location (*Longing* 135). Collections always sever objects from their context and thus produce a sort of mutilation. Johnson's mutilation of the books he relied on for the *Dictionary,* though their owners could not have been expected to appreciate this, merely enacted materially the process of collecting that he was engaged in. In working on Shakespeare, Johnson took what had already been "mutilated" many times and attempted to recollect it, repairing its "mutilations" by replacing what was missing, or redoing the bad repairs made by previous editors with his careful and scholarly best guess: "These corruptions I have often silently rectified; for the history of our language and the true force of our words can only be preserved by keeping the text of authors free from adulteration." If possible, he "restored the primitive diction wherever it could for any reason be preferred" (Preface 331). Restoration, (silent) rectification, the elimination of adulteration: how he managed to do this all the while claiming that he "confined my imagination to the margin" (333) of scholarly footnotes is left to the reader's imagination. The desire to capture national lived experience trumped scholarship, offering a model for a form of desire that attached both Johnson and his readers to the imagined community of the nation.

Efforts to recapture and repair the gaps between the lived experience of the oral world and its representation on the page informed both Johnson's and Macpherson's projects. Both men worked, though with differing levels of commitment and skill, to locate the past and reproduce it in replicable, transmissible form. What they longed for was direct contact with that past. What prevented this contact was their own positioning in a radically different present. Stewart suggests that the souvenir offers direct contact with a remembered experience, an indicia of "authenticity." Unpacking that idea reveals that what fills the gap between past and present is an authenticity *effect,* a textual impression carefully constructed to reduce the appearance of gaps and omissions.[41] Authenticity then is not a quality so much as a comforting impression, produced textually in scholarly notes, "dissertations," and prefaces, in the careful choice of seemingly antique words, phrases, and modes of expression, as well as in impassioned statements of concern with legitimacy and reliability. The authenticity effect is also projected outside the text, through representations of "outscale" versions of magisterial authorship such as we see in Ossian but also in Johnson. Deidre Lynch, as well as Alvin Kernan and any number of others, have pointed to the "complex, outscale individuality of the authorial psyche" as an eighteenth-century development of which Johnson represents the prime example (Lynch, "Beating the Track," 364). Johnson's scholarship, which seemed the natural accompaniment to dictionaries and editions and yet would be completely unnecessary in a perfect world of seamless transmission, was accompanied by a decidedly odder emphasis on authorship—odd in the sense that it is most exaggerated in the works that seem the least original, the collections and editions.

While in *Rasselas* Johnson can joke about "outscale" authorship, he made authorship really matter in the *Dictionary,* a compilation of authors that carried his own authorial name on the title page. Both the format and the production process of the *Dictionary* illustrate Johnson's elevation of authorship and his construction of the relationship of an author to his work as that "solid and fundamental unit" delineated by Foucault. Significantly, the definition of the word "author" in the *Dictionary* focuses on originality, comparing the author to God: "The first beginner or mover of any thing, he to whom anything owes its original." "Owes" seems a key word here: What is the connection between the "thing" and its "original"? Having removed his thing-like words from their origins, Johnson substitutes authorship for that connection. The production process of the *Dictionary* illustrates authorship put to use as an authenticating device.[42] Here diffused, collaborative authorship is transformed into individualized, identifiable authorship. As a collaborative work performed by a number of people who mined the works of multiple authoritative authors for quotations and pressed them into a form suitable for publication, the *Dictionary* would seem more edited than authored, its competing claims suggesting the tension between a compilation process involving

41. See Walter Benjamin for the ur-discussion of authenticity. Subsequent theorists have deconstructed authenticity in a number of different venues.
42. In my discussion of the *Dictionary* throughout this section, I am indebted to Reddick.

many voices and Johnson's overriding authorial voice. Oddly, subsequent abridged versions of the *Dictionary* sometimes omitted the examples and quotations that provide the real evidence for the proper usage of words. Instead, they offered the reader a decidedly unsatisfying *list,* not of texts but of names of the mostly English authors used to illustrate the definitions. The first abridgment of 1756, supervised by Johnson, underscores the point by advertising the definitions as "Authorized by the Names of the Writers in whose Works they are found" (Reddick 86). Here "authorization" stands in for the actual history and process that the quotations of the unabridged *Dictionary* illustrate. In part the problem was one of producing an *English* dictionary. If the author of the great English *Dictionary* proved to be not English but multiple and partly Scottish, the *Dictionary* could not operate as the "national monument" that many immediately claimed it to be (Reddick 2). In the larger sense of the collection, though, authorship substituted for an orality that could never be recovered, offering the voice of one outscale author in lieu of the numerous voices subsumed by the shadowy quotations that themselves stood in for uncollectible orality. Authorship steps in when scholarship fails. Whereas authenticity bridges the gap between past and present, authorship bridges the gaps between the different artifacts in the collection. Thus authorship, that giant trump card, offered a technique, a way of bolstering authenticity, of papering over the gap between the original artifact and its representation. The more difficult the authenticity problem, the more outscale we can expect the author to become. That authorship is a conventional, generic device, one that belongs to a genre we might call the authenticated text, explains both Johnson's careful construction of his own "outscale" authorial persona and Macpherson's expansion of "Ossian."

Macpherson leapfrogged over the complicated processes of authentication and authorial substitution that Johnson had worked out. He thus makes legible the very authenticating devices that Johnson had so carefully hidden, opening them up to question and even to parody. His manner of collecting oral and manuscript sources—he was said to have returned from the Highlands "with two Ponies laden with old Manuscripts" (sometimes they are referred to as two mules)—in itself suggests a comic deflation of Johnson's collecting processes (quoted in Stafford, *Savage* 123). In comparison to Johnson's lengthy account of his processes of collection, Macpherson merely notes that any such account would be "both tedious and unentertaining" (*Ossian,* ed. Gaskill, 51). As Macpherson had it, he easily gathered transcriptions as well as generations of hoarded manuscripts during a quick six-month journey to the Highlands.

He suffered the same problems with corruption, though, that Johnson had endured: what he found was damaged "by wormeating, and other injuries of time, there were here and there whole words, yea lines, so obscured, as not to be read" (quoted in Stafford, *Savage* 124). Like Johnson when editing Shakespeare, Macpherson found that "frequent transcription and the corrections of those, who thought they mended the poems by modernizing the ideas, corrupted them to such a degree" that he was eventually persuaded to publish them in what he claimed to be a more authentic form (*Ossian*, ed. Gaskill, 51). Though no one would place Macpherson in the same scholarly rank as Johnson—he had none of Johnson's intellectual or scholarly resources and few of the historical records that Johnson was able to rely on—he attempted to reproduce the effect of authenticity in the Ossian works, an effort that became more pronounced over time. The two "Dissertations" introducing the 1765 and 1773 editions were bolstered by Hugh Blair's truly scholarly "Critical Dissertation on the Poems of Ossian," with its dozens of Latin and Greek footnotes, appended to most editions after 1765. Macpherson's summaries at the beginning of chapters attempt a sort of academic integrity, while the footnotes that tell us not only the background of the characters' names but also their diminutives, parody an academic, scholarly style. Like Johnson, he made full use of classical references, mentioning Homer more than forty times in his scholarly apparatus, Virgil more than twenty-five, and the Greeks and Romans quite frequently. He peppers the text with footnotes meant to explain etymology, lineage, and the integrity of the various Ossianic story lines.

That *Fingal* was so patently wrong from a historical standpoint made his various gestures toward authenticity even more legible. In this, his second Ossianic publication, Macpherson quite ahistorically plots a multi-level international conflict in which the united power of the Scots saves the weaker Irish from Scandinavian attack. Choosing Ossian as narrator, both because of the traditional association of bards with national and political themes and because the very existence of the "fame of Ossian" imagines an audience already aware of that fame and prepared to celebrate it, Macpherson constructs an internal audience of listeners and admirers even as he assumes an external one that wished to understand and appreciate the traditions on which he bases the stories. The confusing start of *Fingal* allows Macpherson the opportunity to provide copious footnotes in which to explain, for instance, that "Cuchullin, or rather Cuth-Ullin, the voice of Ullin, [is] a poetical name given the son of Semo by the bards, from his commanding the forces of the Province of Ulster against the Febolg" (*Ossian*, ed. Gaskill, 419, note 3). Such remarks establish the characters as historical figures and the bards as historians, but they are bolstered by references to monuments, ruins, and geological structures, those "edifices" which Johnson was to call "the chief records of an illiterate nation" in the *Journey* (73). Macpherson tells the reader eager for the direct encounter with the past that the remains of Cuchullin's palace can still be seen at Skye; more absurdly, a rock that Cuchullin tied his dog to "goes still by his name" (*Ossian,* ed. Gaskill, 419, note 3).

The frequent listing of battles and cataloging of names lends a sense of authenticity to the narrative through sheer specificity of detail reminiscent of real history, but it is the insistence on the presence of an "outsized" bard in the stories which suggests that the events of the story are being accurately observed and recounted. By including the bard, Macpherson tells us the story of how the story will be told, relying on our eventual experience of the story to confirm the work's internal prediction that it will in time be passed down. This is the dynamic of *The Songs of Selma,* which "fixes the antiquity of a custom" of oral transmission, at least according to Macpherson's footnotes. There Macpherson argues that "the bards . . . repeated their poems, and such of them as were thought, by him, worthy of being preserved, were carefully taught to their children, in order to have them transmitted to posterity" (*Ossian* ed. Gaskill, 463, note 1). Had Macpherson forgotten that he had used almost the same language to describe oral transmission in German culture and in regard to the "Yncas of Peru" in his "Dissertation"? If so, he had failed until now to mention this "proof" of oral transmission processes at work in the Highlands (*Ossian,* ed. Gaskill, 50).

The bard's own antiquity reflects the work's concern with a past always on the verge of being lost to history. The poems offer a doubling of the concern with lineage, referring to it in terms of both real history (the lineage of the Scots) and literary history (the lineage of the poems). Many passages insist on the importance of history and continuity and express regret at the ephemerality of life. For instance, "We shall pass away like a dream. No sound will remain in our fields of war. Our tombs will be lost in the heath. The hunter shall not know the place of our rest" (*Ossian,* ed. Gaskill, 97). The very bard himself seems always just about to pass away: "But age is now on my tongue; and my soul has failed. . . . But memory fails in my mind; I heard the call of years. They say, as they pass along, why does Ossian sing? Soon shall he lie in the narrow house, and no bard shall raise his fame" (*Ossian,* ed. Gaskill, 170). What remedies this situation is, predictably, the bard's ability to preserve history in song.

As Macpherson progresses from *Fragments of Ancient Poetry* to the later "epics," his insistence on Ossian as author became more and more pronounced.[43] His growing stress on the bard suggests that he responded to the English privileging of authorship not only by emphasizing and reemphasizing the authorial role of the bard in the tales, but also by constructing the existence of an identifiable single author, whether or not his source material supported that author's existence. He adopts techniques similar to Johnson's, replacing the multiple "authors" of the oral tradition with Ossian, an "outscale" authorial figure who could readily be identified with Scottish national identity. In essence, Macpherson provides the reader not simply with a famous author located in the bardic Ossian, nor with a seemingly authentic text, but with a packaged product in which author and text work together to produce the authenticity effect.

As Katie Trumpener has said in her admirable discussion of Ossian and oral culture, the Ossian poems' central concern is "the vicissitudes of oral tradition" (75). Perhaps Macpherson's most brilliant authenticating device involved the foregrounding of such "vicissitudes," the stylistic attempt to replicate the oral in short, disconnected sentences as well as the intentional inclusion of the gaps in transmission that represented historical distance. Macpherson makes the most of this in the 1773 edition, balancing his new effort to "form a kind of regular history of the age to which they relate" with redoubled efforts to reflect the orality of the original (412). Instead of the dash, he uses full stops; instead of past tense, the present. Both changes emphasized the immediacy of the oral (*Ossian,* ed. Gaskill, xxiii). The newly "authentic" historical frame contrasts wildly with the bursts of expression enclosed within it and further heightens the differences between ancient orality and modern literacy. The poems' orality seems even more natural, more authentic, in comparison to the ornate scholarly frame. This visibility, the pronounced refusal to make the "silent" corrections Johnson had made to Shakespeare's plays, suggests the true collection of oral fragments found in the past and thus promotes authenticity in a way that efforts to paper over the gap between oral and literate never could. But in foregrounding the authenticity of the collection, it foregrounds the collector as well. Such foregrounding almost invited an oppositional scrutiny, one that Johnson provided in his 1773 trip to the Hebrides. In the context of a new edition of Ossian poems, meant to cement Ossian's representation of Scottish national interests, Johnson's transformation of his doubts about Macpherson into a physical and intellectual invasion of Scotland enacted the sort of authentic, materialized authorial presence that Macpherson had tried to provide in the Ossian works.

43. Gaskill points out that in the 1773 edition, Macpherson seems to downplay the role of Ossian, perhaps in response to criticism.

"To Conceive a Little Nation": Johnson in the Hebrides

All of Johnson's frustrated desire for elusive orality came together in the trip to the Hebrides, a trip that could not have been better designed to demonstrate and make visible the gap between orality and literate representation. If Macpherson had filled that gap with "Ossian," Johnson's outscale presence in Scotland provided a modern, fully materialized alternative, an authentic presence to replace Ossian's falsity. Such a reading makes sense of the oddness that the *Journey* is often charged with—its lengthy descriptions of empty landscapes, the assertions that major cities offer nothing to record, the detailing of the mundane with its focus on materiality at the expense of more ineffable qualities. The scant plantings, mocked in the ever-prolonged joke about Scotland's treelessness, troped the larger emptiness Johnson wished to fill and reflected as well the emptiness at the heart of England's own search for an oral, a "natural" national origin. Such concerns emerge in Johnson's compensatory effort to diminish Scotland. Indeed, Johnson's account of the trip seems calculated to demonstrate that Scotland had no separate identity but was merely a lesser, primitive subordinate to England. From the first page, where Johnson emphasizes the antiquity of the Scottish-English alliance, to the last, where he remarks, "After seeing the deaf taught arithmetick, who would be afraid to cultivate the Hebrides?" he emphasizes Scottish subordination rather than Scottish difference (164).

But English hegemony is not the only story told in the *Journey*. From its first pages, one senses Johnson's positive longing for Ossian and all that he signified. Ossian represented the true speech of the people, the orality that Johnson had been attempting to locate throughout his career. The desire to find actual evidence of his existence may have, for a time, outweighed any English need to outdo Scotland. From reading the Ossian poems in books, Johnson progressed to searching for him in the Highlands, retracing the course he imagined Macpherson might have taken more than a decade before. Certainly, Johnson constructed the Highlands as a place of origins, a mountainous country like those that "commonly contain the original, at least the oldest race of inhabitants" (43). Mountains are "the last shelters of national distress," protected places where inhabitants can regroup when under attack (38). The landscape itself was "original," rather than "artificial" and developed (41). Nostalgically he contemplates Scotland as it was before the Union: "It affords a generous and manly pleasure to conceive a little nation gathering its fruits and tending its herds with fearless confidence" (91). This version of community is exactly the opposite of that described in the unhappy Happy Valley of

Rasselas, where men are seduced into entering and prohibited by force from leaving. "To conceive a little nation" means to imagine a nation where men who *might* disperse if they wished—there is nothing to confine them—instead come together naturally "at the call to battle, as at a summons to a festal show" (91).

With imperial certainty, Johnson treats the country as one vast public domain, its history, landscape, and experiences available for his collection. He seems pleased by a song accompanied by a story, advising travelers to take careful note of such remnants of cultural history: "Everything has its history. . . . [N]arrations like this, however uncertain . . . are the only records of a nation that has no historians, and afford the most genuine representation of the life and character of the ancient Highlanders" (50). Johnson never lets readers forget that these stories are fragmented remnants. From the first moment of the narrative, we are alerted to the impossibility of true recollection (Johnson himself cannot remember why he first wanted to come to Scotland), and this is the theme he returns to repeatedly when he is not directly attacking Macpherson's construction of Ossian. Johnson switches rapidly from pleasure to disappointment, from the anticipatory observation that "everything has a history" to complaints about the multiplicity and unreliability of Scottish stories. With unseemly bitterness born from disappointed expectations, he at times rails against the Scots, complaining that first questions are always answered promptly, but answers to second questions "break the enchantment." When faced with a multiplicity of answers to his questions about bardic culture, he shifts ground rapidly: suddenly he finds himself not in the land of the "generous and manly" but afflicted by an "ignorant and savage people" (51). This dynamic—expectation followed by disappointment—echoes his reaction to the Ossian poems. Ossian had suggested that Johnson's dream of a language "perfectly mapped onto the real," as Lynch has put it, could come true ("Beating the Track" 365). His outraged response to Macpherson's blithe claim to have bridged the gap between ancient oral and literate culture and given us intact the original words of a third-century Scottish bard reveals the extent of both his hopes and his disillusionment.

The enchantment broken, Johnson focuses more on ignorance than on generosity in the rest of the narrative. For him, ignorance is the gap that Ossian has filled. "To be ignorant is painful; but it is dangerous to quiet our uneasiness by the delusive opiate of hasty persuasion. . . . If we know little of the ancient Highlanders, let us not fill the vacuity with Ossian" (119). Vacuity is a central figure in the *Journey* as it is in much of Johnson's work. As Johnson says when he arrives at a poorly stocked inn, "The negative catalogue was very copious": "no meat, no milk, no bread, no eggs, no wine," no, as he sums it up, "satisfaction" (48). The country was equally ill stocked. The Scotland Johnson finds suffers from "uniform nakedness," "horrid nakedness," "general barrenness." It is "denuded," a place of "hopeless sterility," "rough, rocky, and barren," "naked of shade," "naked by neglect."[44] As Trumpener has argued, Ossian revealed the Highlands as "one enormous echo chamber, evoking an emphatically oral world"; in a comparison that suggests his own sterile imagination, Johnson found himself unable to hear what was there to be heard (70). In response, Johnson brutally rejected oral culture, a rejection at odds with his pleasure in discovering that "everything . . . has its history" (50). His disillusionment is reflected in his disparagement of the Scottish tradition: "The nation was wholly illiterate. Neither bards nor *senachies* could write or read; but if they were ignorant, there was no danger of detection; they were believed by those whose vanity they flattered" (112). Later he remarks that the state of the Scottish bards was more hopeless than the state of contemporary illiterates: "He that cannot read, may now converse with those that can; but the bard was a barbarian among barbarians, who, knowing nothing himself, lived with others that knew no more" (116). Other comments connect this dismissal of orality to the gaps in transmission that had concerned Johnson for years. A language that "teems" with books makes speech "embodied and permanent." But oral expression, "merely vocal, is always in its childhood. As no man leaves his eloquence behind him, the new generations have all to learn" (115). But the real problem, that which evoked all this anxious anger, can be teased out of the 1782 pamphlet that William Shaw and Johnson may have collaborated on. There Shaw declared that if Ossian "never heard of letters, his poems could therefore only float along the stream of tradition, in which they might be mutilated, corrupted, and confounded with a thousand others; and a traditionary error, once admitted, cannot be corrected" (quoted in Curley 421). The discussion of mutilation and corruption as interruptions to the very stream of tradition seems oddly reminiscent of Johnson's discussion of Shakespeare's plays.

Despite both Macpherson's and his supporter Hugh Blair's freely made admissions that they worked from oral sources, Johnson insisted on framing the debate in terms of text. Johnson's objections to Macpherson, when not focusing on his failure to prove Ossian's authorship, center on the lack of written records. "As there is no reason to suppose that the inhabitants

44. The references to emptiness, loss, "want and misery," ruins, fragments, the sterility of the landscape and waterways ("no fishes are seen, as in England" [39]), and especially the lack of trees are so numerous as to make a complete list of them superfluous.

of the Highlands and Hebrides ever wrote their native language, it is not to be credited that a long poem was preserved among them," he argues (Boswell, *Life* 614). Although at one point he implies that if Macpherson had not claimed to have manuscripts, he "might have fought with oral tradition much longer," other remarks indicate that even the existence of a strong oral tradition would not have legitimated Macpherson's enterprise:

> Why do you think any part can be proved? The dusky manuscript of Egg is probably not fifty years old; if it be an hundred, it proves nothing. . . . There are, I believe, no Erse manuscripts. None of the old families has a single letter in Erse that we heard of. . . . Everything is against him. No visible manuscript; no inscription in the language: no correspondence among friends: no transaction of business, of which a single scrap remains in the ancient families. (Boswell, *Life* 588)

Numerous other comments disparage Macpherson for his failure to provide documents. "I believe there cannot be recovered, in the whole Earse language, five hundred lines of which there is any evidence to prove them a hundred years old. Yet I hear that the father of Ossian boasts of two chests more of ancient poetry, which he suppresses, because they are too good for the English" (*Journey* 117). To be sure, Johnson's focus on literate materiality, on "two chests" of documents, his incongruous attempt to require written documents to authenticate works produced in an oral tradition by a blind poet, picks up on Macpherson's false claims. But it is a move typical of a literate culture, or of one trying to identify itself as such. The Welsh antiquarian Lewis Morris, one of Macpherson's contemporaries, analyzed the desire for text more astutely than most when he recognized that what was important was not so much the writing itself as the existence of a work unaltered since the third century: "If they were handed down by illiterate shepherds or minstrels, without rhyme or numbers, pray what was the *bondage* that kept the words together?" (quoted in Stafford, *Savage* 164).

The depopulation Johnson keeps returning to, an "epidemical fury of emigration" to America (*Journey* 59), figures the loss of Ossianic grandeur. Instead of the vitality of Ossian and his warriors, Johnson finds old women in dirty huts. One, Ossian-like, claims a royal lineage. Like Ossian, she "spins a thread." Unlike Ossian, she is "troublesome to nobody" (8–9). Absence plays out similarly in attacks on Macpherson's works in which the problem of "authenticity" is figured as one of authorship. Boswell quotes Johnson as exclaiming, "The tale of Clanranald has no proof. Has Clanranald told it?" (Boswell, *Life* 588). As the Scottish minister Donald MacQuean put it to Johnson, the question is always whether "Ossian composed that poem as it is now published" (*Journal* 129). At one point Johnson expresses a view remarkably close to what both the Highland report found and twentieth-century scholars believe. "He has found names, and stories, and phrases, nay passages in old songs, and with them has blended his own compositions, and so made what he gives to the world as the translation of an ancient poem," Johnson remarks (Boswell, *Journal* 206). Yet for Johnson such a conclusion, far from suggesting that Macpherson's work may have some value as the authentic record of Scottish culture, merely confirms that Macpherson's Ossian "is not a translation from ancient poetry" (Boswell, *Journal* 204). For the work to promote the Scottish nation, Macpherson must prove that Ossian alone produced the poems and that Macpherson's role was *only* that of a strictly literal translator. As Johnson saw it, "As a modern production, it is nothing" (Boswell, *Journal* 204).

Macpherson's inconsistent response to the demand for authenticity demonstrates his tellingly partial internalization of English values, which can be reconceived as revealing his position astride the oral-literate continuum. Despite his claim to "two ponies" of manuscripts, he hid whatever manuscripts he had. He seemed himself to accept the English devaluation of oral sources. Inviting almost parodic comparisons to Johnson's concerns with Shakespeare's plays, he was known to mutter complaints against bards who had erred in transmission. He thus internalized, even as he tried to defend himself against, the English disparagement of the oral tradition. In doing so, he joined other Lowland Scots like William Shaw, who devalued his discovery of oral evidence supportive of Macpherson's claims, rejecting the oral evidence he found "with indifference and hostility" (Sher, "Percy," 220). Unlike Macpherson, Shaw refused to consider evidence of the Ossian legends when "application was made to some old man, or superannuated fiddler, who repeated over again the tales" (quoted in Thomson, *Sources* 4). In this anti-oral context, no one should be surprised that Macpherson claimed far greater access to written manuscripts than the facts warranted. He never seemed content simply to provide the world with the transcriptions of oral material that twentieth-century scholars such as Derick Thomson praise him for collecting; much of his battle with Johnson centered on his supposed failure to find and display his written records in that locus of literacy, the bookshop. Typical is his response to Thomas Jefferson's request for copies of the manuscripts. Instead of admitting their paucity, he claimed that they were so bulky, so voluminous that he had no time to transcribe them (de-Gategno "The Source" 106–7, note 13).

As if to counter Macpherson's failure to provide textuality, Johnson offered up a textuality of his own. Finding emptiness, he filled the vacuity
with his own writing. In the scene that marks the genesis of the *Journey,*
he describes himself surrounded by mountains that he perversely finds
empty of visual interest: "The high hills . . . forced the mind to find entertainment for itself. Whether I spent the hour well I know not; for here
I first conceived the thought of this narration" (*Journal* 40). The mountains prevented his "eye from wandering," and given his emotional deaf-
ness, there is nothing there for him to hear. In this context, the concluding
incident at the school for the deaf suggests sympathetic identification as
much as condescension. Johnson argues that if even the deaf can be
taught, then Scotland can be modernized. But this seems a cheap shot
meant to distract the reader from noticing that Johnson substitutes the
sterile functions of arithmetic for the lived experience of the ear. In his
imagined modernization of Scotland, one in which Scotland will be made
to resemble Johnson's own England, a strict accounting of numbers that
can always be added and multiplied in the same way to reach the same
answer substitutes for the rich multiplicity of orality, with its frequent revisions and instability.

As Jerome Christensen remarks, Johnson's journey was "designed to
display a learning . . . to demonstrate that the Scots merely pretended to
learning and had nothing valuable to export" (151, note 2). The personal
journey, recorded in multiple documents including Johnson's "book of remarks" and letters to Hester Thrale as well as Boswell's journal signified
a heightened version of authenticity that elevated the author and the written word. Alternatively displaying himself or being placed on display in
Scotland, Johnson embodied a genuine cultural property in opposition to
the inauthenticity of Macpherson and Ossian (Hart, *Samuel Johnson*
150).[45] He represented authorship and print, a walking *Dictionary* and
handbook of aphorisms and proverbs in one. In exchange for Macpherson's *Ossian,* with its tenuous relationship to writing, Johnson offered
himself, dazzling at least some Scots who gathered around to hear what
the great man would say. While Edward Topham had written in 1774 that
Johnson "was looked upon as a kind of miracle in this country, and almost carried about for a shew" (quoted in Hart, *Samuel Johnson* 151),
Johnson himself is backhandedly modest, crediting his "fame" to Scotland's faults, to its emptiness and the absence of incident in the Highlands:
"The arrival of strangers at a place so rarely visited, excites rumor, and

45. See Rogers, "Noblest Savage," for the argument that Johnson's tour involved being
"shown off" as "uncomprehending primitive." Hart offers a nuanced understanding in
which Johnson is both admired and seen as Boswell's property.

quickens curiosity. I know not whether we touched at any corner, where Fame had not already prepared us a reception" (*Journey* 53).

Scots like William Woodfall were less admiring of the man Woodfall referred to as the "literary dictator" (quoted in Rogers, *Johnson and Boswell* 209). Incidents in Johnson's *Journey* suggest that such hostility was connected directly to a sophisticated Scottish critique of Johnson's effort to substitute himself for Ossian. Can anything other than hostility have motivated one of Johnson's boatmen to ask Johnson if he could "recount a long genealogy" and another to declare—perhaps ominously, perhaps humorously—"he heard the cry of an English ghost" (*Journey* 74)? One scene, significantly recounted by Boswell, exposes the intersection between regional and class hierarchies. Boswell's account suggests a comic deflation as revealing as direct hostility:

> The landlady said to me, "Is not this the great Doctor that is going about through the country?" I said, "Yes." "Ay," said she, "we heard of him, I made an errand into the room on purpose to see him. There's something great in his appearance: it is a pleasure to have such a man in one's house; a man who does so much good. If I had thought of it, I would have shewn him a child of mine, who has had a lump on his throat for some time. . . ." Said the landlord: "They say he is the greatest man in England, except Lord Mansfield." (*Journal* 68–69)

Here "greatness," "goodness," and "pleasure" intermingle to provide a symbol of English identity capable of engaging not only a host of Scottish dignitaries but also a reading public symbolized by the landlady. Unfortunately, Johnson—and Englishness—are both quickly demoted. Confused as to fact but not as to metaphoric force, the landlady elevates Johnson only to reduce his self-assigned curative function to potential quackery. Johnson's intervention is reframed surgically; his effort to purify the Scottish voice is remade in the landlady's image of the removal of a ridiculously physicalized lump on the throat. Trying to be helpful as only the conflicted Boswell could, he compounds the problem by explaining that the "great Doctor" is "only a very learned man." Perhaps even worse, the landlord, more educated than his wife, praises Johnson in terms that position him below the Scottish-born Mansfield, held out as "the greatest man in England.[46] Although Boswell claimed that Johnson seemed

46. William Murray (1705–1793) was born in Scone, Scotland. He had a brilliant legal career in England, becoming chief justice of the King's Bench and remaking English commercial law. He became earl of Mansfield in 1776. For his life, see the 1797 biography by John Holliday and the more modern biography by Edmund Heward. Johnson had Mansfield's national allegiances on his mind as early as 1772 when he remarked that Mansfield

"pleased" by the incident, the story suggests how easily Johnson's authorial grandeur could be dismantled: from great author to "only a very learned man," from learned man to traveling quack, the story traverses a number of different class types, suggesting Johnson's tenuous hold on this newly "middling" form of authorship. Meanwhile, the landlord's qualification places "real" law over Johnson's law and suggests a higher and different source of cultural value.

The Scottish Invention of English Copyright Law: Authorship and the Public Domain

If shifts in England's position on the oral-literate continuum were tumultuous in the cultural arena, they were more so in the legal world. As Peter Goodrich has shown, England's claims to a unique or "original" culture were grounded in a judicial system based in orality and memory. Oral roots differentiated English law from Roman and European systems that relied on codification, but orality also "proved" the antiquity of English law just as oral roots "proved" Ossian's ancient origins. Typical of legal mythmaking was Henry Spelman's claim in 1614 that English law predated the Romans. It derived from a "Grecian colony" under orders from Lycurgus "that their laws should not be written, because he would have every man to fix them in his memory; and for that purpose made them short and summary, after the manner of maxims" (quoted in Goodrich, *Oedipus Lex* 84). Fixed in memory rather than in writing, oral law belonged to every man. In this fantasy of identification, each citizen internalized the shared system of governance that differentiated the community from other communities. There is a huge gap, of course, between such fantasies and the actual practice of English law, a practice that had relied on manuscript and printed records as well as memory and oral transmission well before Johnson's time. But during the hundred years preceding Johnson's trip to the Hebrides, the fiction of the orality of English law eroded with extreme rapidity as law was transformed by the flood of print that typified the end of the seventeenth century. Adrian Johns has suggested that written records began to dominate after 1660. Trusting these records as accurate reflections of an oral tradition necessary to national integrity and self-definition was "central to the political order itself" (322). What complicated this scene was the continuing reliance of law on the orality

---

had been educated in England and "much . . . may be made of a Scotchman, if he be *caught young*" (Boswell, *Life* 494). See Harding for a discussion of English concerns about Mansfield's "foreign" birth and training (282–83).

of arguments and traditions, a reliance seen in the constant reiteration of the importance of memory to legal practice. To the extent that law continued to emphasize oral performance and memory, it continued to rely on orality.

The tension around orality suggests that conversations about authenticity, the literate, and the oral have a double meaning in English legal discourse. Attempts in English law to regulate writing always contained a subtextual encoding of concerns about the management of law's own relationship with literacy. If orality is to be rejected, then what of the claims of English law to a unique connection to its people? If incorporated, then how will its authenticity be assured? Questions of orality and literacy vexed English law because they concerned its origins. Such questions could not be confronted directly without risking questions about the authenticity of the system itself. And what might be the results of questioning origins and their authenticity? As Slavoj Žižek suggests in rather startling terms, the origins of law are lawless: any particular evocation of law derives from an exercise of brute power, a fact that it must always hide from itself if it is to exercise authority (205). One way that English law protected itself from questions of origins was by avoiding the literary emphasis on authorship and origins. The law should always be imagined as authorless, or at the very least as authored by a generic and not too specific conception of "the people." As Susan Stewart notes in *Crimes of Writing*, "By establishing a realm of prosecutable actions, laws regarding crimes of writing might be seen to 'spare' such aesthetic practices and at the same time to bracket, and thereby trivialize, their intentions and consequences" (3). But this tells only part of a much more complex story of displacement and distancing. As we shall see in this discussion of law's interaction with Ossian, "bracketing" may have helped English law avoid a direct confrontation with the authentication issues that shaped the Macpherson dispute, but such issues continually resurfaced in discussions that brought law, authenticity, and nation into close proximity.

In producing the Ossian works, Macpherson necessarily came into conflict with ideas of authorship and work inscribed not only in English aesthetic practices but also in English legal systems. But he did not come into conflict with the law. Although Boswell and Johnson fantasized about a trial for forgery, he invaded no copyright when he appropriated old manuscripts or oral works and transformed them into the Ossian poems (Boswell, *Journal* 206–207). Nor was there any formal law prohibiting him from augmenting the Ossian material with his own work. Criminal forgery itself, punishable by hanging throughout most of the eighteenth century, had little in common with Macpherson's acts since it assumed a direct economic motive.[47] Despite the frequently repeated assertion that Macpherson "forged" Scottishness in every sense of the word, in Macpherson's case, these charges were simply rhetorical, a trope for the criminal laws against forgery meant to control the distribution of paper credit.[48] If Macpherson could not be prosecuted formally, his "case" could still be criminalized metaphorically, its transformation into legal language reenacting the transformation of oral to literate that was causing so much anxiety juridically. The 1805 *Report of the Committee of the Highland Society of Scotland, Appointed to Inquire into the Nature and Authenticity of the Poems of Ossian* recirculates compensatory devices— attempts to "fix" orality and assign it an author—already familiar from my earlier discussion of Johnson and Macpherson. Its editor, the attorney Henry Mackenzie, trained in both Edinburgh and London, headed the effort to interrogate witnesses as to evidence of Ossian's authenticity: "Have you ever heard repeated or sung, any of the poems ascribed to Ossian, translated and published by Mr. Macpherson? By whom have you heard them so repeated, and at what time or times? Did you ever commit any of them to writing, or can you remember them so well as now to set them down?" The answers to such questions were to be recorded "with as much impartiality and precision as possible, in the same manner as if it were a legal question, and the proof to be investigated with a legal strictness" (3). Much of the lengthy document consists of what the report refers to as "testimony" and "affidavits." But legal certitude eluded this quasi-legal context; the report simply recycled the same regret that written records that might once have been available were now irretrievably lost. Noting their belief that the oral poetry Macpherson had drawn on existed in "great abundance" and that the fragments located through the search contained "often the substance, and sometimes almost the literal expression . . . of passages given by Mr. Macpherson," the committee members nevertheless concluded sadly that Macpherson had interrupted what should have been an unbroken series of transmissions from the Ossianic past to the *Poems of Ossian* of the present. He had made a practice of "inserting passages which he did not find, and to add what he conceived to be dignity and delicacy to the original composition, by striking out passages, by softening incidents, by refining the language, in short by changing what he considered as too simple or too rude for a modern ear, and elevating what in his opinion was below the standard of good poetry." The committee

47. For a discussion of the crime of forgery and its relationship to literacy and class, see McLynn, *Crime and Punishment* 133–40.
48. See Hart (*Samuel Johnson* 134–36) and Baines for discussions of the relationship between criminal forgery and Macpherson's Ossian poems.

[111]

members declined to decide "to what degree" Macpherson was guilty of these deviations from his sources (151–52).

The vehemence of the accusations against Macpherson, as well as similar concerns with nation, authenticity, and origination, recalls the highly charged language of legal cases against forgers.[49] Forgery cases invoked the national interest directly, that is, economically, and thus required the law's intervention. But law insulated itself here as well, partly by demonizing forgers and thus directing attention away from the operations of law, but also in more complex ways by seizing on forgery as an opportunity for reinforcing the strong bond between author and work that connected works to their nation. Powerful, unquestionable links between author and text reduced or even eliminated the need to examine origins or consider the possibility that "authenticity" might be merely an effect rather than an abstract universal quality. Stephen Roe's account of a 1759 trial warns readers about forgery:

> If you consider the nature and the consequences of this crime, you will shudder and start back at the thought of it! That it is a complicated falsehood and injustice, confounding the distinction of true and false, right and wrong; that it is one of the worst and most dangerous kinds of theft, bereaving a person of his nearest and most undoubted property, even his handwriting, which is the key of all he possesses or enjoys; and destroying all mutual credit and confidence among men. (quoted in Baines 22)

As Roe's comments suggest, criminal forgery threatened the bond between "author" and "work" in the most visceral way possible in everyday life; it severed the hand from the writing and thus undermined public faith in a work's inviolate connection to its origins. In forgery law, anxieties about authenticity and origins were made material, expressed metaphorically in language invoking the body, or worse, were turned literally against the body of the forger. That forgery law operated metaphorically, expressing cultural anxiety rather than any physical danger, can be seen in its internal contradictions. Surely the forgery of a large sum of money threatened the civic order more than that of a small sum. Yet forgery law emphasized authenticity over all else: unlike most theft crimes, forgery did not distinguish between greater and lesser offenses based on the amount of money at stake. A forgery involving a few pence received the same penalty as one involving thousands of pounds: execution. Moreover, the discourse surrounding forgery exaggerated the crime's importance. Given the extreme penalties and the violence of this dis-

49. I am indebted to Paul Baines for this part of my discussion.

course, one might think that forgery presented significant challenges to England's new reliance on paper credit. But as Paul Baines has pointed out, the steep increase in the number of forgery statutes between 1700 and 1800 was not reflected in a rise in indictments or convictions. Despite the perceived need for corrective action deriving from the anxiety about paper credit, the actual conviction rate dropped after 1755 (9–10). Nevertheless, at the very moment Johnson was traversing Scotland to gather evidence against Macpherson, a bill was passed against the counterfeiting of money, declaring that any person who "by any Art, Mysterie or Contrivance, cause or procure the said Words, Bank of England, to appear in the Substance of any Paper whatsoever . . . shall, for such Offence, be deemed and adjudged a Felon, and shall suffer Death" (quoted in Hart, *Samuel Johnson* 134–35). The bill clarifies how national authorship was constructed. For money to have value, it needed an inviolate attachment to its author, the Bank of England. The "Art, Mysterie or Contrivance" of the forger interrupted the link that guaranteed an authenticity of origins and, by allowing anyone to claim to be "the Bank of England," called into question the authority of the nation.

The version of authorship promulgated in copyright law derived from a similar model. Like forgery law, copyright regulations dealt with issues of authenticity by demanding a strong link between author and text in order to promote the nation. Naming the author ensured that national texts could be identified and read as national emblems, while insisting that cultural property be "fixed" in language avoided the sorts of interruptions in transmission that made it difficult to tell who was responsible for what text. To our hyperliterate eyes the association between copyright, authorship, and literacy seems self-evident. What else would copyright law protect but a writing by a particular author? But it was less evident to eighteenth-century thinkers: some saw little difference between oral expression and written work; others thought it unlikely that an author had any right to his or her work at all. Recent research on the ownership of oral traditions has suggested just how culturally egocentric the equation between ownership and writing can be. In the late twentieth and early twenty-first centuries, we have developed a belated sensitivity to oral culture. Thus, Macpherson's "forgery" of Highland materials seems less disturbing to some critics than his appropriation and cultural "enclosure" of indigenous intellectual property.[50] Like Maria Edgeworth's later Irish novels, Macpherson's Ossian poems took local idiom and turned it to his own advantage.[51] Though he exalted it by remaking it as epic, he also di-

50. See Dolan.
51. See Corbett for a discussion of Edgeworth's appropriation of Irish dialect.

vorced it from its original context and disseminated it with little regard for its Highland practitioners. Those of Macpherson's contemporaries who did not see the Ossian poems as forgeries saw them as recuperative, but late-twentieth-century oral history scholars have wrestled with issues of appropriation and ownership, developing a number of strategies that at least recognize the value of oral culture even while at times exploiting it. Increasingly sophisticated indigenous cultures have forced the West to grapple with the idea of cultural rights, to consider who owns oral productions and performances and how to make restitution for their taking.[52]

Common law systems quite often rely on intangible ephemera and protect intangible rights. Why is it then that copyright draws the line between oral expression and expressions fixed in print? A commonplace asserts that copyright protects not ideas but only their tangible expression. "Fixation," required for copyright protection, has always required technology, whether manuscript or print, or in recent times a recording, notation, or video. Linked to proof of the relationship between the author and the work, fixation was codified in English copyright statutes and cases beginning with the 1710 Act of Anne. Locating the regulation of culture in a written form itself assumes the end of the influence of the oral, but the act's anxious efforts to reinforce the literacy of literate culture suggest its own uncertainty about the primacy of the literate world. The act tried to shore up literate culture through its internal preoccupation with the mechanics of writing and printing. Its recording provisions, advertising sanctions, even its penalties ("one penny for every sheet") assert a literate, print culture. Enforcement of the act was predicated on an author's having recorded his or her title in the "register book" of the Stationer's Company and on having provided "nine copies of each book or books, upon the best paper" for the use of the royal and other libraries, the new "repositories" of English culture. The act's intensified emphasis on writing, combined with its timing, only two years after the national identity crisis caused by the Act of Union, suggests that establishing a nation's culture as primarily literate served a legitimating function. One way to ensure that the Union of Scotland and England became an incorporating rather than a confederating event was to reinscribe in law what was very uncertain in fact: the hegemony of a dominant literate, print culture over a less dominant oral culture.

52. For a good summary of critical approaches to oral traditions, see Amodio and Zumwalt. See Gilbert for a postcolonialist critique of academic discussions of indigenous orality. See Pask for a summary of the debates and new legal approaches to indigenous culture.

Fixation continued to be at issue throughout the century, for it marked the separation between oral expression and what the law was willing to protect. While it could be subverted (as Henry McKenzie discovered when an Irish writer copied out the entire manuscript of *Man of Feeling* and claimed it as his own), it implied authenticity and thus seemed a far more reliable way of proving authorship than oral transmission. The majority remarks in *Millar v. Taylor* in 1769 that only through print does the work become "a distinguishable subject of property" and that writing without publication is a "useless sound." Francis Hargrave concludes in his 1774 *Argument in Defence of Literary Property,* an equally strong author's rights document, that

> a literary composition can subsist and have duration, only so long as the
> words, which establish its identity, are represented by visible and known
> characters expressed on paper, parchment. . . . The original manuscript, or
> a written or printed copy, being authenticated, will equally serve the pur-
> pose; but *one* must remain within the power of the person who claims the
> appropriated right of printing the work, or the exercise of the right must
> unavoidably cease from the want of a *subject.* (15)

The law establishes authenticity through "visible and known characters" on "paper, parchment," preferably that of an "original" manuscript. Such concerns link all of the copyright cases to the Macpherson debates.

As with "fixation," we have so naturalized the connection between authorship and ownership that it is hard to imagine life without it. To us, then, the Act of Anne may seem simply to have written into law what everyone already knew. But to at least some late-seventeenth-century thinkers, authors no more owned their works than wits did their witticisms. Lockean theories of ownership that suggested a natural right to the products of one's labor were a novelty. The Act marked the first introduction of authorship into the law, for instance, for the first time allowing authors to register their works under their own names rather than under the names of members of the Stationer's Company.[53] It vested the rights in literary property in the "Authors or Purchasers of such copies" and purported to encourage "learned men to compose and write useful books." While some have argued that the "author" was a rhetorical device put in place by booksellers eager to capitalize on public sentiment, that authors had no interest in the case law construing copyright and no stake in its outcome, this would have been a hard case to make to the authors who wrote and argued about copyright during its periods of con-

53. See Jaszi 468 and Earle 272.

testation (Rose, *Authors* 96). At the very least, it is fair to say that the Act of Anne began a stage in legal history in which disputes about publishing and booksellers' rights were reconfigured through authorship.

Were authorship rights "natural" rights? If so, then authors should own them forever, as men owned land, not just for the term of years covered by the Act of Anne. Those booksellers who held titles to popular works and wished to retain them ignored the term limitations of the act and argued for a natural law or common law right in which authors in fact retained an interest in their works "in perpetuity." But such a system allowed certain printers to have a monopoly on important books, Shakespeare almost always serving as an example. The solution the Act offered was to limit ownership to a term of fourteen years for new books, twenty-one for books already in print, and then return works to the public domain, where they would become available for anyone with a press to reprint. This was the issue that dominated conversations about authorship after the Act of Anne and for most of the rest of the century: Were author and text so inextricably linked that they belonged to each other in perpetuity, or could the state control that relationship, severing it if necessary for the public good?[54] Although it did not become law until *Millar v. Taylor* in 1769, authorship in perpetuity found many adherents, not the least of whom was Samuel Johnson. Given his own borrowing for the *Dictionary,* his vitriolic campaign against literary piracy seems compensatory rather than convincing. The theory that authors "naturally" retained an eternal property interest in their works represented the most extreme example of the idea of author and work as inseparable. Such an idea—promoted in copyright tracts by Francis Hargrave and Catharine Macaulay among others—was fundamentally opposed to the practices of collaborative production and fluctuating open-ended work necessary to the oral tradition. In arguments for copyright in perpetuity, "strong" versions of authorship were repeatedly reinforced. Under *Millar v. Taylor,* for instance, if one could prove that a work was "published without a name" or "not claimed" or with "an author being unknown," one could prove that no literary property interest existed.[55] More metaphorically, Hargrave related ownership to individuality in 1774 as part of his argument for copyright in perpetuity. As he attempted to counter the proposition that literary property was too amorphous to merit protection, he argued for its individualized character: "There is such an infinite variety in the modes of thinking and writing, as well as in the extent and connection of ideas, as in the use and arrangement of words, that a literary work really

54. See Litman and Lange for modern re-expressions of public domain doctrine.
55. *Millar v. Taylor* 224.

original, like the human face, will always have some singularities, some lines, some features, to characterize it, and to fix and establish its identity" (7).

Here fixation and authorship come together, the literary work gaining its unique "fixed" character because it is like a unique individual. Writing that is "really original," that is, with the sure signs of authenticity, will take on the physical characteristics of its author. Such an emphasis on individuality downplays collaborative works while simultaneously building up the strong bond between author and text so as to make them indistinguishable. Under Hargrave's theory, well loved by some of the booksellers who owned copyrights, an author (and thus the bookseller he had sold his rights to) *was* his work. Just as he owned his own body, he owned his work forever. In theory at least, he would always control its use by others, and it could never enter the public domain. In practice, of course, copyright in perpetuity benefited booksellers far more than authors. After buying the rights to a work, they owned them forever, and thus English printers tended to control a monopoly in Shakespeare and Milton, but also in lesser works. As Lyman Ray Patterson points out in his historical study of copyright law, when *Millar v. Taylor* ratified copyright in perpetuity, it represented the apogee of the ascendance of the author-work bond in English law. Here the law gave authors the most exclusive rights in their works, allowing either the author himself or his assigns, usually booksellers, to preclude others from printing his works indefinitely.

Millar v. Taylor held for only five years. By May 1773 even Samuel Johnson had rejected copyright in perpetuity and come to a more measured view, one he shared with Boswell:

> There seems to be in authours a stronger right of property than that by occupancy; a metaphysical right, a right, as it were, of creation which should from its nature be perpetual; but the consent of nations is against it, and indeed reason and the interests of learning are against it; for were it to be perpetual, no book however useful, could be universally diffused amongst mankind, should the proprietor take it into his head to restrain its circulation. . . . For the general good of the world, therefore, whatever valuable work has once been created by an author, and issued out by him, should be understood as no longer in his power, but as belonging to the publick. (Boswell, *Life* 546)[56]

But the English courts did not hold against authorship in perpetuity in a vacuum. The Scottish courts, advised by a group of lawyers that included

56. Johnson's position on copyright was complex and variable. See McAdam 10–14, 167–69.

Boswell, beat England to the punch in declaring for public domain in *Hinton v. Donaldson*. Drawing on Ossian—and subliminally on Johnson—as examples and thus making legible the connection between public domain and the oral tradition, they argued that literary property was little different from oral expression, and thus no one owned it in perpetuity. As Mark Rose has pointed out, Scotland was keenly interested in breaking up the London print monopoly and opening a larger market for Scottish printers. The question of authorship in perpetuity "played out in the form of a national contest between England and Scotland" (*Authors and Owners* 92). To say as Rose does that *Hinton v. Donaldson* sounded a "patriotic note" understates its national theme. Each justice reaffirmed Scottish autonomy: the law of England "ought to have no influence"; it was "in many particulars special to itself"; English law is "foreign law"; "we can have no rule . . . but the law of Scotland"; Scotland was not "bound" by English law"; "the law of England . . . I pretend not to know." The judges repeated these sentiments almost ritualistically. *Hinton* clarifies what remains buried in other literary property cases: disputes over literary property are embedded in questions of national and cultural identity. However "non-national" such disputes may seem at times, they have serious consequences for the survival of national and cultural traditions and thus are construed through a national lens.[57]

Most telling is Ossian's presence in the *Hinton* case. As Boswell's own father, Lord Auchinleck, argued against authors' rights and in support of a strong public domain: "Anciently very valuable performances were preserved only by the memory. It is said Homer was so, and Ossian. When that was the case, what privilege could the author have?" The Scots repeatedly returned to the oral-literate continuum, emphasizing the similarities rather than differences between oral and literate expression. No man owns his own speech. The moment a thought becomes words, it becomes common property. If literary property was to be owned in perpetuity, then the law might as well allow "the author of every wise or witty saying, uttered even in conversation" to have a monopoly over it. Oral performances should not be owned, but should be free to all. "The poem of Chevy-chase, so much celebrated, and upon which we have a criticism of Mr. Addison, was, in my remembrance, repeated by everybody. Was

57. The Union of Scotland and England in 1707 merged the Scottish and English parliaments, giving the Scots only limited representation at Westminster. After the Union, as T. C. Smout remarks in his history of Scotland, "there was little to stop England from totally absorbing Scotland, except those parts of the treaty guaranteeing the separate existence of the Church of Scotland and the Scottish law courts." The Scottish justices' emphasis on separatism survived to make the court system a "rallying point of national consciousness today" (Smout 216).

there a copy of this little heroic poem? What privilege could the author have in it?" (Boswell, *Hinton* 5). If speech was common property, print was even more so: "When a man publishes his thoughts, he gives them away still more than the man who utters them in conversation. The latter gives them only to his hearers, but the former to the whole world" (Boswell, *Hinton* 3). The court was quick to point to dictionaries as inconsistent with any holding for authorship in perpetuity. Perhaps thinking of Johnson's well-articulated concern with "the general good of the world" or more likely of "Dictionary Johnson's" recent journey through Scotland, the judges attacked English law for its inconsistency. The English claimed to enforce copyright in perpetuity, they said. But their own national works could not have been published given such a system. To publish a dictionary, for instance, "the works of a hundred authors are ransacked; out of them is produced, as the sages express it, an entire new work" that copyright in perpetuity would never have allowed (Boswell, *Hinton* 7).

Hinton first wrote public domain into law. The copycat English case *Donaldson v. Becket,* decided in 1774 only a few days after Boswell distributed copies of his account of the *Hinton* decision in London, ratified this subtler understanding of the interaction between authors' rights to their literary property and more public, cultural rights. While the English justices voted for copyright in perpetuity, their vote was only advisory to the House of Lords, where Lord Camden played a central role in arguing for a new public domain. Camden's views echo those of the Scottish court: "Most certainly every man who thinks, has a right to his thoughts, while they continue HIS. . . . But what if he speaks, and lets them fly out in private or public discourse? Will he claim the breath, the air, the words in which his thoughts are clothed?" (32). He mentions no dictionary writers with disrespect, but instead restates the problem of scholarship as one involving a general fund of learning: "Knowledge and science are not things to be bound in such cobweb chains" but should instead be common to all (55).

The fact that the Scots celebrated the *Donaldson* decision with bonfires and fireworks could only have brought home to the English that adopting public domain for English national law created the risk of blurring English national identity, of accepting an ever deeper Scottish incursion into the heart of Englishness.[58] Moreover, creating an English public domain opened up questions about originality and authenticity, about the vastness and uncontrollability of archives, that the English legal system pre-

---

58. Rose quotes Ian Simpson Ross, *Lord Kames and the Scotland of His Day,* in describing the Scottish reaction to the case (*Authors and Owners* 97).

ferred not to confront. Yet authorship in perpetuity, as the Scottish jurists had so dismissively pointed out, created a different and equally serious problem: it made it much more difficult to produce collective projects, those monuments of national learning such as Johnson's *Dictionary.* An open public domain seemed necessary to national literature, but to support it the English judges had to "English" it, making it their own and yet bracketing the issues of authenticity it inevitably raised. The surprising turn the *Donaldson* case report takes at its end makes sense only in this context of national anxiety. There Lord Effingham Howard suddenly raised the issue of freedom of the press. Copyright in perpetuity endangered the English press, he argued, for a government official under attack could buy up the copyrights to those works critical of his policies and thus prevent them from ever being reprinted, "securing in his closet the secret which might prevent the loss of freedom to the subject" (59). The maneuver aptly connected the new law of public domain to English immemorial custom. By trumpeting, "I am satisfied in myself, that the Liberty of the Press is of such infinite Consequence in this Country, that if the Constitution was over-turned, and the People enslaved, grant me but a free Press and I will undertake to restore the one and redeem the other" (*Cases* 59), Effingham Howard associated public domain with the liberty of the English constitutional subject and thus distanced it from all the questions that might have called the foundations of English law into question.

Effingham Howard's contribution tended to erase Scotland's—and Ossian's—impact on English copyright law. Making legible Ossian's intersection with the most central of English institutions reveals the highly politicized origins of abstract legal concepts such as authorship and work and calls into question their naturalized status. Far from evidencing "the law of nature and truth, and the light of reason, and the common sense of mankind," as Judge Aston claimed in *Millar v. Taylor,* literate ideas of author and text were carefully constructed to advance the nation through a politicized literature. In Macpherson's case, the quasi-criminalization of his work as forgery and the refusal to acknowledge its value in recuperating the Scottish oral tradition reveals more about the English desire to avoid depending on orality with all the uncertainty that this entailed than it does about the Ossian poems themselves. As Girodet's painting suggests, Ossian with his outstretched arms embraced both literate and oral culture, both the old and the new, and reached even into England's most national institution to direct English law's construction of national authorship.

[3]

Nation Engendered: Catharine Macaulay's "Remarkable Moving Letter" and *The History of England*

> Letters, the most intimate sign of the subject, are waylaid, forged, stolen, lost, copied, cited, censored, parodied, misread, rewritten, submitted to mocking commentary, woven into other texts which alter their meaning, exploited for ends unforeseen by their authors. Writing and reading are always in some sense illicit intercourse—not only because they may be expressly forbidden, but because there is always the possibility of a fatal slip between intention and interpretation, emission and reception.
>
> TERRY EAGLETON, *The Rape of Clarissa*

For a brief period in the 1770s, women seemed poised to move into a more prominent role in the life of the nation. Linda Colley points out that opportunities were opening up. The position of British women was "in flux"; as men increasingly laid claim to the full rights of citizenship, the question of what to do about women became more pressing (*Britons* 239). That women seemed more plausible as citizens than they had in the past may have been partly the doing of Catharine Macaulay, England's first national female historian, a prominent intellectual of her day, and a woman who came as close to being a national spokesperson as a woman could during her era. Perhaps more than any other famous woman of her time, Macaulay's career demonstrates the "flux" to which Colley refers.

From 1763 until 1779, Macaulay may have been one of the best-known, most respected women writers in England.[1] Certainly she was the only woman famous for publishing a national history and other political and philosophical tracts, including—significantly for this story—the only tract on copyright written by an English woman during the century. An advocate of English rights and the "liberty of the subject," held up as the "antidote" to Hume's poison in Parliament, she was the subject of numerous portraits and engravings, at least two wax models, a large marble statue, and any number of prints, both admiring and satirical (Davis, "Two Bodies" 11). Whereas the first volume of David Hume's *History of England* sank (as he said himself) "into oblivion," Macaulay's *History* was so popular it was republished as a serial (quoted in Hill, *Virago* 43 and 50). She was admired by Joseph Priestly for her "masterly performance" (Peardon 60); other reviewers suggested that her style would "bear the test of the strictest scrutiny: nay, it is so correct, bold, and nervous, that we can discover no traces of a female pen" (Review 375).

But in 1779, Macaulay's career effectively ended. A year earlier, Macaulay, then a forty-six-year-old widow, had been living in Bath with her elderly patron, Thomas Wilson (Looser 139). While at Wilson's Alfred House, she was treated by the Scottish physician James Graham. In December she married Graham's younger brother, William, who was twenty-one and, perhaps even worse, a Scot. It was a marriage that scandalized Hannah More and offended even Horace Walpole.[2] To avert Wilson's fury she wrote him what seems to have been a conciliatory letter, now lost. "Litera Scripta Manet" (letters once written remain fixed), Hugh Blair opined in his masterpiece on rhetoric, but this was not the case with Macaulay's letter (quoted in Favret 24). Instead, Wilson seems to have taken Macaulay's letter, passed it around to friends, allowed copies to be made, and even started trying to have it published. Immediately misappropriated, distributed to those it was not intended for, advertised as part of a forthcoming collection of scandalous letters, parodied in popular tracts, prepared for an unauthorized publication, and almost certainly misinterpreted, the letter—reinscribed in numerous misogynistic pamphlets though never recovered—undermined Macaulay's career morally and intellectually but also generically. It loomed large enough in subse-

1. Lucy Martin Donnelly's 1949 article reintroduced Macaulay to twentieth-century scholars. Bridget Hill's biography has been invaluable to me in writing this chapter. Other serious studies of Macaulay include Boos and Boos; Natalie Zemon Davis, "Gender and Genre" and "Two Bodies"; Ditchfield; Fox; Staves; Withey; Schnorrenberg, "Brood-Hen" and "Opportunity Missed"; Mazzucco-Than; Guest; and Looser. Pocock has written favorably of Macaulay in "Catharine Macaulay: Patriot Historian."

2. Hill, *Virago,* quotes Hannah More at 144. See Walpole 165 for his opinion that the marriage was "uncouth."

quent discussions of her life and marriage to damage her reputation in England and taint her career.

After the marriage, Macaulay continued to be revered by a few English radicals such as Mary Wollstonecraft, as well as in America and France.[3] Praised by George Washington and Thomas Jefferson, she was instrumental to Mercy Otis Warren's decision to write a history of the American Revolution. In France, where copies of her history were eventually offered as school prizes, Michelet rhapsodized, "Few were the women of letters then who did not dream of being France's Macaulay. The inspiriting goddess is found in every salon" (quoted in Gutwirth 257). But the trouncing she took in the English popular press for the marriage—most of it focusing on the mysterious letter to Wilson—was something she never overcame in England. Mocked in tracts that took up the issue of the letter ("A Bridal Ode," "The Female Historian to the Patriot Divine," "A Remarkable Moving Letter"), she traveled much over the next twelve years, publishing the remaining volumes of her *History* to little effect, and died in 1791. As the *European Magazine* remarked in 1783, "Perhaps there never was an instance, where the personal conduct of an author so much influenced the public opinion of their writings." The letter to Wilson, "if really existing, has been suppressed, though it would probably excite the public curiosity as much as anything which has fallen from her pen" ("Account" 334).[4]

That Macaulay's missing letter so excited "the public curiosity" is not surprising. Epistolary theory notes the connections between letters and a woman's body, between letters and private life. While functioning to make the private public, the late-eighteenth-century letter offered a material manifestation of interiority, of the body and its desires, but also of individual emotional life.[5] That the contents of Macaulay's letter were inaccessible made it more mysterious and desirable. Lost letters even more

3. See Hill, "Links," for a discussion of Macaulay's relationship with Wollstonecraft. In a letter to Macaulay, Wollstonecraft wrote admiringly, "You are the only female writer who I coincide in opinion with respecting the rank our sex ought to endeavor to attain in the world" (quoted 177).

4. The letter continues to "excite public curiosity," as Bridget Hill's 1995 article on her effort to obtain Macaulay's private papers at auction demonstrates. As Hill relates, most of Macaulay's papers were thought to have been lost in a fire at her family home in the early twentieth century. More recently, some came on the market at private auction. The Gilder Lehrman Collection in the Pierpont Morgan Library includes 190 letters, but many of them are from Macaulay's correspondents (Looser 136). In a conference paper titled "Challenging Eighteenth-Century Boundaries," Barbara Schnorrenberg has suggested that few letters ever existed, citing evidence from Macaulay's daughter's correspondence that Macaulay seldom wrote letters (13).

5. I am indebted to Cook, Eagleton, Favret, and Kauffman for their work on epistolarity.

than available ones tend to provoke curiosity, to reinforce the questions of presence and absence that letters in themselves evoke. For Macaulay, the stolen private letter signified more still: it figured the return of what had been repressed throughout a career devoted to offering a newly integrated, linear model of national history.[6] Throughout her career Macaulay had suffered the inevitable gendered attacks launched against most women intellectuals of the period. Still, until the stolen letter became a matter of public gossip, such attacks remained muted, subtext rather than text. The letter prompted a vicious and public series of attacks that concentrated on Macaulay's sexuality. While the letter provoked fantasies about her private sexuality (and its misappropriation suggested the violation of that sexuality) incompatible with the public image Macaulay had so carefully wrought, it also retroactively contaminated everything she had written by interjecting, as Mary Favret has put it, the specters of "heterogeneous medley" and "formal disorientation" (95). For just as Macaulay had tried to write a sequential national history, some of it in epistolary form, the stolen letter represented what national history abjected: "secret history," a genre typified by the inclusion of anecdotal, personal, often sexual information, which brought the private to bear on public life and in doing so disrupted the linearity of national history.

If nations "imagine" themselves into being, constructing themselves as unified, whole, and rich with content, they do so partly by manipulating their histories and implying a seamless continuity with a national past.[7] Like other genres, the best-known example being the novel of the 1750s, national history had to reinvent itself for Englishness, to elevate itself above its discontinuous "foreign" and low associations with secret history, and thus resituate itself in the generic hierarchy. Indeed, history as a genre became respectable in the eighteenth century to the extent that it suggested continuity between the origins of the nation and contemporary public life (Phillips, "Adam Smith" 318). That generic advantage could be maintained only to the extent that history could reject aggressively its low origins in secret history. Secret history originated in Procopius' *Arcana Historia*, first published in England in 1624. Taken up by any number of English writers writing in the first twenty years of the eighteenth century, it was a popular, novelistic form thought to be particularly se-

6. Peardon points to the importance of linearity for "nationalist" historians who have "tended to emphasize historical continuity more strongly than their predecessors" (182).

7. As Eric Hobsbawm observes, "Modern nations and all their impedimenta generally claim to be the opposite of novel, namely rooted in the remotest antiquity, and the opposite of constructed, namely human communities so 'natural' as to require no definition other than self-assertion" (Hobsbawm and Ranger 15). See also Anderson, *Imagined Communities;* and Berlant.

ductive to women.[8] The escape from secret history relied on abstraction, on the elision of individual particularity and its accompanying risk of scandal.

Secret history, with its anti-linear deviations, both sexual and textual, had a special relationship with the letters and private papers it often relied on as evidence. David Jones argued in 1697 in *The Secret History of White-hall* that the genre was best presented in epistolary form: "There is a very engaging part naturally couched under such a method of bringing State-Arcana's to light by way of Letters, which, in the very Notion of them carry something of secrecy" (quoted in Mayer 99). Rejecting the use of letters and other personal, subjective accounts, the new national history stressed official records (Peardon 59). David Hume, Macaulay's immediate predecessor and rival, exemplified an extreme version of this view, relying more on previous histories than on records of any kind. He did little or no primary research, but "anticipated the modern synthetic historian in uniting and enlivening the sometimes ponderous research of others" (E. C. Mossner 316). Although it may not be true that he refused to leave his couch to check a source across the room, he made a virtue of rejecting primary materials, asserting that he included "no original papers, and enter'd into no Detail of minute, uninteresting Facts" (quoted in E. C. Mossner 316). For Hume, the letter—which in other histories often provided the contents for the footnotes and citations that Hume rejected—seems to have represented the incidental, decorative, superfluous artifactual information that threatened to undermine sequential history. But even Hume was susceptible to its allure. Though he had avoided the archives of the British Museum, on discovering that Macaulay had found an important letter there, he used it in writing later editions of his *History* (Kenyon 55).

Both metaphorically and literally subtextual, the letter, with its allusions to secret history, lurked in the margins of historical writing. Disruptive generically, it contained disruptive information as well—information about the body and emotions of individuals thought improper for inclusion in the new national history. That the letter had such implications for historical writing suggests a new understanding of Macaulay's misappropriated letter and its explosive impact on her career. Saturated with generic meaning, that letter represented not simply a revelation about Macaulay's private life, but revelations about all that history repressed in order to yield

8. Robert Mayer offers an excellent discussion of secret history, and I am indebted to him for this part of my discussion (94–112). He lists the obvious examples such as Defoe, Haywood, and Manley, but also Jones, Crouch, and Oldmixon. John Richetti discusses secret history as "popular fiction," listing a number of intriguing titles as well (120, note 1).

a seamless narrative of national progress. Thus the lost personal letter—because it revealed personal, scandalous information about a prominent woman historian of England—provided a powerful metonymic challenge that threatened to undo not just Macaulay but national history itself.

National history inevitably implicated legal history; the two were intertwined in discussions of the constitution and the rights of the subject. Thus, the narrative of the misappropriated letter offered a very particular and pointed critique not only of national history but of national legal history as well, undermining Macaulay's own representation of that institution. The version of English legal history that Macaulay had constructed in *The History of England,* despite its supposedly radical leanings, was widely accepted as defining Englishness against foreign autocracy. As she had argued in the introduction to the *History,* the English "enjoy privileges unpossessed by other nations," most particularly "the liberty of the subject, [which] is as absolutely instituted as the dignity of the sovereign" (1:ix, xiv–xv). Thus the law's failure to protect her literary property called into question one of the fundamental arguments Macaulay and many others had made for England's uniqueness: her argument for liberty and equality based in national law. For copyright law the problem of letters—how to construe ownership in light of their informality and easy dissemination—condensed a host of anxieties, concerns about the author's physical link to the text evoked by the letter's relationship to the body, but also about the contrast between the ephemerality of literary property and the materiality of print. But these issues had presumably been settled and resettled in the decades since Pope's successful 1741 battle to defend his personal letters. In interrupting Macaulay's private ownership of her own correspondence, Wilson ignored what had been English law since 1741, the author's right to control the dissemination of private correspondence. Such a misappropriation of a woman's letter in clear contravention of the law challenged the commitment of English law to equality, suggesting how gendered even its seemingly gender-free operations were.

Literary property was not *literally* gendered, of course. Although we may note today that the 1710 Act of Anne aimed to encourage only "learned Men to compose and write useful books," the omission of "and Women" would hardly have signified a gendered exclusion to the eighteenth-century reader. While unmarried women (the *feme sole* of legal discourse) could produce and sell literature, on the deeper level of metaphor, illegitimate literary property was consistently feminized, legitimate property masculined. This gendering of literary property in order to "shrink" it or render it insignificant becomes clear only when we reread the copyright law system in light of the controversies surrounding it. Mainstream literary figures regulated their opponents by gendering battles that seemed on the surface to be perfectly gender neutral. Richardson, for instance, feminized that "limed bird" Faulkner, as surely as Lovelace used gender against Clarissa. Johnson, too, with his great oak stick, that "manly" beater of schoolteachers, reader of "all ancient writers, all manly" (Boswell, *Life* 30, 44), threatened book pirates both textually and sexually in a passage worth quoting at length:

> We shall lay hold, in our turn, on their copies, degrade them from the pomp of wide margin and diffuse typography, contract them into a narrow space, and sell them at an humble price. . . . We shall, therefore, when our losses are repaid, give what profit shall remain to the Magdalens; for we know not who can be more properly taxed for the support of penitent prostitutes, than prostitutes in whom there yet appears neither penitence nor shame. (Boswell, *Life* 244, note 2)

Shrinking the text is here equated with a reduced status: book pirates, it turns out, are lower than prostitutes, as they have no "penitence nor shame." In Macaulay's case, gender discrimination defined her career in the most obvious, even blatant ways. Her literary property was gendered from its inception, in part because of the role gender played in making her larger political arguments. But gender also operated more surreptitiously, rising to the surface in the law's failure to protect even a prominent woman—ironically, the only English woman who had written seriously and at length on the importance of copyright for authors—from an invasion of her literary property. Pierre Bourdieu has concerned himself with the hinges between law and society, with the way the "juridical field" exerts its magnetic power over large populations. Macaulay's story encourages us to look at this relationship in reverse. Perhaps more than any other episode in this book, the story of Macaulay's stolen letter suggests the power of culture over law.

The Secret History of History: Gender and Historiography

Macaulay set gender against genre when she decided to write history, flying in the face of a tradition that bound up the gender of history's readership with the generic conventions of national history. The misogyny of national history—its assumption of masculine authorship and its relegation of women to casual rather than serious readers—was a social fact rooted in women's exclusion from education and literacy training, but it was also a deeply embedded generic convention. As a social fact it had a complex history itself. As D. R. Woolf points out, women had long participated in "the social circulation of historical knowledge" broadly defined. Moreover, educated women such as Elizabeth Montagu and Charlotte Lennox had written history of a sort, as had Europeans such as Christine de Pisan.[9] But those women who became actively engaged with history were most often associated with family history, antiquarianism, and gossip, leading Addison to mock them in 1710 in a general characterization of "one of those female historians that upon all occasions enters into pedigrees and descents, and finds herself related, by some offshoot or other, to almost every great family in England" (quoted in Woolf 655).

Any attempt to trace women's "real" relationship to history writing soon encounters such anecdotal mockery, which had more to do with the bolstering of the generic conventions of the new national history than with an understanding of women's actual writing and reading practices. Writing gender into history helped establish the superior position of national history in the hierarchy while also reinforcing its claims to the transparent reinscription of the real. Because gender seemed so natural, it helped hide the constructed nature of the hierarchy.[10] By associating secret history with the feminine and the new national history with masculinity, the more professionalized eighteenth-century historians created a space for a serious history of the nation, one that focused on a masculinized narrative of progress and avoided the asides and distractions of secret history. While the latter foregrounded its own bias, sources, and writing process, making them visible on the very surface of the text, the seamless narrative that national history attempted suggested that the nation's existence was a powerful abstract entity with a pleasingly progressive organic life of its own. The rejection of secret history, with its political bias and patched-together source material, made the new national history seem natural.

In light of this, Peter Whalley's reliance on gendered imagery in his 1746

9. Although women before Macaulay did write history, they tended to limit their sphere of attention. Margaret Lucas, for instance, noted that by writing such a "particular" history, she avoided the need to "preach on the beginning of the world nor [make] long observations upon the several sorts of government." Women historians writing after Macaulay include Charlotte Cowley, Mary Hays, Lucy Aiken, Charlotte Smith, Helen Maria Williams, and Hannah More (Kucich 450). Natalie Zemon Davis discusses Macaulay as one of a number of female historians in "Gender and Genre." For more recent work on women historians, see Looser, Bonnie Smith, and Woolf.

10. I am indebted here to Wai Chee Dimock, who has helpfully articulated this point: "Gender does its symbolic work primarily by restoring a natural order to a newly denaturalized political order. . . . [G]ender works with the solidity of a natural fact" (238).

discussion of history, written at a tense historical moment right after the Jacobite invasion, can be seen as part of a larger effort to naturalize national history's progressive tendencies: "History is a manly composition, and should accordingly be appareled with such ornaments as are consistent with the boldness of its nature. Lucian very aptly compares an History effeminated by trifling, incongruous Circumstances, to Hercules in a Woman's Dress, submitting to the Dominion and Discipline of his Mistress Omphale" (22). Whalley details the qualities necessary to the historian, such as virtue, objectivity, and "Integrity of Heart" (10). He rejects the methods of the "romance" writer, arguing that while romance revels in "unwarranted Excess . . . which might be apt to descend to low Minutenesses," history should be "temperate and sparing" (20). Meanwhile, he associates "ambitious ornaments" or "trivia," which he sees as typical of romance, with effeminacy. Choosing the overtly gendered Hercules-Omphale image (an ornamental device in itself), Whalley adopts Lucian's argument that historical facts should be "dressed" in an appropriately masculine style because Herculean history deserves masculine attire.[11] Rather than submit to "the feminine"—a catchall term for romance, ornamentation, secret history, and disruption—history, Whalley says, should distance itself from the confusion of "trifling, incongruous Circumstances."

Hume's historiography and his *History of England,* to which Macaulay's *History* was frequently compared, offer a good example of Whalley's theories in action as well as a helpful context for understanding just how anomalous Macaulay must have seemed to the eighteenth-century reader. A detailed analysis of both his philosophical and historiographic comments on gender and genre suggests a historiography surprisingly dependent on gender difference.[12] Far from being a stereotypical misogynist, Hume believed that men and women share a basic sexuality as well as similar intellectual potentials. Although he found most English women to be poorly educated and thus poor companions, his intellectual relationships with French women demonstrated a deep respect for female intellect. But as Annette Baier has argued in an intriguing series of articles,

11. For an introduction to the Hercules-Omphale narrative, see the entry for "Hercules" in the *Oxford Classical Dictionary.* Hercules was required to serve Omphale for a period of years to atone for acts that are described differently in different sources. She purportedly dressed him as a woman and required him to perform women's tasks. Some accounts claims that he wore a brassiere. This story was recounted in various classical texts and was taken up by a number of artists and sculptors. At least one eighteenth-century play, *Hercules and Omphale: A Grand Pantomimic Spectacle in Two Parts,* draws on the theme; see also Galinsky and Kampen.

12. Much work has focused on the connections between Hume's philosophical and historical writings. See especially Norton and Popkin xxxii–lv.

Hume also believed that social utility rather than natural difference required society to treat women quite differently from men.[13] For instance, he grounded his demand for absolute female chastity not in any argument about the "essence" of women but in an appeal to the proper functioning of society. In Hume's discussion of gender difference in the *Treatise of Human Nature,* the major concession to a gender of essences involves biology as related to paternity: a woman will always know whether a particular child is genetically her own, whereas a man's knowledge must rest on a woman's protestations. If men cannot be sure that their children are their own, they will refuse to support them, thus destabilizing patrilineage and the structure of the family. As Hume posits, "From this trivial and anatomical observation is deriv'd that vast difference betwixt the education and duties of the two sexes" (*Treatise* 571).[14] The "trivial" nature of the distinction is belied by its impact on women and on society at large. For based on this difference, one that creates an "inequality of trust" between men and women and thus threatens to upset all of society, women must be held to a special, higher standard of chastity and modesty. Like men, women are not naturally chaste or modest, but unlike men, women (or at least most women—Hume creates an exception for prostitutes) must be socialized into absolute chastity lest men be discouraged from supporting children and society lapse into chaos. "Woman" disrupts the linear generational progress of the family and, because of the family's metaphoric connections to national and racial continuity, disrupts their progress as well.

Undergirding this utility-oriented theory of gender traits lies a more subtle association of women with disruption. In the *Treatise,* Hume ends "On Morals" by setting up a dichotomy that any present-day feminist will recognize. Remarking that the obligations of men "bear nearly the same proportion to the obligations of women, as the obligations of the law of nations do to those of the law of nature" (573), he argues that male moral obligations in the sexual arena are much less essential than female obligations. Here Hume associates women with nature, an entity that he has earlier described as disruptive in that it is "independent of our thought and reasoning" (168). Nature, it turns out, though composed of "but few and simple" principles (182), evokes Whalley's discussion of history in that it "is compounded and modify'd by so many different circumstances,

---

13. My account here is heavily indebted to Baier's numerous articles on Hume. See "Good Men's Women," "Hume: The Reflective Women's Epistemologist?" and "Hume, The Women's Moral Theorist?"

14. Annette Baier's work influenced my discussion of this passage. See "Good Men's Women" 6–7.

that in order to arrive at the decisive point, we must carefully separate whatever is superfluous" (175). The "laws of nature" are seen to govern the circumstantial superfluity that tends to blind us to them, just as moral obligations placed on women regulate feminine excess and irregularity and thus protect the institution of the family.

The association between masculinity and linearity, and between femininity and superfluity, has obvious consequences for the writing of a historical narrative founded in a model of linear progress. As Luce Irigaray suggests, the oft-noted conflation of "void" with "feminine" elides the real consequences of the feminine for historical linearity.[15] The tendency to equate woman with "lack" reveals male anxieties about women's "insatiable hunger, a voracity that will swallow you whole," but simultaneously cloaks the far more threatening possibilities presented by female multiplicity—possibilities that Hume recognized when he urged women to accept a more restrictive moral code. Irigaray helps us understand that what the culture imagines as female "really involves a different economy more than anything else, one that *upsets the linearity* of a project, undermines the goal-object of a desire, diffuses the polarization toward a single pleasure, disconcerts fidelity to a single discourse" (29–30; emphasis added).

Hume takes up history's relationship to linearity and multiplicity directly in *The History of England* in several key discussions of historical method. In his account of Henry III, Hume argues that

> history also, being a collection of facts which are multiplying without end, is obliged to adopt such arts of abridgement, to retain the more material events, and to drop all the minute circumstances, which are only interesting during the time. . . . What mortal could have the patience to write or read a long detail of such frivolous events . . . which would follow, through a series of fifty-six years, the caprices and weaknesses of so mean a prince as Henry? (2:3–4)[16]

Like Paul de Rapin-Thoyras, who had suggested that history should "be a continuous narrative, with nothing distracting or superfluous," Hume deals with the anxiety about disruptive, and surprisingly *reproductive*, "facts which are multiplying without end" by advocating a historiography of elimination (Levine, *Battle* 269). In general, as Hume suggests, "minute circumstances" and "frivolous events"—both associated with

15. See Irigaray, *This Sex Which Is Not One*, for this argument.
16. This frequently discussed passage was first brought to my attention by Price, *David Hume* 89.

[131]

the feminine—should be elided. The historian should focus on what Whalley constructs as Herculean history and Hume calls "general theorems" (*History* 2:3). Even though the method was as old as Lucian, it was newly suited to the goals of national history. As Hume argued, "If no man is to know the English story but by perusing all those monuments, which remain of it, few will be able to attain that useful and agreeable erudition." Historians must consolidate the records, eliminating their superfluous elements, or "what must foreigners do to get some notion of our history?" (*Letters* 1:284–85).

But the elimination of feminine superfluity in favor of seamless linearity worked better in theory than in practice. Superfluous details, the incidental and decorative, threatened linearity even when they were being most forcefully rejected. A crucial moment in the early chapters of volume 5 of Hume's *History of England* demonstrates the problem. Passing over the infamous physicality of James I's infatuation with Robert Carre, Hume dispatches in a few lines the rumors that "the monarch, laying aside the sceptre, took the birch into his royal hand, and instructed him in the principles of grammar." Rather than pursuing this interesting topic, Hume breaks off into a defensive explanation, abruptly declaring that

> such scenes, and such incidents, are the more ridiculous, though the less odious, as the passion of James seems not to have contained in it any thing criminal or flagitious. History charges herself willingly with a relation of the great crimes, and still more with that of the great virtues of mankind; but she appears to fall from her dignity, when necessitated to dwell on such frivolous events and ignoble personages. (*History* 5:53)

In the passage, Hume equates a moment of homosocial disorder with the feminized fall of history. But he also demonstrates the contradictory complications involved in rejecting "frivolous" scenes. By placing frivolity against the "dignity" of history, the "birch" against the "sceptre," Hume amuses readers while impressing upon them the seriousness, virtue, and centrality of his historical project. But here, as in Whalley's discussion of Omphale, the "ridiculous" image that draws the reader's attention to its moral also threatens to displace it.

A similar problem vexes Hume's gendered model of historical study in "Of the Study of History," an essay addressed "to my female readers" (*Essays* 563–68). In the essay, Hume reiterates his views of the purposes of history while emphasizing the disjunction between masculinized history and feminized secret history. He argues that female students of history will be benefited "much to their quiet and repose" in part because they will learn that they have much less impact on men than romances and novels may have led them to believe. From reading history, women will learn that "love is not the only passion, which governs the male-world, but is often overcome by avarice, ambition, vanity, and a thousand other passions" (564). Men are motivated by desires, not necessarily virtuous, but removed from female influence. Although Hume suggests that both men and women can benefit from reading history, he creates of women a special case, detailing "how well suited it is to every one, but particularly to those who are debarred the severer studies, by the tenderness of their complexion, and the weakness of their education" (565). Without studying history, "a woman's mind is so unfurnished, 'tis impossible her conversation can afford any entertainment to men of sense and reflection." Halfway through the essay Hume admits that these remarks constitute "raillery" (565), the admission underscoring the boundary between the feminine, which prompts levity, and the historical, which does not. In the final section Hume shifts to a masculine norm, suddenly remarking that "a man acquainted with history may, in some respect, be said to have lived from the beginning of the world." Leaving questions of female inadequacy behind and turning to "Machiavel," Horace, and the generic "man of business" for his examples, Hume seems to forget the gendered theme with which he began (566–68). Although Hume may be able to forget the "raillery" in which he indulged, we should not: it reappears often when his historical views confront the gendered reader.

For instance, Hume also opens "Of the Study of History" with raillery. In an anecdote that sounds more like secret history than "real" history, he relates:

> I remember I was once desired by a young beauty, for whom I had some passion, to send her some novels and romances for her amusement in the country; but was not so ungenerous as to take the advantage, which such a course of reading might have given me, being resolved not to make use of poisoned arms against her. I therefore sent her PLUTARCH's lives, assuring her, at the same time, that there was not a word of truth in them from beginning to end. She perused them very attentively, 'till she came to the lives of ALEXANDER and CAESAR, whose names she had heard of by accident; and then returned me the book, with many reproaches for deceiving her. (*Essays* 564)

Immediately after this interpolated "teaser," Hume attacks the "secret history" for its falseness and triviality. But his use of its techniques and motifs—personalization of the famous, revelation of desire, a lexicon of potential seduction—in an essay that explicitly and emphatically de-

[133]

nounces the form suggests a dynamic similar to that relied on by writers of secret history. Unlike Whalley, who finds redeeming characteristics in the romance, associating it with "fable" and the "greater Kinds of Poetry" (5), Hume redeems romance only to the extent that it turns women into readers of history. He may have associated secret history with romance and novels, by authors such as Madeleine de Scudéry, Aphra Behn, and Mary Delarivier Manley.[17] But, like secret history writers, Hume seduces his readers with a personalized, sexualized anecdote. While the essay places the trivialized interpolated romance against a linear and progressive history associated with truth, impartiality, virtue, and manliness, the seductive opening refuses erasure. In granting secret history a lingering presence, Hume reinforces proper history's seriousness and "manliness" but also suggests its susceptibility to secret history's appeal.

Throughout his career Hume tended to gender his readership female, subordinating it to his own masculinized authority.[18] But in certain key passages he claimed two readerships, one masculinized and one feminized. Thus, the famous passage in which Hume equates the "interesting" with the feminine: "The first quality of an Historian is to be true & impartial; the next to be interesting. If you do not say, that I have done both Parties Justice; & if Mrs. Mure be not sorry for poor King Charles, I shall burn all my papers, & return to philosophy" (*Letters* 1:210). What a comfortable image: the male reader critiques the text's truth and fairness, its rational linearity, the female reader its "interesting," excessive, more human qualities. But what if the female reader was also a historian? As David R. Stevenson suggests, Hume tended to respond to ambiguities, either historical or personal, by resort to irony, or as Hume might put it "raillery" (217). Raillery registers Hume's discomfort, his inability to come to terms with the ambiguity of irreconcilable ideas, but it also suggests a digressive veering away from the issue at hand. Such flirtatious raillery seemed particularly inappropriate when Hume applied it to Macaulay herself: "Had those principles always appeared in the amiable light which they receive both from your person and writings," he wrote to her after the publication of *The History*, "it would have been impossible to resist them" (quoted in Norton and Popkin 408). Macaulay recognized such devices for the hierarchical jostling that they were, referring to Burke's similar reliance on "chivalry" in *Reflections on the Revolution in*

17. For representative examples, see Madeleine de Scudéry, *Artamène, ou Le Grand Cyrus* (1650–55) and *Clélie* (1658–62). Behn's *History of the Nun* (1689) and Manley's *Secret History of Queen Zarah and the Zarazians* (1705) are both collected in Backscheider and Richetti. For a comprehensive study of the relationship between romance and the novel, see Doody, *True Story*.

18. See Christensen for this argument.

France as an attempt to "enslave our affections." Chivalry, she said, is "methodized sentimental barbarism" (*Observations* 22).

"Defects of the Female Historian": Footnotes, Letters, and Historical Narrative

Historiographers have reacted in various ways to Macaulay's work, some, such as Thomas Peardon, arguing that it "is really only a masterly example of how not to write history" (60), some praising her but not making her work central to their studies.[19] Such indifference did not characterize her own time. From the mid-1760s until her second marriage in 1778, the English public ranked Macaulay as highly as any other eighteenth-century historian (Wexler 23). In part, they seized on her so enthusiastically because she was a curiosity. As Walpole so famously wrote, "She is one of the sights that all foreigners are carried to see" (*Letters* 5:146). As a woman writing what purported to be national history, she represented a radical departure from the norm and thus could carry a suggestion of scandal without doing anything particularly scandalous. Nevertheless, her *History of England,* despite its female authorship,

19. It is interesting to speculate about the intersection between Macaulay's "scandalous" behavior and twentieth-century evaluations of her work. Typical is the notation in the University of Virginia library copy of Peardon's 1933 work, where someone has penciled in the word "rubbish" next to the observation that Walpole regarded Macaulay's history as "the best extant history of England" (79). The dearth of serious critical reflection on Macaulay's career (at the time of writing, fewer than twenty scholarly articles, only one slim biography, and one chapter in a study of eighteenth-century women historians) suggests that modern critics have adopted at least some of the negative attitudes prompted by the scandal. Even Macaulay's largely sympathetic biographer Bridget Hill devotes two pages to an apology for airing what she sees as Macaulay's embarrassing behavior, her "dirty washing" (103–4). The scholarly void is often excused by the assertion that Macaulay wrote partisan history. But as Victor Wexler demonstrates in his book-length study of Hume's *History,* in his own time Hume was criticized as frequently as Macaulay for partisanship. John Kenyon makes an important point about Macaulay's contribution when he suggests that her work on the seventeenth century was better than Hume's, "more extensive" and "deeper" (58). The flood of excellent work on eighteenth-century historiography offers little analysis of Macaulay. J. G. A. Pocock's *Barbarism and Religion,* a powerful synthesis centered on Gibbon, does little with Macaulay despite Pocock's assertion elsewhere that "she was quite simply, very good at [writing history]" ("Catharine Macaulay" 243). Joseph M. Levine's works do not deal with Macaulay's period. Mark Salber Phillips unaccountably disposes of Macaulay in less than a page, despite his claim to deal with historiography from 1740 to 1820. Phillip Hicks praises and dismisses Macaulay in a few paragraphs. Works that take up the relationship between historiography and fiction but do not deal with Macaulay include those by Patricia Zimmerman and Robert Mayer. Devoney Looser's valuable survey of historical writing by British women writers focuses on Macaulay's short *History of England from the Revolution to the Present Time in a Series of Letters.*

was eagerly awaited by a public that perceived a need for national *English* history during the period Hume famously called "the historical age" (*Letters* 230). Whereas late-seventeenth-century intellectuals had complained that there was no decent national history—Sir William Temple remarking in 1695, for instance, "that so ancient and noble a Nation as ours . . . should not yet have one good or approved general History of England" (quoted in Levine 292)—by the mid-eighteenth century, complaints centered on the fact that the nation's history had not been written by *British* writers (Looser 11). Even Hume's *History of England* (1754–62) did not really solve the problem for those who wanted Englishness to define what it meant to be British. Could Hume's Scottishness have provoked the London author of *Directions for a Proper Choice of Authors to Form a Library* to complain in 1766 that "his own countrymen" had failed to produce a history of England?[20] Certainly Hume saw his Scottishness as a problem: "I do not believe there is one Englishman in fifty, who, if he heard that I had broke my Neck to night, woud not be rejoic'd with it. Some hate me because I am not a Tory, some because I am not a Whig, some because I am not a Christian, and all because I am a Scotsman" (*Letters* 1:470). Writing in 1765, he ascribed his reluctance to extend his *History* to modern times to English xenophobia. "This Rage against the Scots which is so dishonorable and indeed so infamous to the English nation" had "made me resolve never in my Life to set foot on English ground" much less to publish even more controversial material on English history (*Letters* 1:491). Macaulay stepped into this gap. Born Catharine Sawbridge, though she married "Scotsmen" twice, Macaulay had unassailable English credentials in the politically well-connected Sawbridge family and thus offered the first respectable English history written by an author firmly rooted in English soil. What she produced was a history made national not only through the usual xenophobic concerns about the "other" of foreign nations and customs, but also in much more complex ways through its relationship to linearity, origins, and national character.[21]

Macaulay emphasized the personal in the introduction to the *History*, even admitting the "defects of the female historian." Her authorial and generic choices reinforced the nature of her national and republican project and yet always threatened to undo it. By advertising the *History* as

20. See Looser for a paraphrase of this text (11).

21. Macaulay herself exhibits a xenophobic insularity typical of her time and yet peculiarly tailored to her "Patriot" cause in her rejection of the "tour of Europe" as the "finishing stroke that renders educated Englishmen useless to all the good purposes of persevering the birth-right of an Englishman." The "gaudy tinsel of a superb court," by which she means almost any foreign court, blinds the English to the benefits of civil liberty (*History* 1:xv–xvi).

written by "Catharine Sawbridge Macaulay," English citizen and participant in the nation, she capitalized on her authorship, making the connection between author and work speak for the work's ability to represent the nation. Unlike Hume, who avoided the personal and thus deemphasized his Scottish roots, Macaulay introduced her *History* with her personal history:

> I think it incumbent on me to give the public my reasons for undertaking a subject which has been already treated of by several ingenious and learned men. From my early youth I have read with delight those histories that exhibit Liberty. . . . Studies like these excite that natural love of freedom which lies latent in the breast of every rational being, till it is nipped by the frost of prejudice, or blasted by the influence of vice. (*History* 1:vii)

Making public her private "early youth" in the hotbed of Sawbridge radical politics, she refers to her "delight" and excitement, projecting her own "natural love" of freedom into the "breast of every rational being." Against her better judgment she has ventured "into a path of literature rarely trodden by my sex," motivated by "the cause of liberty and virtue" (x). In these passages her gender takes on a particularly significant role. Her very identity—as a woman subverting established gender categories—performs a sort of cultural work that no amount of declamation could replace. Apologizing for those "defects of a female historian," she invites close investigation: "If the goodness of my head may justly be questioned, my heart will stand the test of the most critical examination" (ix). In the long run, of course, the public's "most critical examination" of her heart offered her no advantage. In the short run, however, by subordinating head to heart, Macaulay put her gender to good use. Exempted by sex from the politically interested group of "wicked men" and "time-serving placemen who have sacrificed the most essential interests of the public to the baseness of their private affections," she lays claim to a form of disinterested authorship emanating from a true affection for liberty and virtue. Gender inversion suggests the possibility of historical revision, as Macaulay places herself above and beside those insiders, "men to whom tyranny is profitable" (vii–viii).

Macaulay's *History* refused the neat categories represented by antiquarianism on the one hand and philosophical history on the other.[22] But this was the inevitable result of her desire to write a national history

---

22. See Levine, *Humanism and History,* for the battle between the antiquarians' concern with the minute details of the nation's past and the philosophical history of writers such as Hume.

grounded in republican principles. Like Gibbon, but in a work devoted to England and thus to quite different effect, Macaulay collected the materials of the nation. The *Monthly Review* recognized this in 1763, noting that she had "tread the path of history," accomplishing "the laborious task of collecting and digesting the political fragments which have escaped the researches of so many learned and ingenious men" (372). In doing so, she answered complaints levied against Hume's methodology, such as that by Joseph Ayloffe in 1772 against the "too common . . . practice with historians hastily to transcribe from the writings of others, and upon their credit to state facts without trying the truth of them by that test, from which alone they can absolutely be ascertained." Research into what Ayloffe called "proper materials" flew in the face of decades of public scorn for the dusty work of antiquarians (quoted in Peardon 292). Yet Macaulay embraced what Hume had referred to as the "dark industry" of primary research, acquiring over five thousand primary documents of the seventeenth and eighteenth centuries by the time of her death (Hill, *Virago* 47–48). The collective nature of her production process, one assigning the same weight to primary materials as to analysis, reaffirmed the message of her *History,* in part because it gathered together a virtual archive of national artifacts, and in part because it allowed readers a direct encounter with the materials that made up national history.

Macaulay's interest in all sorts of margins—women, radical politics, the heart, and, as we shall see, footnoted letters—reflected and reinforced her politics, something few readers seemed to think about when they praised the early volumes for their celebration of "liberty" and yet criticized them for extensive footnoting. To the extent that a truly national history is a history of the people, Macaulay's was more national than most. In order to foreground nation, she leveled other identity categories such as gender and class, imagining the connections among English men and women laterally rather than as mediated through a monarch.[23] Thus she emphasized personality and character, an emphasis that demystified the elite while implying the rise of the common man. In the process, both footnotes and footmen were elevated, as the famous story that pits her against the always hierarchically inclined Johnson demonstrates. As Johnson told it to amuse his conservative friends: "I put on a very grave countenance, and

23. Mary Poovey explains this dynamic: "The process by which individuals or groups embrace the 'nation' as the most meaningful context for self-definition necessarily involves temporarily marginalizing other rubrics that could also provide a sense of identity. Because other classificatory systems and interests persist even in periods of nationalistic fervor, however, and because they often compete with or even contradict 'national' values, national identity is always a precarious formulation for every individual who shares the nationalist sentiment as well as for the nation as a whole" (197).

said to her . . . 'here is a very sensible, civil, well-behaved fellow-citizen, your footman; I desire that he may be allowed to sit down and dine with us.' I thus, Sir, shewed her the absurdity of the leveling doctrine. She has never liked me since" (Boswell, *Life* 317). Boswell, of course, omits Macaulay's response, but according to Macaulay, she ably defended her principles: "I was speaking only of political distinctions; a difference which actually does not exist between us, for I know of no distinctions of that kind which any of the commoners of England possess" (*Letters on Education* 167). As Susan Staves argues, Macaulay's leveling principles were based in rights rhetoric, not in ideas involving economic equality. Macaulay's revision of the story—a revision that reestablishes her as speaking subject—demonstrates what she felt most important to the *History* and to her construction of England as a nation: that commoners, even footmen, had rights so long as England's law permitted no inequality other than the economic. Her imagined England did not quite bring footmen to the table, but at least it offered them access to equal rights.

Comparing Macaulay's histories to other histories of the period reveals the formal consequences of imagining a nation of equal national subjects. Take, for instance, the digressive and interruptive footnote. Its history suggests that throughout the eighteenth century writers were struggling with its implications.[24] Hume tended to avoid long notes, preferring to integrate extraneous material into his narrative, but Gibbon provided lengthy notes until faced with complaints. Then he relegated them to the end of the work so as not to interrupt the thread of his argument (Grafton, *Footnote* 101–3). In comparison, Macaulay's extensive interruptive footnotes offer perhaps her history's most legible formal device. Through these lengthy notes that only pretend to confine themselves to the bottom of the page, Macaulay provided the reader with a heteroglossic mingling of voices drawn from many documents but especially from letters, evoking a vivid sense of a nation in dialogue with itself. After volume 5 she attempted to reduce the number of footnotes in response to public criticism, clarifying their relationship to sequential history when she noted that she had "woven into the text every part of the composition which could be done without breaking into the thread of the history" (quoted in Donnelly 190). But the footnotes of the earlier volumes provide a perspective that Hume often ignored. Quite often they quote extensively from otherwise obscure and inaccessible letters. In volume 1, for instance, the first footnote includes what she calls a "curious passage in a letter which [King James I] wrote from Edinburgh" (1:2). Only a few pages later we find

24. Anthony Grafton has written a detailed history of the footnote.

her analyzing epistolary conventions, suggesting that a letter addressing James as "Right high, right excellent, and mighty prince" gave him "romantic notions of his present fortune" that led to subsequent abuses of royal power (1:14–15). In later passages describing Anne of Denmark, Macaulay demonstrates the importance of the queen, again by including a letter in a footnote. Whereas Hume barely mentions James I's queen, emphasizing instead James's distaste for women, Macaulay's inclusion of Anne's letters to James and to his favorite, Villiers, serves both to present a more complex view of court life and to insert a woman's voice into the narration. Macaulay disowns Anne's acts by remarking that her letters are included to demonstrate her lack of "taste or propriety." But the letters themselves speak for Anne's power over and intimacy with the king. Here Anne, referring to Villiers, tells James how glad she is that her "dog does well, for I did command him that he should make your ear hang like a sow's lug, and when he comes home I will treat him better than any other dog." In a second letter to Villiers himself, Anne is revealed as a behind-the-scenes manipulator, exhorting Villiers to be loyal to the king (1:153). Such details significantly revise Hume's representation of James's complex loyalties and provide insight into his character. In doing so, they also reveal the continuing threat that secret history posed to sequential history, the possibility that an endless set of new and intriguing facts—particularly "private" facts—could undermine any progress at all. Indeed, the length and richness of Macaulay's footnotes tend to draw the reader's attention downward; subtext here is always on the verge of becoming text, of controlling the meaning of the larger text and thus relegating sequential history to a secondary role.

What might it mean to take the epistolary subtext out of the notes and bring it into the text itself? Macaulay experimented with the radical potential of epistolarity in only one historical work, written shortly before she issued the infamous personal letter to Wilson. In 1778, the same year Frances Burney's best-selling *Evelina* suggested that a woman could "expose" herself by writing letters to a man, Macaulay reversed her usual procedure of emphasizing linear prose and relegating letters to the notes when she published *The History of England from the Revolution to the Present Time in a Series of Letters to a Friend* and dedicated it to the seventy-five-year-old Wilson.[25] The *History in Letters* represented a break with tradition in more ways than one. In writing it, Macaulay broke up the chronological progress she had established, interrupting volumes 5

25. Looser also points out the connection between the *History in Letters* and *Evelina*'s publication date. I follow her practice of referring to this work as *History in Letters* rather than by its full title.

(1648–60) and 6 (1660–74) and skipping forward to the more recent present.[26] She broke with generic patterns, too, adopting an epistolary form more commonly used for secret histories and novels than for national history and anticipating by a decade the renewed use of the epistolary form to signify political activity.[27] In part, she drew on the familiar epistle of classical rhetoric, a form that would not become popular in England until more than ten years later. As Mary Favret points out, Burke used the same form in 1790, thus suggesting "a fiction . . . based on the classical virtues of 'consistency' and 'equipoise,' on stable interpretive structures and on a smooth transition between generations" (26).[28] Macaulay operated between that mode—somewhat unstable for Burke, who occasionally departed from it—and the more intimate style of personal address, turning the "smooth transition between generations" on its head by addressing her older patron. Far more than simply a didactic or framing device, the notion of epistolary exchange saturates this work. Macaulay wonders if Wilson is "entertained with my narration"; she mentions (no doubt for the reader's benefit) "your many compliments on the unaffected style of my narrative, which, you assure me conveys to you a very full idea of the temper of parties, and the humor of the times" (*History in Letters* 31–32); and she introduces arguments by first remarking on Wilson's position (32).

The perplexed reviewers who found the narration "singular" and "peculiar" confirm the disruptive nature of this method. Calling Macaulay and Wilson "platonic lovers," the *Critical Review* wondered what was behind the *History in Letters* and why she had chosen the epistolary form (Looser 147). But the biggest secret the *History in Letters* held was that there was no secret—at least with regard to Wilson. If Macaulay romanced anyone in the *History in Letters,* it was her national public. True, the assumption that these were love letters on some level might have been forgivable, given the suggestive titles of works involving letters published during the 1770s.[29] Moreover, she adopted a personal, conversational

26. She had meant to publish two volumes extending from 1660 to her own moment but ended in 1733 (Hill, *Virago* 45).

27. While epistolary histories were written, especially for a juvenile audience, Phillips, noting the rarity of the device, refers to only one other respectable historical work written in epistolary form (*Society* 93).

28. Favret refers to the "genre of the familiar epistle" as a sign for political activity during the years immediately preceding and during the French Revolution (34). See Deidre Lynch's discussion of the *Oxford English Dictionary*'s use of "correspondence." She argues that the definition of correspondence as "'intercourse or communications of a secret . . . nature' has priority over the definition that understands it as 'congruity, harmony, agreement'" (*Economy* 42–43).

29. A list of titles bolsters the critical claims for the connection between letters and interiority, particularly female interiority: *Letters to a lady, with her genuine answers. Both*

mode, beginning with an encomium to Wilson, praising his "virtues," "moderation," "patience and fortitude," and finally "the munificent favors you have conferred on me," an unfortunate choice of words given the loaded meaning of "favors." But she ends the preface by tethering his passion to the nation rather than to herself. "Love" for the nation is his "only ruling passion," and thus she will endeavor to "fix [his] attention" through a historical account. Letters provide a textual body in substitution for absent physicality, or make absence presence, as Samuel Richardson pointed out long before postmodernists theorized epistolarity.[30] If the *History in Letters* had been meant to compensate Wilson—or Macaulay's larger readership—for her missing body, then Macaulay provided a pretty good idea of what form that compensation might take. Defining her readers' "ruling passion" as exclusively historical, she then offered them the body of history in the guise of her own body to fulfill that desire. The true secret of the history was this offering up of herself as an affective substitute for national history.

In the *History in Letters,* Macaulay provided a more approachable and accessible version of history, but also of the historian.[31] The much-criticized "familiar style" of the *History in Letters* served a number of functions, not least of which involved an ideological reversal in which readers were placed on the same level as historians (quoted in Looser 147). In part, she reversed the gender of her readers. If the traditional letter writer "masters his effemination by feminizing his public," as Favret suggests, Macaulay played with these possibilities by emphasizing her own gender in writing to Wilson (14). Such an ideological reversal was particularly appropriate to Macaulay's topic. Here form and content merged. She saw the Glorious Revolution as the moment when the people came to control

---

printed verbatim from the originals (Dublin 1752); *Genuine copies of all the love letters and cards which passed between an illustrious personage and a noble lady, during the course of a late amour* (London [1770?]); *The embarrassed lovers or, the history of Henry Carey, esq. and the Hon. Miss Cecilia Neville. In a series of letters,* 2 vols. (London 1775); *The memoirs of Miss Arabella Bolton. Containing a genuine account of her seduction, and the barbarous treatment she afterwards received from the Honourable C—— L——, the present supposed M——r for the county of Middlesex. . . . The whole taken from the original letters of the said C—— L—— to Dr. Kelly* (London 1770); *Original love-letters between a lady of quality and a person of inferior station* (Dublin 1784); *A copy of a love-letter from a yong gentleman [sic] in this neighborhood, to the lovely nymph in Mosely-street; with the young lady's answer; and a copy of verses in praise of the young lady. They were found in Drury-lane, near the new play-house by a gentleman last night, who ordered them to be printed, to gratify the curiosity of the public* (London 1795).

30. Cook also points this out: "Writing a letter can be understood as the attempt to construct a phantasmatic body that in some measure compensates for the writer's absence" (26).

31. For a discussion of fantasies regarding national icons and accessibility, see Berlant 22–28.

the power of the Crown and represented that moment in an epistolary form that implied hierarchical reversal and public accessibility. Her "un-affected stile" reflected the "humor of the times," as she said (*History in Letters* 31–32). But it also reflected the *History in Letters'* immediate po-litical agenda. Epistolary fiction imagines an "archive" subject to inter-pretation by the activist reader (Phillips 92). Such had been Macaulay's method from the beginning: she had imagined a readership capable of di-rect contact with the historical archives, able to analyze what it found there. Now she tried a different tactic, offering readers a window into the historical conversation. Readers must have felt themselves a party to the making of historical discourse as Macaulay chatted informally with her mentor. By bringing epistolarity into the text, she lent history a less for-bidding form. But in doing so she exposed her "heart" to close analysis. Because it was addressed to Wilson and composed of letters, the *History in Letters* became evidence itself, the raw material of secret history. Thus when Macaulay's private letter with its mysterious contents surfaced a short time later, her career imploded. The private letter retroactively brought the *History in Letters* and then the previous volumes of the more traditional *History of England* under suspicion. A Macaulay sexualized was a Macaulay particularized and gendered, one disruptive rather than productive of national history.

Britannia's Treatment: Macaulay and the Body of History

That the lost letter could have such a negative impact on Macaulay's career demonstrates just how fragile her public image had been from the beginning. Caught between the gender stereotypes that governed histori-cal writing and the needs of a republican historian, Macaulay struck a very delicate balance, one easily upset by the multiple threat represented by the missing letter. By putting forward a personalized version of au-thorship as constitutive of national identity, Macaulay invited public in-spection and comment, as she said, "the most critical examination" (1:ix). But given her politics, this was never simply a disadvantage to be over-come. Instead, her status as "man-woman" represented a challenge to all forms of hierarchical stratification.[32] By destabilizing gender categories, she constructed a powerful—perhaps *too* powerful—internationally known symbol of Englishness in which her frequent shifts between "mas-

32. For the argument that transgression in one cultural sphere affects our understanding of other cultural arenas, see Stallybrass and White.

culine" pen and "feminine" Britannia suggested the possibility of radical change.

That she presented a threateningly ambiguous gendered public figure was apparent from the moment of her first publication. As the 1763 *Monthly Review* reaction to her work reveals, Macaulay's publication of the first volume of the history subverted gendered generic traditions in ways that were difficult for her audience to articulate. Arguing that men should do history and women should sew, the reviewer suggested that even though Livy and Tacitus could have learned to sew if they wanted, "no one would allow it to be a natural and becoming accomplishment for two such grave historians. . . . [T]he soft and delicate texture of a female frame, was no more intended for severe study, than the labourious drudge, Man, was formed for working of catgut" (Review 373).[33] One of the earlier suggestive comments appears in the *Review*'s discussion of "one Phatheusa, the wife of Pytheus," who "thought so intensely during her husband's absence, that, at his return, she had a beard grown upon her chin." This is followed by a warning that study "is in every way danger-ous for the fair, for while they are wrapt in a profound reverie, they may lose——We don't know what they may lose" (373). What will the study of history do to ladies? Perhaps it will result in their masculinization: the signs of "severe study" will appear on their bodies. Perhaps it will result in a loss of virginity or even (perversely enough) in a phallic loss, one that the reviewer finds impossible to narrate. Although women were often told to better themselves by *reading* history, the serious study of history, the *writing* of history, apparently blurred the boundaries between gender (who shall sew) and sexual identity (who shall grow beards). Significantly, the "ladies" subject to the elided violation were silent ones. The reviewer imagines them "wrapt in a profound reverie" rather than as active speak-ing subjects.[34]

The redoubled gap that occurs when the reviewer tries to imagine what women historians may lose during a "profound reverie," a gap in con-sciousness underscored with the reviewer's multiple textual dash, reveals an inability to express what may have been gained as well. The reviewer

33. Macaulay in *Letters on Education* seems to provide an oblique response to this cri-tique when she argues in favor of teaching sewing to both girls *and* boys. A handicraft such as "forming a button" is far better for boys than "spending whole days in hunting down a harmless animal, both at the hazard of their necks, and at the expense of their benevolence" (65).

34. See Berlant for the ways in which a silent woman's body can represent national unity. As Berlant points out, the "female icon's" power emanates from silence: the Statue of Lib-erty's "immobility and silence are fundamental to her activity as a positive site of national power and fantasy" (27).

here fails, as Claudia Johnson has put it in a different context, "to imagine the as yet unimaginable—a thinking woman whose desire is not narratable" (50). Like other nonnarratable desires, Macaulay's desire lacked a home, an available discursive field through which to represent itself and within which to make meaning.[35] To remedy this lack, both Macaulay and her public struggled to locate her discursively, "swerving" from one identity to another and finding all of them unsatisfactory.[36] Anchoring the public understanding of Englishness in a private body made public, she attempted to offer a contradiction in terms: a speaking version of Britannia, the well-known historical figure that naturalized governmental institutions by linking them to the body (Lynch, *Economy* 25). Thus she made of herself a public symbol of a female intellectual, and she was often referred to as Britannia or Clio, and portrayed as such in engravings, paintings, sculptures, Derby ceramic figures, and wax museum casts. Even if one brackets the contrast between her status as speaker and the silent, passive nature of the available images, none of these categories was particularly stable. Indeed, their very passivity released a sexual commentary that might otherwise have remained cloaked. For instance, references to Macaulay as Clio, apparently innocent on their surface, suffered from a context in which Clio appeared in various inviting sexual postures.[37] Britannia too, despite or perhaps because of her increasing visibility in a world of British imperialism and commercial success, was subject to sexualization. In a typical print, "Britannia's Treatment," published in 1770, Britannia appears with a spear to the breast, disrobed, the Magna Carta torn and tattered at her feet (Dickinson 82). As Madge Dresser argues, mid-eighteenth-century images reveal a "salacious prurience" evident in the way in which "Britannia is variously dismembered, buggered, ridden, and even flogged naked with a 'ScottishThistle'" (34). Other associations were just as sexualized. Macaulay was often referred to as an Amazon, but even Amazons could be eroticized, as Johnson's references to her reveal. In 1765, well before the second marriage, Johnson "began to grow very great [drunk]; stripped poor Mrs. Macaulay to the very skin, then

35. I am indebted to Claudia Johnson's use of Eve Kosofsky Sedgwick. Johnson and Sedgwick speak of sexual desire, or more particularly of the desire to construct a particular sort of sexual identity category "too liminal to be represented" (Johnson 50). In Macaulay's case, authorial desire stands in the place of sexual desire. She longed for an authorial identity that had no predecessors and thus found herself hunting through the various available categories in search of something suitable.

36. Johnson asks, "How far can or will an already gendered and physically very localized desire swerve, how radically will it misrecognize itself, in its need to join a preexisting current of discourse through which to become manifest, to be fulfilled, manipulated, or even frankly repressed—to become, in short, meaningful?" (50).

37. See Fox for a discussion of Clio's representation.

gave her for his toast, and drank her in two bumpers" (Boswell, *Life* 344). In 1775 he found her "like the Amazons of old; she must be courted by the sword" (Boswell, *Life* 607–8).

Samuel Foote's 1768 play *The Devil on Two-Sticks* offers a good example of the potential for destabilization that the woman intellectual presented. On the whole, the play demonstrates the powerful appeal Macaulay's man-woman status held for the public. The *London Chronicle* reported that "this character is said to be drawn for a celebrated Female Historian, who has greatly distinguished herself in the cause of liberty" (quoted in Hill, *Virago* 21). Noting that he could not buy a seat the first time he tried to see the popular play, Walpole remarked that on June 17, more than two weeks after the play was first performed, Macaulay attended "to see herself represented." As Elizabeth N. Chatten notes in her work on Foote, the satiric thrust of the play was "mild, probably because, aside from her being a female intellectual, there was little to ridicule" (89). In *The Devil* Foote most clearly points to Macaulay when "Margaret" describes an author she knows: "Liberty has already a champion in one of my sex: The same pen that has dar'd to scourge the arbitrary actions of some of our monarchs shall do equal justice to the oppressive power of parents!" But Foote also limns Macaulay directly in the character of Margaret, a republican patriot who reads "Machiavel, Montesquieu, Locke, Bacon, Hobbes, Harrington, Hume . . . Alberoni and Cardinal Richlieu . . . the pragmatic Sanction . . . the Vinerian professor," causing her brother to cry "mercy on us" (3). Margaret's defining characteristic—she seems drawn from Mrs. Western in *Tom Jones* and, as we shall see later in this chapter, provides a model for the bookseller's wife in Paul Jodrell's post–second marriage play—is that she applies the discourse of civic republicanism to domestic events, causing her brother to complain, "If you want money to pay off my bills, you move me for further supplies; if I turn away a servant, you condemn me for so often changing my ministry, and because I lock up my daughter. . . . [I]t is forsooth an invasion of the Bill of Rights and a mortal stab to the great Charter of Liberty" (2).

The play constructs a comic opposition between the arbitrary power associated with the English past and Macaulay's by now famous footnotes. Margaret threatens to have her brother's "despotic dealings properly and publickly handled" in London: "I may, perhaps, be too late to get you into the historical text; but, I promise you, you shall be soundly swinged in the marginal note" (6). Macaulay herself was "swinged" in the margins of the play. The play's emphasis on the virtue associated with civic republicanism contained a veiled reference to private vice. Hinting at the allure exerted by Macaulay's man-woman persona, the play's "devil" displays a print of "Britannia a-dying," noting that "her disease is a lethargy." While a doctor holds a "draught to her mouth . . . to lull her faster to sleep," another man "rouses Britannia, by tickling her nose with that straw . . . you see, Britannia is delivered from death" (34–35). The embedded tableau conflates an "aroused" Britannia—one capable of speaking for the nation—with an eroticized Britannia, thus indicating the conflicting images at play in Macaulay's persona, but also somewhat eerily pointing to Macaulay's eventual relationship to the Graham brothers, whom she did not meet until 1775.[38] As the play demonstrates by matching comic power to comic disempowerment, to the extent that the female body could be figured as powerful, it could also be distorted, sexualized, and violated.

This covert identification of Macaulay with low forms of sexuality reflected a larger cultural undoing of intellectual women. To control the radical instability her authorial persona evoked, Macaulay and her supporters relied on heightened claims to republican virtue with its accompanying discourse of corruption. In this revisionary Machiavellian world, virtue controlled the tendency of liberty to run rampant while corruption debased liberty and thus caused political disorder. Claims to virtue had a double cultural valence when made by historians. Most historians represented their claim to authority, to "truth," as originating in "virtue." As Michael McKeon points out in his study of the English novel, "questions of truth and virtue begin to seem not so much distinct problems as versions or transformations of each other, distinct ways of formulating and propounding a fundamental problem of what might be called epistemological, social, and ethical signification" (266). Both Hume and Macaulay engage with this discourse, setting history and virtue against fiction and vice. Hume argues, for instance, that historians are the "true friends of virtue," poets "advocates of vice" (*Essays* 567), while Macaulay recommends that children study history but avoid novels, for while novelists "are in general ranged on the side of virtue . . . they are apt to deceive" (*Letters on Education* 143). But when used to authorize a republican history, concepts of "virtue" became inextricably interwoven with the discourse of classical republicanism, a discourse that, though it could legitimate Macaulay's republican version of English history, would have created problems for any female historian. In the complicated transition in which the English began to assume political agency in the public sphere, virtue played a central part. As J. G. A. Pocock explains, an "equilibrium

38. See Chatten's discussion of the play for a different interpretation.

of virtue and powers" was essential to maintaining stability in a republican system: "States and nations, like individuals, might rise and fall as ambition condemned them to mount upon the Wheel, but only the republic obliged the individual to pit his virtue against fortune as a condition of his political being. Virtue was the principle of republics" (*Machiavellian Moment* 349–50). As republican thought developed, "virtue" contended with "corruption" rather than "fortune." Civic virtue had a heavy weight to bear.

Like other political women of the 1760s, Macaulay relied on virtue for her authority. The dynamic undergirded almost all discussions of Macaulay's cultural and historical role, especially those that imagined her in national contexts. In William Robertson's poem of 1768, she fights "Corruption, Luxury, Venality, / Division, Vanity and fell Oppression" (quoted in Hill, *Virago* 21).[39] In Hannah More's poem of 1774, she is associated with a list of authors in whom "female virtue joins with female sense" (quoted in Hill, *Virago* 20). The poem "Atti Dell'incoronazione de Corilla Olimpica" suggests virtue's function, its tense relationship with agency. Here an aggressive and outspoken Macaulay is chosen over Anna Barbauld, Hester Chapone, Elizabeth Montagu, and Elizabeth Carter as the English woman writer best able to compete with Italy's Maria Maddalene Morelli:

> To plead with warmth in Freedom's sacred cause,
> Defend my people, and support their laws;
> To shew Corruption in her vilest light:
> To speak with boldness and undaunted write;
> To tear the shackles from the Briton's wrist;
> And from his eyes to clear the northern mist;
>
> . . . .
>
> If such be merit, such deserve our praise,
> MACAULAY, come, and take the well-earn'd bays.
>
> (quoted in Staves 174)

Virtue balanced Macaulay's willingness to "speak" with a "boldness" that would inevitably emphasize her body and person, a duty she bore more than willingly, for like Johnson himself, she apparently enjoyed celebrity.[40] That boldness itself, however, suggested the very excesses that republican virtue was supposed to counteract.

39. William Robertson (1704–83) was a pupil of Francis Hutcheson who eventually became a proponent of Unitarianism (Hill, *Virago* 20–21).

40. Paula McDowell's work on late-seventeenth-century women writers suggests that women's celebrity status was related to the new visibility they enjoyed in a burgeoning print

As a political and intellectual woman with republican leanings, Macaulay inevitably found her virtue under attack.[41] Claims to virtue were easily destabilized when made in conjunction with an argument for liberty, especially if made by a woman. As Diana Donald notes, prints of the 1760s opposed "manly virtues" to female corruption and suggested that the corruption of virtue posed a threat to British liberty.[42] Civic virtue had always been associated with the ownership of landed property, with reason, and with the carrying out of various public duties. The virtues of the body—its proper husbanding, so to speak—were displaced onto women, who bore the cultural responsibility for constraining improper sexual passions. As Macaulay well knew, female virtue invoked a duty to family lineage, which in turn immediately invoked the body. In the *Letters on Education*, Macaulay complains bitterly about the inequitable way "virtue" was applied to the sexes: "There is but one fault which a woman of honour may not commit with impunity; let her only take care that she is not caught in a love intrigue, and she may lie, she may deceive, she may defame, she may ruin her own family with gaming, and the peace of twenty others with her coquettry, and yet preserve both her reputation and her peace" (210–11).

This bitter stance, developed after Macaulay's second marriage, was figured differently in her treatment of politically active, petitioning women in the *History*.[43] Here we see Macaulay negotiating the same virtue-aggression axis that governed her own career. Petitioners, as Hume said, were "the authors of liberty to the nation" (*History* 5:495), but in their active demonstration of political equality they also represented the possibility of violent and even revolutionary activity. Thus scenes of petitioning provided apt sites for the discussion of national virtue and vice,

---

culture. As she says, these women were "caught up in a circuit of property values, and a host of new consumer items (encomium poems, frontispieces, engravings, busts) transformed the female writerly body itself into an *objet d'art*" (227). In Macaulay's case, such consumer items were given renewed meaning as national icons.

41. The currency of such attacks is demonstrated by a print from 1784 depicting the duchess of Devonshire—famously active on Fox's behalf—holding a "shield of virtue" to fend off arrows from the press labeled "malice," "envy," and "woman hater" (Donald 126–27).

42. See Donald for a short discussion of the print "An Essay on Woman," no doubt a reference to John Wilkes's obscene publication of the same name (78). The print is inscribed "He that tastes woman ruin meets," perhaps a veiled comment regarding the temporary "ruin" Wilkes encountered when prosecuted for the "Essay on Woman" in 1763. See Peter D. G. Thomas for an account of the essay's impact on Wilkes's career (4).

43. For discussions of the primary role petitioning played, see Mark Knights's "London's 'Monster' Petition of 1680," and "Petitioning and the Political Theorists," as well as Patricia Higgins, "The Reactions of Women." I am indebted to Susan Staves, "The Liberty of a She-Subject," for drawing my attention to the issue of petitioning.

of liberty and corruption. Arguing that petitions perform a communal function, one in which the nation appears to speak with one voice, Macaulay makes a point of quoting John Pym's melodramatic response to the large number of petitions initiated during the early 1640s: "In these petitions, my lords, said he, you may hear the voice, or rather *the cry of all England;* and you cannot wonder if the urgency, the extremity of our condition, produce some earnestness and vehemency of expression more than ordinary; the agony, terror, and perplexity, in which the kingdom labours is *universal*" (*History* 3:190; emphasis added). Whereas Macaulay emphasizes the collective nature of petitioning, Hume focuses on the dangers of improper petitioning, defining petitions as "a new method of framing and dispersing libels . . . invented by the leaders of popular discontent" (5:296). Hume notes the royalists' claims that many petitions included forged signatures: "A petition was first framed; moderate, reasonable, such as men of character willingly subscribed. The names were afterwards torn off, and affixed to another petition, which served better the purposes of the popular faction" (5:296). The "torn" petitions—petitions that divorced virtuous men from their reasonable goals to reassociate them with disorderly factions—suggest the dismembering of the body politic which Hume saw as endemic to the process of petitioning itself.

To recuperate petitioning after Hume, Macaulay distinguishes between effective petitioning by modest, moderate, and virtuous women and disastrously ineffective petitioning by women who are immodest, importunate, and frivolous.[44] In volume 3 of the *History* she offers an example of the "good" women petitioners who "prayed [to Parliament] to be secured from the cruelty and persecution of Papists" in 1641. According to Macaulay, these women

> expressed their resentment on the cruelties committed in Ireland, in very pathetic terms: they apologized for this their uncommon act, on the principle that they were sharers in the common calamities that oppression produced: "On these grounds, conclude the petitioners, we are emboldened to present our humble desires to this assembly, not regarding the reproaches which may and are by many cast upon us; we do it not out of any self-conceit or pride of heart." (3:197–98)

Successful petitioners, well treated by Pym, these women were met at the "door of the house," the threshold of political power, only to be encour-

44. For an overview of seventeenth-century petitioning incidents involving women, see Higgins.

aged to return home with their prayers. Such a result, though not satisfying to the twenty-first-century reader, mediated the relationship between women and civic virtue through religious agency. Worse responses could be imagined, as Macaulay suggests in the marginal note. There she defends the female petitioners by comparing them to petitioners in ancient Rome. The government of Rome, she says, was never influenced by "loose and vicious women," but did esteem those who "exhibited any symptom of public virtue." When Roman women were rebuked for petitioning, it was because they petitioned on "subjects that concerned themselves," what Macaulay calls "the improper object[s] of their desire" (3:196). Opposing public virtue to private, female "desire," Macaulay redeems the "uncommon act" of petitioning but also suggests the scrutiny imposed on women who claim their political rights. Vulnerable to the rumors of secret history, to deviation from the linear text of patrilineal descent, female virtue was always about to be undermined, even in Macaulay's own marginal notes.

Like that of the female petitioners, Macaulay's right to public commentary was plagued by marginal deconstructive gestures. Prefiguring her final undoing in 1778, visual marginalia complicated Macaulay's vulnerable public image—an image under revision in numerous porcelain figurines, theatrical portrayals, paintings, frontispieces, and satirical prints.[45] Whereas in the earliest paintings and Derby porcelains she tends to hold the Magna Carta or other symbol of the people's law, in later images she holds a dedication to Wilson. The 1774 painting by Robert Edge Pine provides a good example. Unadorned and desexualized, Macaulay appears in robes that sweep from her neck to the floor. Her hair is pulled back from her face. The viewer's gaze is drawn not to any mark of gendered sexuality or feminized display, but to the large intelligent eyes, gracefully elongated nose, and high forehead. As Natalie Zemon Davis points out in reference to the portrait, Macaulay represents herself and is represented as "muse," "liberty," and "Macaulay" ("Two Bodies" 18). Davis relates the elisions between these constructs to "the tension between the living historian and the eternal body of history," a tension recreated in Macaulay's case by the continual undermining of the "body of history" by the historian's body. In the portrait, the artist conflates self, virtue, republicanism, and the nation, as Macaulay leans her writing arm on the volumes of the *History of*

45. Using the secondary literature, I have counted over thirty images of her person or her history, from the painting *Nine Living Muses*, to the Derby porcelains now at Winterthur and the Metropolitan Museum in New York, to the crude reproduction of her face on a medallion in a satirical print featuring James Graham. See Fox; Donnelly; and Hill, *Virago*, for discussions of her pictorial and other public representations.

England, which in turn are supported by a short pillar inscribed with the words "Government a power delegated for the happiness of mankind, conducted by wisdom, justice, and mercy." In one hand she holds a quill, emblem of authorship. But in the other she holds a card printed with her patron Thomas Wilson's name, thus foreshadowing her future deflation. While her authorship rests on a recitation of ideas of civic virtue, of a government untainted by personal interest or faction, the card in her hand suggests that such associations could be undone by the private interests that would eventually destroy her reputation.

That deflation began even before the second marriage, for the famous statue Wilson erected to Macaulay contained its own deconstructive gesture (figure 2). The statue itself was innocent enough. Called *History,* it depicted Macaulay in a posture typical of her portraits, holding a pen in one hand and leaning on the volumes of her *History.* But Wilson's inscription immediately provoked shocked comments among Macaulay's contemporaries. Drawn, interestingly enough, from a secret history, *The Correspondents: An Original Novel; in a series of Letters* (1775), the inscription praised Macaulay as "a kind of prodigy" and "proof that genius is not confined to sex," but ended with a plea that "we want no more than one Mrs. Macaulay." Even worse, the source of the quotation, misattributed by Wilson to the respected Lord Lyttelton (George), was actually George's disreputable son, Thomas, whose letters to the aptly named "Apphia Peach" were the basis of *The Correspondents.*[46] Whether this was Wilson's idea of wit or simply a mistake, the implications were immediately apparent.

Macaulay performed herself at her infamous forty-sixth birthday party, an event that becomes legible only in light of the unnarratability of Macaulay's identity and her resulting tendency to "verge" in and out of a variety of unsuitable alternatives.[47] Such displays were not unprecedented. Charlotte Lennox had been publicly feted under far more compromising circumstances. But Macaulay's party was a public relations disaster.[48] Placed in a "conspicuous elevated situation in front of the company," mostly male, she was presented with a gold medal, reminiscent of

46. I have drawn on Hill, *Virago* 100–101 and Guest 198–99 for this account.

47. The celebration was orchestrated in part by James Graham, in part by Wilson, but Macaulay assented to most of its details, thus placing the stamp of approval on what could only become a public demonstration of her power.

48. Although Macaulay's party sounds quite self-promotional even in our age of advertising, Johnson staged an even more egregious celebration in honor of Lennox's first novel. During the party, Johnson "directed that a magnificent hot apple-pye should make a part of it, and this he would have stuck with bay-leaves, because, forsooth, Mrs. Lennox was an authoress, and had written verses; and further, he had prepared for her a crown of laurel" (quoted in Bate 270). The occasion is mentioned as an example of Johnson's spirit, not of Lennox's conceit.

Fig. 2. J. F. Moore, Catharine Macaulay as *History* (1778). Courtesy of the *Warrington Guardian*.

the medallion-type engraving used as the frontispiece to the histories. Thus adorned with the histories as well as her elaborate and fashionable clothing, she was set above the men at the gathering. The recitation of six odes composed for the occasion by various poets—later published with the notation that they commemorated "an event so pleasing to the true friends of literature and liberty in these kingdoms"—only increased the ensuing public ridicule. The verses associated her with Britannia:

> 'Tis She, 'tis She, 'tis She!
> The Child of Liberty!
> To whom Britannia gave the prize,
> Oh! Sound her triumph thro' the skies.
> (quoted in Hill, *Virago* 96–97)

But they also suggested that she had explored Britannia's "secret springs" in order to expose the "self-created powers usurp'd by Kings." Macau-

[153]

lay's own "secret springs" were repeatedly invoked as well—in comments regarding her "cure" by William Graham's brother James, the quack doctor already achieving fame for his use of electricity as a medical treatment.[49] Although the poets may have conflated the celebration of Macaulay with the celebration of Britain, her health with the health of the nation, those who read of the party in the Bath papers did not. The reactions ranged from "extreme disgust" to Elizabeth Carter's remark that "I think one never heard of anybody, above the degree of an idiot who took pleasure in being so dressed out . . . like a queen in a puppet show" (quoted in Hill, *Virago* 95).

Macaulay's being "dressed out . . . like a queen in a puppet show" drove the most vicious of the pre-marriage attacks against her. In a satirical print produced in 1774, Macaulay is shown facing a mirrored dressing table (figure 3). Unlike almost all other pictorial representations of Macaulay, satiric or serious, the print contains neither books nor direct references to the *History*. Instead of a pen, she holds a makeup brush; rather than working at a writer's desk, she is painting herself at a dressing table littered with makeup bottles and powder containers reminiscent of those in Swift's poetical dressing room scenes. The satirist endows her with an enormous headdress, associating her with the exaggerated femininity of the elaborate hairstyles that were the fashion at the time. But this headdress contains a miniature hearse and team of horses, and behind Macaulay sits the figure of Death—an arrow piercing his groin—grinning demonically as he turns over an hourglass. The caricature, titled "A Speedy and Effectual Preparation for the Next World," associates excessive femininity with a debased reference to historical writing in the image of Macaulay's brush-holding hand. The hearse bearing down from above marks not only her own approaching old age and death but also the death of the *History* itself. Placing Macaulay with her face to the mirror and her back to the death-signifying skeleton with his hourglass in turn suggests a relationship between the death of history and the move toward a "feminine" worldly vanity. By emphasizing private vice rather than public virtue, the print associates Macaulay with the very traits she had rejected in the *History*'s petitioning scenes.

The print attacked every available fissure in Macaulay's public persona. Its emphasis on fashion and paint intersected with veiled and not so veiled commentary on Macaulay's performative femininity. The competitive

49. Within the next few years, Graham would open his London "Temple of Health," later renamed the "Temple of Hymen," which showcased the "Grand State Celestial Bed" where electricity was used to cure impotence and infertility. See Schnorrenberg for a discussion of James Graham's reputation and methods.

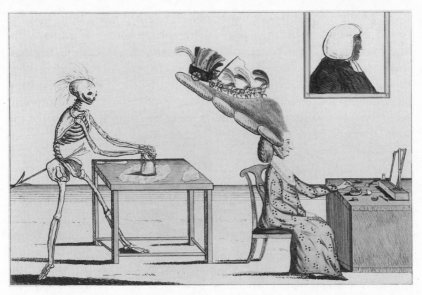

Fig. 3. Matthew Darly, "A Speedy Effectual Preparation for the Next World" (1777), a caricature of Catharine Macaulay. Copyright © The British Museum.

Elizabeth Carter had suggested the anxiety that gathered around Macaulay's fashionable image as early as 1757 when she recorded a meeting in which Macaulay's dress caught her attention: "I should have been mighty cautious of holding any such conversation in such a place with a professed philosopher and scholar, but as it was a fine, fashionable well-dressed lady, whose train was longer than anybody's train, I had no sort of scruple" (quoted in Boos and Boos 50). Noting that she was "much more learned than becomes a fine lady," Carter juxtaposes Macaulay's person and conversation with that of a generic young woman present at the party, who listened to Macaulay "for a considerable time with the most profound attention to a discourse, which must have been for the most part as unintelligible to her as if it had been delivered in Arabic" (Hill, *Virago* 11). In the vignette, Carter critiques the extremely narrow range of acceptable behavior available to Macaulay: ironically claiming that it was Macaulay's clothes that permitted their conversation, Carter simultaneously asserts the association between fashionable dress and mental vacuity.

The competitive threat adhering to a train "longer than anybody's" suggests the larger dynamic driving Macaulay's allegiance to fashion and cosmetics. Metonymic to fashion of all kinds, the train was a sign of femininity, of a heightened commitment to dress, ornamentation, and frippery, and thus seemed unnatural when harnessed to intellect. Yet because

[155]

it was phallic and overpowering, it also represented aggression. Johnson had recommended cosmetics as a benign replacement for Macaulay's political projects: "She is better employed at her toilet, than using her pen. It is better she should be reddening her own cheeks than blackening other people's characters" (Boswell, *Life* 749). But by the 1770s, the dressing table image, with its cosmetics, mirror, and portrait of self-absorption, evoked not just vanity and fashion but the threat women presented to the social order. In part, the fear of newly discovered female political agency was enacted through the association between political expression and hair styling. A typical French print of the period shows a French woman putting a male servant to work on her hair while she reads a book. As such commentary indicates, moralists saw fashion as "the means by which men were entrapped and emasculated" (Donald 85–86). Women's elaborate hairstyles were often used as signifiers of an exaggerated, aggressive femininity, one that came to stand for excess of every kind. In the satiric 1771 print "Proportion," the opposed sides of a half-male, half-female figure are marked mainly by their difference in hairstyles. And in "The Ladies Contrivance or the Capital Conceit," a print of 1777, the lady's coach is distinguished from the gentleman's coach by its elongated roof, meant to accommodate her elaborate hairdo. But hair was also an emblem of national identity, even of national excess. In "The Flower Garden" of 1777, a woman's hairdo supports the carefully tended gardens and fields of England. And in "Bunker's Hill or America's Head Dress," a print of 1776, an American satirist turns these images against the English themselves, placing a scene of cannon, fighting troops, flags, artillery, and tents in a woman's hair, which here signifies English weakness. The soldiers, all of whom are British, are shown shooting directly at one another.

The reaction to Macaulay's "train" and all it signified thus registered a high level of anxiety in which the aggressive performance of femininity intersected with concerns about political expression, consumer behavior, and corruption. As the *Lady's Magazine* had complained in 1773, women's fashion encouraged women to think of themselves performatively: "The world is now nothing but a masquerade, wherein everyone wears, not the dress which suits her character, but the most pleasing to her fancy, and under which she thinks she shall be best concealed" (quoted in Donald 88). If gender was a performance, it was not supposed to call attention to itself as such. Exaggerated performances, like overwrought stage acting, suggested gender's unnaturalness. "Fashion plugs the body into consumer culture," as Erin Mackie has suggested (xiii), and in the late eighteenth century, consumer culture represented corruption and dissipation. If the public imagination made fashionable women bear the weight of the entire culture, this was an image that Macaulay had actively sought. She had marketed herself as a commodity, lending her image to frontispieces and portraits for public consumption. The cosmetic painting of her face for the public represented only another form of the painted portraits that were already available for viewing. But to be associated so closely with commodities as to *become* a commodity risked being redefined in terms of corruption. As Laura Brown has argued, "it is only one quick step from the equation of women and commodities to an attack on the hypocritical female as the embodiment of cultural corruption" (430). Macaulay's fashionable attire served numerous purposes: fashion "plugged" her into a resistant discourse in which women turned fashion and commodity culture against men, using it as a sign of their power. Macaulay may also have relied on it as a gesture that compensated for the supposed masculinizing tendencies of history. Finally, it served as a class marker, protecting her from identification with hacks and scribblers, from being leveled herself to a class from which she could not make authoritative historical pronouncements. But in adopting the elaborate hairstyles and makeup of her class, Macaulay also risked becoming an objectified representative of the excesses that a male-dominated elite wished to distance itself from.

The satirical references to the cosmetics table thus divorced Macaulay from the historical pen and reassociated her with consumption, undermining the connection between historical writing and virtue and suggesting that her own historical writing covered up underlying corruption. This was a powerful attack in part because the success of the *History* had rested on her efforts to merge self and work and promote a unified image of what would eventually be revealed as impossibly dissonant ideas. To sustain the illusion of unity, she needed to assert her authority, to undermine hierarchy but not to advocate disorder. Any attack that divorced her from her pen undermined that unity. Although she and her *History* aimed to suggest national integration, this symbol's consolidating value relied on her ability to maintain the unbroken relationship between her person and her literary property, in order both to legitimize her project and to underscore continually the connections between virtue and republican values, and between those values and Englishness. Macaulay managed to maintain an uncertain equilibrium until her second marriage. Despite all of her earlier behavior, it was the misappropriated letter in which she explained the marriage that provoked the most powerful attack on her ability to represent the nation. Perhaps it consolidated all of the doubts that had dogged her career for years. In combining sexual images representative of female disintegration with the disruption of the relationship she had established between gender and genre, between her authorial self and her work, it disassociated her from her pen and reassociated her with the corruption of femininity.

"A Remarkable Moving Letter": Gender and Literary Property

When Macaulay married James Graham's younger brother William in 1778, she was forty-six years old; he was twenty-one. An odd marriage, many thought, although as Mercy Otis Warren pointed out, Macaulay might have imagined she could marry "an inoffensive obliging youth with the same impunity a Gentleman of three score and ten might marry a Damsel of fifteen" (quoted in Fox 141). Those who knew her would not have been surprised had she married her patron, Wilson, who in buying Alfred House in Bath was said to have "purchased and presented her with a mansion . . . a library, servants, and every article of luxury" ("Account" 332–33). When she turned to Graham instead, her public was scandalized. In the picture "The Auspicious Marriage," printed in *Town and Country Magazine* shortly after the marriage, a miniature Graham leads Macaulay away from Alfred House toward the altar of an embarrassed Hymen; discarded on the ground lie the staff of Liberty, Macaulay's pen and ink, and the volumes of the *History*. The distortion of Macaulay's frame (she is all fashionable bustle, double chins, and massive hairpiece decorated with feathers and fool's cap) suggests the distorted body politic; her proportions overwhelm the much smaller frenchified Graham. The text suggests that she has rejected writing for passion.

Yet her marriage might have remained a small private affair rather than becoming a career-destroying public scandal had Wilson kept her letter to him private. Instead, he transformed it into the "remarkable moving" production imagined in one of the parodies. It was misappropriated for publication by Wilson, quoted by John Wilkes, passed around to writers such as Paul Jodrell and probably to others eager to lampoon Macaulay. Even Elizabeth Montagu and Elizabeth Carter, always quick to criticize Macaulay, were familiar with the letter (Guest 199). Wilson, with the aid of Wilkes (who may have imagined himself her rival, as he was writing a history himself), helped shape the public reaction to Macaulay's marriage by threatening to print that letter along with others he had received or acquired from a maid who was supposed to have burned them (Hill, *Virago* 120). Despite clear legal standards that prohibited the reprinting of private letters, by September 1779, Wilson had formed an agreement with

Macaulay's own publisher, Cruttwell of Bath,[50] to publish not only the lost letter, this "formal vindication" of the marriage ("Account" 334), but also the other letters Macaulay had written, a collection that Wilkes, ironically given his obscene *Essay on Woman,* thought "too gross for the public eye" (quoted in Hill, *Virago* 112). What did the letter actually say? The parodic response it evoked has created such a dense fog of misogynistic misinterpretation that it is impossible to restate any of the letter's contents with certainty. She may have apologized to Wilson for what she supposedly called her "slip"—the marriage to Graham. Those who saw the letter claimed that she affirmed her love for Wilson, but explained that his advanced age made it impossible for her to marry him. Her proposal to tend her "honored parent" to the grave with the help of her new husband added insult to injury (Donnelly 188).

Did Macaulay send an indelicate letter? If so, she may have done so confident that her right to control its dissemination would be respected. In 1737, Pope had complained that weak copyright protection encouraged "any domestick or servant, who can snatch a letter from your pocket or cabinet" to profit from the crime. But the law had changed since them. Justice Yates's comments in *Millar v. Taylor,* decided in 1769, affirmed the prevailing belief in the right to protect one's "sentiments": "It is certain every man has a right to keep his own sentiments, if he pleases. He has certainly a right to judge whether he will make them public, or commit them only to the sight of his friends" (198, note 2). The protection of such sentiments—at least when they were embodied in letters—had been law since 1741. Indeed, Wilson and Wilkes's plot seems even more reprehensible, more invasive, in light of well-publicized law clearly protecting personal correspondence. That the ownership of letters was controlled by their author had already been decided in two celebrity cases, both of which must have been known to Wilson and Wilkes. As early as 1741, Pope had manipulated the court and literary property systems to his advantage in *Pope v. Curll,* a particularly important case because it wrote the concept of incorporeal literary property into the law. As Mark Rose argues, Pope's case against the printer Edmund Curll resulted from the mid-eighteenth-century confusion about whether literary property was material or immaterial. If material, ownership would lie with the recipient of the letter; if immaterial, ownership would lie in the author. Under the earlier system prior to the Act of Anne, an author owned his manuscript, "yet once the material object left his possession, the author's rights in it were at best tenuous" (Rose, "Author in Court" 478). Before Pope,

---

50. Macaulay never published with Cruttwell again.

the author was generally thought to have the right to control publication as a matter of "honor and reputation consistent with the traditional patronage society" but not as a matter of law (Rose, "Author in Court" 478–79). The *Pope* court decided unequivocally that the recipient of a letter might own the paper it was written on, but not the right to reprint its actual words.

Pope's case was widely known since it placed two major literary reputations (Swift's and Pope's) in the hands of the notorious Curll. But even if Wilson and Wilkes had been unaware of it, they could hardly have claimed not to have known of the famous Chesterfield letters case, decided only a few years before the threatened publication of Macaulay's letters. In this 1774 decision, known as *Thompson v. Stanhope,* the court reiterated the principle that the author owns the copyright in his letters. After public advertisements announcing the publication of Lord Chesterfield's letters to his son Philip, Chesterfield's executors moved for an injunction to prevent his son's widow from printing the letters. Despite the fact that when the widow had mentioned possible publication of the letters during Chesterfield's life, Chesterfield had replied only that "there was too much Latin in them" (*Thompson* 476), the court held that without Chesterfield's (or his executor's) unequivocal consent the letters could not be published.

For eighteenth-century booksellers and authors, these cases represented episodes in a contested field rather than legal edicts presumed to control behavior. But despite their uncertain regulatory status, they suggest that the stakes involved in connecting authorship to ownership extended to epistolary productions. Moreover, they indicate the magnitude of the violation Macaulay suffered as a result of the misappropriation of her letters. That violation seems even greater because Macaulay herself had written about copyright in 1774, taking a strong authors' rights position in her tract "Modest Plea for the Property of Copy Right." Now the miscreants who had benefited from the theft of Macaulay's private letters mocked even her copyright tract in the parodic pamphlets. "The Female Patriot, An Epistle" (possibly by Jodrell) footnoted Macaulay's "Modest Plea," arguing that "its appellation was peculiarly proper, as it was intended for the instruction of all the learned judges of England, when the final decision of that important cause was to be ultimately determined in the House of Lords" (9). Attacking her audacity in light of her apparent ignorance of the legal process, Jodrell located the desire for authorial self-possession in the widow's sexualized "plea" to take a younger husband.[51]

51. The attack on Macaulay's legal prowess was unfair. The case did eventually come be-

But Macaulay's copyright tract did not deserve the attack. While some believed it a poor effort, it was quoted extensively and favorably in one of the reports on the *Donaldson* case and took its place among the many pamphlets and commentaries published during the copyright debates of the 1770s. Its "immodesty" inhered in its expression of authorial control over literary property, a position Macaulay held along with other authors. Indeed, she took the position once assumed by Johnson, calling for rights to a work to remain with the author in perpetuity, unless assigned to a bookseller or other agent. Of course, like Johnson's position, her's was inherently contradictory. Authorship in perpetuity was at odds with her own collectivist projects. Perhaps she was supporting her bookselling friends (many thought the booksellers would be ruined if they lost their long-running copyrights); perhaps she was demonstrating another manifestation of a lifelong desire to control her own texts. In any case, the tract focuses its energies on national authorship rather than on the more technical arguments of the law. Macaulay begins and ends with disclaimers meant to protect her from charges of overreaching. Despite "the heavy oppression of sickness, and languor of body, and at the distance of above a hundred miles," she has taken up her pen, she says, to protect "the welfare of many worthy members of society, and thousands yet unborn" (*Modest Plea* v–vi). Demonstrating in miniature her faith in the moderate and virtuous "petition" to make palatable even the most disruptive claims of right, her apologies frame a radical claim for the rights of the author.

The *Modest Plea* clarifies the national aspects of copyright. Although Macaulay does deal with the economics of copyright, she focuses mainly on the English national interest. Emphasizing writers' connections to the common people, she democratizes authors who, like other people, are interested in owning their own property because "literary merit will not purchase a shoulder of mutton, or prevail with sordid butchers and bakers to abate one farthing in the pound of the exorbitant price which meat and bread at this time bear" (15). Nor can "sublime flights of poetic fancy" compensate starving authors in the same way a good dinner might (17). Authorial independence and control over the work form the core of her argument, and yet they are never separated from the public sphere. Demanding that Parliament give writers permanent rights in their works so that "men of independent tempers [can] employ their literary abilities

---

fore the House of Lords, but the justices were advisory to the House, their views important in that although they did not prevail, they had much influence over the direction of the final decision.

in the service of their country," she argues that "if the positive law does not lend its aid to the support of the tottering state of literature in this country, this decision will be a more mortal stab to the freedom, virtue, religion, and morals of the people of England, than the unthinking multitude in general at present apprehend" (25). Lack of national support for authors' rights will result in the "indelible disgrace of the country" (25), the end of a period in which the country benefits from "better paper, better print, and more elegant editions of English authors, than I believe were ever known, since literature flourished in England" (31).

Arguing in favor of copyright in the same terms in which she argues against class privilege, Macaulay creates a discursive link between "strong" authorship rights and the national interest. Virtue and the democratic spirit form the underlying structure of an argument that advocates individual rights and bases the perpetual ownership of literary property in principles of "THE ETERNAL RULE OF RIGHT, AND MORAL FITNESS OF THINGS." Like Richardson twenty-five years earlier, Macaulay grounds authorial ownership in the dyad of "genius" and effort, an effort that should be exercised didactically for the public good: "If there is anything which an individual can properly call his own, it is . . . those high gifts of genius and judgment, with which the Almighty has in a peculiar manner distinguished some of his creatures; gifts which, if they are properly exerted for the service of mankind, deserve the respect, the care, and the attention of society (29). Also like Richardson, she links class interests to national interests. Thus she objects to the limitations public domain places on authors' rights partly because such limitations will increase class stratification: "If literary property becomes common, we can have but two kind of authors, men in opulence, and men in dependence" (37). Such men will never write disinterestedly, but will flood the English markets with works calculated to please the public or their patrons. Placing national authorship between "opulence" and "dependence," Macaulay reinforced the role of the "middling" in representing the nation.

Macaulay does not emphasize gender in the *Modest Plea*. It was left to the story of Macaulay's stolen letter to reveal the gendered secret history of copyright. For while Macaulay could only watch as her personal correspondence careened from reader to reader and was refracted through one satirical publication after another, Pope had managed the dissemination of his letters even while claiming they had been stolen. Unlike Macaulay, Pope was in absolute control of the alleged "theft" of his letters, which he slyly referred to as "so great and growing an evil" (quoted in Rose, "Author in Court" 482). As early as 1735, Pope had tricked Curll into publishing a supposedly unauthorized version of his personal correspondence, at least in part to avoid charges of personal vanity. Although Pope protested that such acts were in the nature of "betraying Conversation" and "the greatest breach of honor," his expert manipulation had the desired results (quoted in Rose, "Author in Court" 481–82). As Maynard Mack points out, "It was part of his effort to set the record straight, garner up the fruits of his career, project an edifying image to the after time, communicate his deep belief in the social worth of the poetic function, and erect a monument to himself and the gifted group of writers he had known" (660). In the face of a society that saw self-publication of letters as impermissible self-aggrandizement (Mack 657), Pope succeeded not only in publicizing himself, and not only in making himself appear the honorable victim, but also in obtaining an important legal right for authors. From the moment of this "immoral act" through the publication of his letters, Pope—never in danger of having a single unfavorable word reach print—exercised a masterful level of interpretive control.

The invasion of Macaulay's literary property—coming as it did shortly after her public proclamation of authors' rights—turned Pope's nexus of plotting and law inside out. Whereas Pope had edited and prepared his letters before arranging to have them "stolen," Macaulay's unedited letters were meant for Wilson's eyes only. Whereas Pope himself plotted the mock invasion that resulted in further fame and glory, Macaulay's artless efforts resulted in an actual invasion, not only of her literary property but also of her privacy. Whereas the publication of Pope's letters had served as a "monument" to his literary fame, the threatened publication of Macaulay's letters was accompanied by the dismantling of an actual monument, the statue Wilson had erected in her honor, as well as by the metaphorical dismantling of her reputation.[52] And whereas commentators on Pope's case focused on the immorality of the theft, those who remarked on Macaulay's situation focused on the immorality of her own behavior as revealed in her letters.

Such reversals suggest how gender invested letters with different meanings. In the introduction to his own letters, Pope had argued that for a third party "to open letters is esteem'd the greatest breach of honor; even to look into them already open'd or accidentally dropt, is held ungenerous, if not an immoral act. What then can be thought of the procuring them merely by Fraud, and printing them merely for Lucre?" (quoted in Rose, *Authors and Owners* 61). Pope's commentary elides the commercial value of "honor," a value recognized in slander laws that made attacks

---

52. The statue was eventually moved to the public library at Warrington (Hill, *Virago* 99–110).

on male but not female virtue a criminal offense. Protecting the "honor" of women was far more problematic. As Hume had argued, women's "honor" was generally constituted through sexual virtue. Since it was important to monitor that virtue, directives involving women's letters dictated an openness, a willingness to reveal unstudied interiority. Richardson urged Sophia Westcomb to banish "diffidence" and then asked, "Who then shall decline the converse of the pen?" meanwhile imagining her presence in the summerhouse, the scene of Pamela's fictional seduction. Correspondence might make up for the physical distance Sophia's "hoops" placed between them. "The pen that makes distance, presence; and brings back to sweet remembrance all the delights of presence; which makes even presence but body, while absence becomes the soul," Richardson rhapsodized, implying a tantalizing confusion of body and soul in an epistolary correspondence that always threatened to escape the bounds he himself placed on it (Carroll 65). In an age in which popular novels associated women's letters not only with their souls but also with their bodies, the theft of Macaulay's letters suggested a symbolic physical invasion not present in the theft (whether real or manipulated) of Pope's letters.

Macaulay's letters, of course, could not avoid a fictional tradition that associated letters with the erotic. Richardson's *Pamela* and *Clarissa* had codified the erotic potential of letters in works that made such codification part of English culture. Such powerful associations between the epistolary and the erotic ensured that almost any woman's lost letter would be read in that context. To turn briefly to *Pamela* is to see the relationship between letters and eroticism made explicit as Mr. B's near rape of Pamela takes second place to the theft of letters hidden about her body. After asking whether her letters are "above" and being answered that they are, in a sense, "below" in the garden, Mr. B threatens to "begin to strip my pretty Pamela; and hope I shall not go far, before I find them" (204). Richardson conflates sadism and the law in repeated references not so much to discipline as to torture. "But let me know where they are" says B, "and you shall escape the question. . . . If a criminal won't plead with us here in England we press him to Death or till he does plead. And so now, Pamela, that is a punishment shall certainly be yours, if you won't tell without" (203). The treatment of epistolary eroticism in Burney's *Evelina,* suggests that almost any letter, no matter how innocuous, could be eroticized. Evelina's peace and health are threatened when she writes a perfectly innocent letter only to have it stolen. The forged response she receives in return reinterprets her epistle in unfairly sexual terms, leading her to regret ever having written at all. In a society informed by bestsellers like *Pamela, Clarissa,* and *Evelina,* not to mention the lesser epistolary novels that flooded the market during the period, the theft of Macaulay's private letters helped transform her from an intellectual authority to a beleaguered and comically elderly "Pamela," subject to examination, misinterpretation, and trivialization.

Eventually suppressed by Macaulay's brother John Sawbridge, the letters never saw publication. But they were advertised as "an authentic narrative of the conduct and behaviour of Mrs. M——y now Mrs. M——y G——m during her residence at A——d house, B——h; containing a succinct and faithful history of the extraordinary means made use of by that lady to obtain such a profusion of expensive gifts from her benevolent patron the REV. Dr. W——n." The publication was to be padded with stories of her trip to Paris, her trip to Leicester, and her marriage "with all the original letters, notes and anecdotes." Significantly, Wilson and Wilkes planned to attach to the production "a dissertation on swindling," suggesting a level of corruption that deconstructed all of Macaulay's efforts to associate herself and her works with virtue (Hill, *Virago* 112–13). Privately Wilkes described the letters as "indecent, insolent, mean, fawning, threatening, coaxing, menacing, and declaratory. Such words I believe never escaped a female pen" (quoted in Hill, *Virago* 111). Once having escaped, such words could not be recaptured. Wilkes and Wilson's efforts to disseminate them resulted in at least three direct parodies of the letter printed in 1779. Whereas Macaulay had used footnotes to marginalize "ornamental" sexual and personal details, the parodies foreground both these devices and their sexual content, making such digressive material the central focus. Words like "moving," "trembling," and "shaking" were meant to imply sexuality, a Shandean example appearing in the lines "Here faithful Hist'ry ends. / Britain must to her Centre shake!" (*Bridal Ode*). But they also evoked the instability of Macaulay's letter, its openness to uncontrolled dissemination and interpretation. The parody "A Remarkable Moving Letter, which was Suggested by an Extraordinary Epistle Sent by Her on her Second Marriage to Her Clerical Admirer" assumes that Macaulay's abandonment of Wilson and marriage to Graham resulted from the uncontrollable passion of an aging widow. In it the Macaulay character writes Wilson:

> Hadst thou possess'd (shame checks my falt'ring pen)
> The pow'rs that Heav'n allots to younger men,
> My frailer nature had not dar'd to rove,
> But politics had paved the road of love.
>
> (6)

As Devoney Looser points out, Macaulay's "epistolary pow'rs," powers most recently demonstrated in the *History in Letters,* are caricatured here as the powers most likely to reassert Wilson's sexual "Historic energy" (129).

Another parody, *The Female Patriot, An Epistle from C——t——e M——c——y to the Reverend Dr. W——l——n* ON *her late Marriage. With Critical, Historical, and Philosophical Notes and Illustrations,* probably written by Jodrell, mocks both the *History in Letters* and Macaulay's earlier work within the frame of the supposedly rediscovered lost letter. The main text parodies the dedication Macaulay had written to Wilson in the *History in Letters.* Macaulay here addresses Wilson as "honour'd parent." In the notes, Jodrell explicates the details of the unprinted private letter, claiming that Macaulay had informed Wilson that he was "an entire stranger to the glowing nature of her constitution; that she must pass the delicious hours of amorous dalliance with her beloved husband." In the end, Jodrell suggested that to follow Macaulay's lead would mean to "freely give my birthday suit, / And all the world beside to boot" (30). Given the many caricatures of the Scottish Bute as a boot, the last line provides an aside on Macaulay's national betrayal in marrying a Scot.

That Jodrell took a second swing at her in his 1779 play *A Widow and No Widow,* demonstrates the currency of Macaulay's scandal in popular venues. Jodrell's claim in the dedication to the play that "NOBODY respects an Author" may have been meant to sum up his own situation, but it also slyly referred to Macaulay's far more respectable authorial career.[53] Macaulay was worse than a "nobody" by 1779, her career as a historian in shambles, her personal reputation shot. The play ignored the fifteen years of celebrity Macaulay had enjoyed and made no reference to the respect paid her as England's historian. Anyone seeing the play—in which Macaulay is represented as the avaricious fraud Mrs. Sharp—would have been astonished to learn that she had been cited favorably in Parliament, praised by the *Critical Review,* the *European Magazine,* and *Monthly Miscellany,* and accepted by a wide circle of male historians and politicians as one of their own (Hill, *Virago* 49–50). Jodrell buries in the plot's past an image of Macaulay, a Mrs. Roundhead who "never thought of any thing but the Revolution" (63). But those familiar with the story of the second marriage would have recognized Macaulay in the avaricious widow Sharp, a like-minded admirer of Milton, but one who plots fraud rather than history. Never identified as an author or historian, Mrs. Sharp announces early on that "once a woman has blinded a man by love, she can pick his pocket at her leisure" (4). Rather than writing, Mrs. Sharp spends most of the play defrauding a Scottish author, a frenchified English

53. Susan Staves relates that Jodrell was the "son of the solicitor-general of the Prince of Wales, a lawyer, and later a Tory MP" (176).

fop, and the elderly Dr. Alfred (a parody of Wilson), all in order to elope with a fellow schemer, the Irish O'Kite. Mrs. Sharp thus juggles a number of different national "types" throughout the narrative, manipulating them for their money. Particularly notable is the relationship with Dr. Alfred, whom she finally turns away remarking, "My good Doctor. At your time of life, to think of marriage!" (67) drawing on the excuse Macaulay purportedly included in the letter she had written to Wilson. The play ends when all the men converge, discovering one another, but also disclosing to Mrs. Sharp that they are "all counterfeits." The fop's jewels are false; the Scot's bills are "drawn on the bank of air"; even Alfred's notes are worthless.

The play thematizes writing as plotting, making much of the exposure of paper credit as false credit. But writing intersects most legibly with nation in a scene in which the Scot Macfable tries to sell a bogus history to Splash, an opposition bookseller. In Splash's shop, values that Macaulay revered, those of English "liberty" and "freedom of the press," represent instead the freedom to be libelous and stupid. Elevating secret history over other genres, Splash rejects what he thinks is a true history of the "Great Mogul" for the marginality of political pamphlets, low satire, even "something loose and pretty; a sentimental, amorous novel, with a few real characters" (47). Although Splash demands absolute "liberty" in conducting his own affairs, he tyrannizes his wife, who repeatedly asks what good such liberty does *her*. In this little scene, Jodrell tells us that female advocates of liberty may "marry" print culture, but their views are unlikely to be met with respect. Overall the play, with its multiple representations of plagiarizing, forging authors and its obsession with national origins, provides a veiled commentary on Macaulay's career, while the sexualized portrayal of Mrs. Sharp points to the gender issues involved in her authorship of a national history. Imagined not as a historian but as an unsuccessful and sexualized plotter, her own "history" reduced to lies and extortion, Jodrell's Mrs. Sharp embodies Macaulay's loss of control over constructions of authorship and literary property, a loss that destroyed not only her career but also her ability to represent the nation.

Such ridicule after the marriage devalued her historical works, at least in Britain. Wilson himself publicly declared that the histories—even the one dedicated to him—were full of errors (Hill, *Virago* 115). John Taylor's remark that the marriage came "at a time of life when she ought to have been wiser, and then lost all her historical reputation" conflated without comment the two seemingly unrelated events (quoted in Hill, *Virago* 118). By 1780 even the medallion she had received at her forty-fifth birthday party had been devalued and reassociated with the more disreputable of

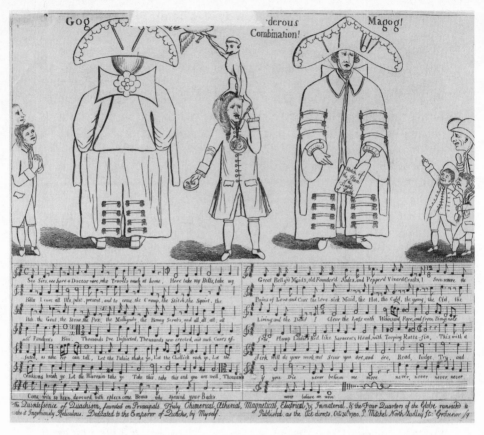

Fig. 4. Anonymous, "The Quintessence of Quackism" (1780), a satirical print showing Dr. James Graham wearing a portrait medallion of Catharine Macaulay. Copyright © The British Museum.

the two Graham brothers, James, who by then was operating his notorious Celestial Bed in London. A print titled "The Quintessence of Quackism" depicts Graham wearing a medallion with Macaulay's picture on it (figure 4). Reduced to a merely supplementary position to make a point far removed from any ever made in her *History of England*, Macaulay's image had become a footnote to Graham's spotty career. As the *European Magazine* noted in retrospect: "We perceive no diminishment of the powers she formerly displayed and was allowed to possess, yet the ridicule which has been thrown out against her, on occasion of her marriage, has totally extinguished all curiosity about her opinions on those important subjects which she formerly discussed, with as much credit to herself, and we think, with as much advantage to the world" ("Account" 333).

The juridical failure to protect Macaulay from public scandal reestablished the order her status as a public intellectual had violated. Peter Stallybrass and Allon White have famously argued that "psychic forms, the human body, geographical space and the social order" are linked (3). Upsetting one hierarchy inevitably upsets others. In writing history, Macaulay had upset the accepted relationship between gender and genre, precariously balancing that liberty-asserting transgression with claims to civic virtue. But in the tradition of republican virtue, "liberty" suggested an out-of-control threat to the political order, to constitutional and juridical culture. Macaulay's letter represented liberty gone wild, as the parodies that took up the letter suggest. Refusing to correspond with any of correspondence's generic conventions, the letter was written out of turn, interrupting the proper order that letters were supposed to follow just as the marriage interrupted expectations about familial and marital progress.[54] Those expectations defined the family as one that provided a "natural" and "organic" image of how public life should work. But the family that fueled national imagery was not the new family that Macaulay created in marrying Graham. Macaulay's marriage rejected the image of the paternal father who ruled over his wife and children, children who would grow up, establish new lives, and form families of their own. This normative ideal of generational progression domesticated change, defanging it by suggesting that even radical change fell within the natural scheme of things (McClintock, "Family Feuds" 63, 64). Such a comforting construction of the family would have been reinforced if Macaulay had married Wilson. An older husband united with a younger wife (or nurse) raised no eyebrows; it offered no threat to historical progression. Indeed, one of the parodies had celebrated that possibility by fantasizing that a marriage between Wilson and Macaulay would have produced a set of historical twins. But traditional ideas about family were thrown into disarray by the marriage to Graham, with its complex realignment of age, class, regional, and gender issues, indeed of almost every possible identity category. Perhaps because Macaulay's symbolic value focused on history, age tended to trump the other issues raised by the marriage. When Macaulay married a much younger man, she enacted the possibility that the past could suddenly reappear in the present, even have sex with it. As in *Tom Jones,* to choose one of the best-known examples, incest motifs

---

54. I am indebted to both Elizabeth Heckerdorn Cook and Janet Gurkin Altman here. As Altman argues, letters from women to their lovers are supposed to follow a particular pattern of reaction to male agency, the pattern in which, as Altman suggests, "the heroines of countless epistolary fictions are locked into erotic dramas that turn primarily around the agency and power of entrepreneurs on whom their destiny depends" (173).

involving lascivious older women signified a digressive and even regressive disorder that had to be reversed by the marriage of the hero to a younger woman, not to the aging widow. Thus the parodies of Macaulay's letter relied on an image of history disrupted by an out-of-turn "correspondence." As author of the mysterious letter, Macaulay represented an English past that refused to stay past but instead leapfrogged into a future of unnarratable possibilities.

The law's passivity in response to Macaulay's stolen letter reveals the limitations of English claims to equality. In embedding her understanding of English identity in equality and liberty, Macaulay was far from alone. Though no twentieth-century democrat, her contemporary William Blackstone made similar claims in the *Commentaries* (1765–69). He opens with the plea that readers

> only reflect a moment on the singular frame and polity of that land, which is governed by this system of laws. A land, perhaps the only one in the universe, in which political or civil liberty is the very end and scope of the constitution. This liberty, rightly understood, consists in the power of doing whatever the laws permit; which is only to be effected by a general conformity of all orders and degrees to those equitable rules of action, by which the meanest individual is protected from the insults and oppression of the greatest. (1:6)

This fantasy of an England superior and unique because of its commitment to equality undergirded most national texts of the second half of the century, not least of which was Macaulay's *History*. English law made much of its construction of individuals as equal subjects with free agency, and yet it also feared equality and freedom. Unlike civil law systems with their codes, the common law of England was thought to have derived from the contingent circumstances of the discrete individualized conflicts that, when brought to court, became cases. The system—at least arguably rooted in the actual experience of "the people"—thus lent itself to identifying Englishness with liberty and the rights of the subject. In contrast, European systems could be imagined as top-down and autocratic. Yet widespread agency suggested an ungovernable contingency as well as the multiplicity and threats to linearity that national history rejected. Thus the very flexibility of the English legal system, its responsiveness to contingent circumstances, led to anxiety about its cohesion and unity. Every "case" differed slightly and thus was subject to interpretations and argumentation. Such differences threatened the stability and coherence of the legal system—its linearity—and resulted in an unresolved anxiety that was played out in fears about the proliferation of laws and the unreliability of legal texts, but was also displaced onto women. As Peter Goodrich has argued, the figure of the woman or "femininity" played a crucial role in keeping anxieties about contingency at bay.[55] Long associated with passion, irrationality, and uncontrollable forces, the feminine offered a convenient location for concerns about the contingent origins of law.

Thus it is hardly surprising that the law would fail to protect Macaulay's lost letter. She herself represented one of the "contrarieties" that Blackstone found impossible to resolve while the letter embodied all that was contrary about her. In offering no help to Macaulay, the law elided the threat the feminine presented to law's linearity and unity, a threat embodied in Macaulay's career, her politics, and her unconventional personal life. Simultaneously, Macaulay's spectacular humiliation operated to reinstate the traditional position of women during a period when a national rhetoric of equality and inclusion had created the possibility of real change. While Macaulay could argue in the *History* that equality of rights typified the English system and made it unique, the history of the letter told a different story. The law protected letters; it protected Pope's letters in 1741 and Lord Chesterfield's letters a few years later. Yet the fiction that women's letters were common property—promulgated throughout the culture—exerted an extrajuridical force powerful enough to undermine any legal protection Macaulay could have claimed. These extrajudicial forces also effected a powerful rewriting of Macaulay's "true history." Despite recent historians' efforts, Macaulay has been more frequently represented as an infamous woman than a public intellectual. Reframing the story supposedly told *in* Macaulay's letter as the story *of* the letter—its misappropriation and illegal circulation—is thus a corrective gesture. It makes legible the alternative histories cloaked by Macaulay's "scandal," the true history not only of gender and historical genre but also of gender and law. In Macaulay's context, the legal fiction of equal access and equal rights central to English legal history turned out to be simply that: a fiction.[56]

<hr />

55. See Goodrich, *Oedipus Lex* and *Law in the Courts of Love*.

56. In suggesting the dichotomy between the story in the letters and the story of the letters, I draw on Cook's discussion of Todorov (127).

[4]

Libels of Empire: Mary Prince
and British Slavery

> Libel
> 1. A little book; a short treatise or writing
> 2. A formal document, a written declaration or statement.
> 3. a. *Civil Law.* The writing or document of the plaintiff containing his obligations and instituting a suit. b. *Eccl. Law.* The first plea, or the plaintiff's written declaration or charges in a cause. . . .
> 4. A leaflet, bill, or pamphlet posted up or publicly circulated; *spec.* one assailing or defaming the character of some person.
> 5. *Law.* Any published statement damaging to the reputation of a person. In wider sense, any writing of a treasonable, seditious, or immoral kind.
>
> *Oxford English Dictionary*

Mary Prince, an enslaved West Indian woman, testified at length in a British libel case in 1833, an act so overwhelmingly transgressive that even literary critics quite invested in her cause get it wrong.[1] Born enslaved in Bermuda sometime around 1788 and traumatized from her earliest days, Prince does seem an unlikely woman to have drawn the attention of the

---

1. Helena Woodard, in an otherwise insightful analysis, remarks that Prince "was forbidden by law to give court testimony in order to fend off . . . charges of libel" (135). See Moira Ferguson's introduction (28) and the *London Times* of March 1, 1833, appended to Ferguson's edition of Prince's narrative for an account of Prince's testimony. It does not seem to have been uncommon for Africans to testify in such cases. See Oldham for a transcript of Thomas Lewis's testimony drawn from Chief Justice Mansfield's trial notes. Lewis, an African living in London, testified as to his kidnapping and the attempt to return him to enslavement in Jamaica in 1771 (50).

British judiciary.[2] As an enslaved child and young adult, she endured separation from her family, frequent beatings, ten years in the salt mines on Turk's Island, crippling illness, and a course of insults, threats, and disciplinary measures that would have completely silenced most people.[3] In 1828, at her request, her owner, John Wood, brought her from Antigua to London with his family. Though Prince had hoped that the English climate would help her rheumatism, she found the conditions in London worse than those in Antigua and became determined to return to Antigua a free woman. After a prolonged battle with the Woods, she left their household, eventually finding help from Thomas Pringle, a prominent abolitionist already known for his South African adventures.[4]

Prince became a cause célèbre for the abolitionists. After Pringle unsuccessfully petitioned the House of Commons for her freedom, he helped her publish her story as *The History of Mary Prince: A West Indian Slave Related by Herself*. It appeared in London and Edinburgh in 1831. Once in print, the story, perhaps because it involved a woman and contained thinly veiled hints of sexual abuse, intrigued and scandalized the public. Abolitionist readers sympathized with Prince's plight, while the plantocracy raged at her claims of mistreatment. In one of the most vitriolic attacks, the anti-abolitionist James Macqueen assailed Prince, Pringle, and the abolitionist cause in *Blackwood's Edinburgh Magazine*. In return, Pringle, perhaps seeing a chance to further promote the abolitionist cause, sued Macqueen's London publisher, Thomas Cadell, for libel. Meanwhile, John Wood sued Pringle for remarks recorded in Prince's narrative, even-

2. All who study and teach Prince's narrative are indebted to Moira Ferguson for her work on Prince. For this brief account of Prince's history, I draw on Ferguson's introduction to her edition of *The History of Mary Prince,* first published in 1987 and revised in 1997, as well as on her critical work, *Subject to Others.* I rely also on James Walvin's various works and Peter Fryer's account in *Staying Power.* All subsequent references to Prince's narrative are taken from Ferguson's 1997 edition.

3. To emphasize the agency involved in enslaving others, I have avoided "slave" when possible, using terms such as "an enslaved person" to describe victims of the British slave system. The word "slave" should not be used as an identity category. As Peter Goodrich remarks, "Our identity is a feature of belonging to and participation in a particular narrative of our place and purposes," not presumably of participation in a narrative thrust violently upon us ("Poor Illiterate Reason" 9). For slightly different reasons, I prefer "enslaver" to "slave owner," since "enslaver" places agency where it belongs, on those who chose to own other human beings.

4. Thomas Pringle (1789–1834) defined himself as a poet as well as an abolitionist. Born in Scotland, he spent six years in South Africa before returning to Britain to serve as secretary of the Anti-Slavery Society in 1826. Important publications include *The Autumnal Excursion and Other Poems* (1819), *Some Account of the Present State of the English Settlers in Albany, South Africa* (1824), *Ephemerides: or Occasional Poems, Written in Scotland and South Africa* (1828), *Glen-Lynden: A Tale of Teviotdale* (1828), and *African Sketches* (1834). For biographies, see Doyle and Meiring.

[173]

tually winning because Pringle could not bring the witnesses he needed from Antigua to bolster the truth of Prince's narrative. Other writings by those who had experienced slavery such as Phillis Wheatley had been threatened with legal and quasi-legal proceedings, but Prince's narrative was attacked directly in the English courtroom.[5] The resulting affidavits, court appearances, and newspaper accounts created a collective text that struggled to control a complex challenge to British national and thus imperial ideology. That these varied materials have been collected in subsequent editions of the narrative enacts textually the interdependency of the different forms of national culture the Prince story brought together. These forms ranged from the juridical, or as Lauren Berlant puts it, the "official culture" of the nation, to working-class and domestic cultures much less official but just as powerful in their impact on national identity.

I turn now to Prince's narrative to suggest the national function of print spectacles and their manipulation of scandal in an era of emerging mass culture.[6] Abolition efforts helped reestablish national respect in England after 1776, serving to trump American claims to liberty. The first major antislavery petition occurred in 1788, the one hundredth anniversary of the Glorious Revolution (Colley, *Britons* 354). By 1831, England's abolition movement was playing a powerful integrative function, partly by drawing in the elite and the working classes, women, and domestic labor. The community formed around the issue was not only wide but also deep in the sense that house-to-house canvassing helped spread the word. By the 1820s, large groups of women who engaged in "tireless neighbourhood visiting and assiduous fund-collecting" were involved in the antislavery movement (Colley, *Britons* 278). At a time when Britain's population was about 12 million, as many as 1.5 million signed petitions against slavery (Walvin, *England* 126). But the movement went beyond print. To reach the public so widely and deeply, abolitionists engaged every imaginable technique, relying not only on public lectures that drew huge crowds but also on devices that implicated all of the senses. London's white community was invited to experience slavery through viewing the famous slave ship pictures and displays of chains and manacles, wearing the Wedgwood cameo of a slave in chains, and associating the taste of sugar with slavery.[7] Prince's scandal, with its

5. See Gates, *Figures in Black* chap. 1, for a discussion of the charges brought against Wheatley.

6. See Drescher, "Public Opinion," for a helpful discussion of antislavery as a "mass movement" or, alternatively, a class movement.

7. See Drescher, "Public Opinion," for a discussion of the many diverse ways in which public opinion was expressed. See Walvin, "Propaganda of Anti-slavery," for a discussion of public lectures as a propaganda tool. See Wood, *Blind Memory,* for a comprehensive work on the many different representations related to slavery and abolition.

published narrative, resulting newspaper battles, and spectacular court appearances, brought the titillating lived experience of an enslaved black woman to bear on such emblems of slavery and in doing so helped radicalize the abolition effort (Blackburn 442).

The Prince scandal, perhaps more than any other discussed in this book, brought print and spectacle together to foreground the role of "the people" in forming national culture. As I argued at the beginning of this book, the fact that the scandals I have discussed encompassed both print and spectacle implies that the construction of nation has a more populist and less elitist base than much work on nation might suggest. While most would agree with Benedict Anderson that print culture is crucial to national formation, print is generally seen as an elite form, accessible only to a small minority of a nation's population, its impenetrability at odds with the very idea of nation as lateral and democratic. Because of the elitism of print, some theorists argue instead that the nation is experienced primarily through spectacles attended by the masses.[8] But Prince's case provides a good example of the way print and spectacle not only coexisted but also intersected to create the powerful print spectacles that mark modern culture. Even as the written reports and news articles surrounding Prince's case reached the literate elite, the theatricality and visibility of the law evidenced in the trials for libel created a public spectacle that encompassed both popular and official culture.[9] Whereas the other literary scandals I discuss in this book implicated popular "low" cultures primarily through the incorporation of ludic, violent, and sexualized images drawn from those cultures, the Prince scandal drew on both print and public spectacle to reach a broader range of people more directly. It thus made legible the combined operations of print and spectacle to reach across gender, class, and regional boundaries.

Prince's case also allows us to see how print spectacles operate in an explicitly imperial context, how they translate from the London metropolis to the West Indies. The legal cases her narrative generated placed the West Indian plantocracy in close proximity to the London center—already decentered because the narrative's promoter, Thomas Pringle, was a Scot with strong connections to South Africa. The dynamic of containment and resistance in such a setting seems particularly complex and interesting.[10]

8. See McClintock, *Imperial Leather* 374, for one such view.

9. See Lerer for an account of the importance of law's theatricality during the medieval period.

10. See Young for a discussion of theories of resistance and containment. Prince's actual resistance—her arguing, fighting, and final escape—tends to get lost in discussions of covert, symbolic resistance. On a more theoretical level, while Stephen Greenblatt pessimistically argues that Renaissance subversion was articulated only because it could be contained, Homi

Because these legal cases furthered the abolitionist cause, perhaps contributing to England's emancipation of 750,000 enslaved people in the West Indies shortly after Prince's case came to court,[11] Prince's story suggests that print spectacles—even at their most repressive—had the potential to serve progressive agendas, that they could give marginal figures a voice not otherwise easily heard.[12] Some have argued that Prince was victimized by the controversy over her narrative, and particularly by the libel suit brought against Pringle on account of it.[13] Certainly the detailed analysis of the libel cases that I offer later in this chapter demonstrates the power of law to reconstitute disruptive narratives. Prince dismantled certain English ideals, only to find them reestablished in the juridical setting. In the end, what Prince's "libel" has to tell us (and I use "libel" here in all of its senses, as a writing, as a legal pleading, and as a defamatory statement) is that print spectacles cut in both directions, preserving traditional markers of identity, but also opening up new ways of thinking about the national self. While Prince's case revisits issues encountered in the previous chapters—"national" issues of difference, colonization, the domestic and the foreign, the construction of family, as well as "literary" issues of authenticity, literacy, and authorship—it also complicates the larger argument of this book, suggesting that the repressive hypothesis that has driven previous chapters offers only one limited way of understanding the workings of print spectacles in what by Prince's time was rapidly becoming modern print culture.

"Related by Herself": The Challenge to English Norms

Prince's narrative was far from the only well-publicized story of mistreatment under the slave system. The various abolition societies special-

---

Bhabha suggests that resistance can escape containment. Gary Boire offers one way to think about Prince's story as a form of resistance: as he suggests, "Resistance, in an inescapable logic, never exists 'outside' its own oppression; 'resistance' is itself a mirrored series of constant re-arrangements, re-alignments and re-negotiations" (212). Prince's case brings to light the tension between "containers" (the actions for sedition and defamation) and resistance, but also suggests that "containers" can sometimes serve as a form of resistance.

11. The reasons for abolition's eventual success have been debated extensively since Eric Williams published *Capitalism and Slavery* in 1944. For more recent approaches to the issue, see Thomas Bender; Drescher, *Capitalism and Antislavery*; and Solow and Engerman.

12. I draw on Homi Bhabha here, who argues that a political position is "not simply identifiable as progressive or reactionary . . . outside the terms and conditions of its discursive and textual address" ("Commitment" 8).

13. Ferguson suggests that in lieu of becoming embroiled in the controversy, Prince could have lived the remainder of her life in peace (introduction to *Prince* 27); Woodard wrongly claims that John Wood "brought charges" against Prince (135).

ized in such stories; Pringle even attaches one, "The Narrative of Louis Asa-Asa, a Captured African," to Prince's account. Why then did Prince's narrative go into three editions the year it was published, become the subject of so much commentary in the abolitionist and anti-abolitionist press, and eventually fuel two expensive and well-publicized libel suits? In part, the public attention garnered by the narrative resulted from its challenge to deeply held convictions about Englishness—convictions grounded in beliefs about liberty, domesticity, class hierarchy, and authorship. That the narrative exposed domestic "private" life to public scrutiny, making of intimacy a spectacle, gave it an extraordinary disruptive power.[14] But more globally, by simultaneously calling a number of powerful notions about Englishness into question, Prince's narrative forced the English to confront their own internal contradictions. Like all good disruptive colonialist texts, it forced an imperial "center" sure of its moral and ethical rectitude to confront the signs of its own disintegration, signs made visible in the form of Prince's deteriorated body.[15]

Because the narrative was an as-told-to tale by an enslaved black woman living in London, it offered an unusual perspective on abolition. Prior to 1789, Africans in Britain seemed well on the way to producing an influential body of work. Ignatius Sancho, James Gronniosaw, Phillis Wheatley, Ottobah Cugoano, and Olaudah Equiano had published widely read poetic, autobiographical, and political works. As Henry Louis Gates suggests, their work formed "a literature that was propelled by the Enlightenment demand that a 'race' place itself on the Great Chain of Being primarily through the exigencies of print" (*Slave's Narrative* v). On the eve of the 1790s, Africans in Britain seemed poised to enter a truly productive period in which their writing could be instrumental to the antislavery movement and the general trend toward abolition. But after 1789, such works seem to have dwindled in importance. Even though between ten thousand and twenty thousand blacks—some described as "ladies" and "men of color in the rank of gentleman" by Hester Piozzi in 1802—lived in Britain, literary production by Africans in London virtually disappeared during the first decades of the new century.[16] In part, the publica-

14. I am indebted to Chase and Levenson for this insight.

15. Like Gary Boire, I argue that colonialist texts tend to be disruptive to the extent that they force the center "to gaze agonizedly, not at the external sign of its triumph, but at the displaced symbol of its own inevitable and internal disintegration" (211).

16. One in forty people in Britain in the mid-1760s may have been black (Walvin, *England* 46), while by the end of the eighteenth century, as much as a quarter of the British navy was composed of Africans (Gilroy, *Black Atlantic* 12). Linda Colley sets the black population in Britain at twenty thousand in the early nineteenth century (*Britons* 355), though according to James Walvin estimates range from three thousand to fifteen thousand (*Black*

tion gap may be explained by the politics of the French revolutionary era and the reaction that followed, in part by the poverty and illiteracy of Africans living in London. Perhaps, too, the abolitionist movement absorbed such tales, providing a venue for them in the numerous tracts and pamphlets published in the 1820s and early 1830s. But the explanation may also lie in the challenge such print works presented to English identity. African writers like Equiano were so proficient, so quick to pick up the English language, that they threatened the utility of language as a national marker. Although a common language is often resorted to as the ultimate sign of national integration, such a sign is always flawed because linguistic proficiency can be acquired too easily to perform the sort of exclusionary work that nation requires. If even highly differentiated outsiders such as enslaved Africans could make proficient use of the English language, then the use of proper English as a marker fails and some other identifier must be found (Balibar and Wallerstein 99). Johnson's *Dictionary* and similar projects that associated the English language with Englishness were thus called into question by the intelligent expression of the African cause in published writings by Africans in English. Not surprisingly, Wheatley, Equiano, and Prince had more in common than their narratives: neither Wheatley nor Equiano was dragged into court in efforts to regulate their writing, but both were threatened with judicial or quasi-judicial repression. Wheatley was subjected to a mock trial for supposed plagiarism, while Equiano's authorship, his credibility, and even his African origins were attacked throughout the 1790s (Equiano 181–84.)

Prince's narrative—in the first person, rough, colloquial, yet eloquent at times, far longer and more personalized than the third-person narratives of the abolitionist papers—erupted from those papers, took on a life of its own, and disrupted the components of identity that defined Britain and England at a crucial moment in abolitionist history. The narrative's "as told to" form confounded categories of oral and literate, suggesting an alliance between popular, working-class culture and "high" or elite culture.[17] Meanwhile, its intermingling of historical and geographical detail,

---

and White 46–47). The fact that this number may have been exaggerated suggests that the black population, whatever percentage of the total population it may have represented, loomed large in the public imagination (*Black and White* 46–47). Despite the large number of blacks in London between 1789 and 1831, Davis and Gates list only one narrative by an enslaved or formerly enslaved person published there during those years (*Slave's Narrative* 320–21).

17. Prince may have been able to read and write a little, but her story was dictated to Susannah Strickland, a self-described bluestocking associated with abolitionist circles. She claimed to have taken down the story more or less verbatim. In a letter she noted, "I have been writing Mr. Pringle's black Mary's life from her own dictation and for her benefit ad-

political purpose, and personal (at times explicitly sexual) history suggested an equally confounding conflation of low and high. Prince's complicated and repeated overlayering of supposedly disparate ideologies,
images, and identities (literacy versus orality, white editor versus black
speaker, choice versus compulsion, economic difference versus racial difference, domestic intimacy versus public politics) articulated the central
contradictions contained by late-eighteenth-century and early-nineteenth-
century "Britishness." Most compellingly and obviously, the narrative
shocked the public because it brought slavery home to England, partly by
telling the story of Prince's importation to London and her treatment there,
but also by repeatedly exposing the dissonance between British ideals of
liberty and rights and the practices of slavery.[18] Although it was not true
as Prince argued that "few people in England know what slavery is" (64),
her assumption throughout the narrative that the personal account of
slavery she brought to England would automatically dictate English support for abolition underscored the challenge slavery offered to British
ideals.

If Britain's identity rested on claims of liberty and individual rights,
those claims were antithetical to slavery. But English liberty had not always been felt to exclude the possibility of slavery. As late as 1600, the
common law assumed that Englishness and slavery were, while perhaps
not fully compatible, at least not antithetical (Baker, *Common Law* 334).
Only in the century to follow was English liberty's intolerance of slavery
transformed from a mere suggestion into a well-worn cliché. Perhaps the
cliché was compensatory: it seemed to increase in power even as the slave
system grew throughout the seventeenth century (Walvin, *England* 17).
Whatever purposes the cliché served, the logical incongruity between English "liberty" and English reliance on slavery could be ignored only so
long as Africans stayed in the colonies. The grossest brutalities of slavery
were thus necessarily kept at bay, relegated by and large to the colonies,
imagined in important ways as "foreign" rather than domestic.[19]

---

hering to her own simple story and language without deviating to paths of flourish or romance" (quoted in Haynes 22). For more information on Strickland and her later career as
a Canadian writer, see Whitlock.

18. As Walvin points out in *Black Ivory,* "The particulars of the slave cases were often
shocking, but shocking *only* because they had taken place in England" (13).

19. Marcus Wood offers a particularly intriguing example of the abjection of colonial
slavery in his reading of the "abolition map" that accompanied Thomas Clarkson's 1808
work on the abolition movement. The map uses cartographic imagery to provide a genealogy of English and French abolitionists whose names branch off from what appear to be
several large rivers. As Wood points out, no enslaved people are included; "Africa is off the
map," even though Clarkson intended the map to allow readers interested in abolition "to
comprehend the whole of it at a single view" (*Blind Memory* 2–5).

African writers themselves drew heavily on the myth of English liberty. Equiano, for instance, had made the yearning for a specifically English form of liberty the primary leitmotiv of his autobiography.[20] His intense Anglophilia can be understood as an attempt to force England to abide by its own sense of self. Prince too seemed to yearn for England, though at least on the surface only because she thought it would ease her physical ailments. "I was willing to come to England," she wrote. "I thought that by going there I should probably get cured of my rheumatism, and should return with my master and mistress, quite well, to my husband" (86). Prince's references to bodily suffering locate her text in the tradition of the "humanitarian narrative," a narrative that draws on the body to bring home images of suffering to the powerful few in a position to help.[21] But bringing home such images was hardly an innocent act if "home" was England and the images were images of the suffering of the enslaved. Deploying images of bodily suffering, Prince emphasized the relationship between labor and physical deterioration in a way that evoked deeply rooted English working-class concerns. She also evidenced a sophisticated understanding of the link between the treatment her body had received and her political and geographical position. Throughout the narrative, she underscores the relationship between the physical location of her body and the conditions of slavery, for instance, telling her master, "Mr. D," that in England he could no longer beat her because "Sir, this is not Turk's Island" (77). Thus, her references to illness and the body functioned as references to labor in the context of the slave system, references that reverberated with working-class radicals quick to draw comparisons between enslaved and working-class cultures. Her rheumatism—no doubt the result of long immersion in the salt ponds of Turk's Island—troped the harshest conditions of enslavement in the colonies; its cure would be a cure for the evils of slavery itself.

By displaying her ruined body in England, Prince confounded England's sense of itself as an isolated island. Perhaps the one factor that most allowed England to think of itself as unified and "national" was its geographical isolation. But the spatial sense of self produced by the continuous natural boundary of the shoreline, by England's geographical insularity, is easily disrupted by face-to-face encounters with empire.[22] Signs of

20. Wheatley and other African writers of the eighteenth century showed more subtle signs of Anglocentrism in their adoption of English literary traditions.

21. See Laqueur for a discussion of the humanitarian narrative. Hans Turley draws on this discussion in his book on piracy (136).

22. I am indebted to Ian Baucom's analysis of national space for this part of my discussion. As he tells us about modern Britain, "Once the post-imperial frontier is drawn in Bristol or London, once white Britons can no longer ignore the fact that they share their streets with the 'strange races' of empire," space loses its "identity-determining magic" (23).

empire had to be continually distanced from what was seen as naturally occurring within England's geographical boundaries if the fiction of Englishness was to be sustained through recourse to England's island status. By entering London and then making an issue of her bodily presence, Prince inserted a living sign of destabilization into the very center, even the juridical center, of Englishness, a sign that disrupted the disciplinary structures meant to keep an insular center safe from destabilization by colonial stress. Her insistent presence redrew the frontier, making it impossible for Britons to ignore slavery and changing their relationship to national space. One of the structures she challenged was the structure of "inside" and "outside" that allowed the English to define themselves by looking both inward and outward, a dynamic seen in exaggerated silhouette during the abolition crisis of the 1830s. Although nations probably do tend to define themselves by looking both inward and outward, they find it hard to look in both directions at once as Prince forced them to do. She took the "outward" edge of Englishness and brought it to the center of English life, thus forcing a simultaneous inward-outward view.[23]

No wonder, then, that the narrative made much of the spectacular presence of Prince's body in London, a body subject to personal inspections later recorded in affidavits attached to her narrative. Prince told a story of beatings and whippings in the narrative in such a way as to undermine the didactic narratives of improvement[24] often used to bolster the enslaver's cause:

> The next morning my mistress set about instructing me in my tasks. She taught me to do all sorts of household work; to wash and bake, pick cotton and wool, and wash floors, and cook. And she taught me (how can I ever forget it!) more things than these; she caused me to know the exact difference between the smart of the rope, the cart-whip, and the cow-skin, when applied to my naked body by her own cruel hand. And there was scarcely any punishment more dreadful than the blows I received on my face

23. In *Britons,* Colley puts this in historical terms when she points out that by 1815 the British Empire included one fifth of the world's inhabitants. "The question of how these millions of men and women who were manifestly not British, but who had been brought under British rule by armed force should be treated and regarded thus became inescapable. What responsibilities, if any, did the mother country have towards them? Did they have any claim on those vague but valuable freedoms that so many Britons considered to be peculiarly their own? Or could British subjects also be slaves as long as they were black and safely overseas?" (322).

24. One need not go far to find justifications of slavery based on the supposed need of "savage" Africans for education. See Dabydeen 28. James Macqueen drew on this argument in his diatribe against Prince's narrative.

[181]

and head from her hard heavy fist. She was a fearful woman, and a savage mistress to her slaves . . . for I was licked, and flogged, and pinched by her pitiless fingers in the neck and arms, exactly as they were. To strip me naked—to hang me up by the wrists and lay my flesh open with the cow-skin, was an ordinary punishment for even a slight offence. (58)

Such an account resisted easy dismissal because it lent itself to immediate juridical authentication. In the appendix to the third edition, Pringle included an affidavit attesting to two "inspections" of Prince's body by Susannah Strickland, by Pringle's unnamed wife and sister, and by Martha Browne. According to the ladies' report, "The whole of the back part of her body is distinctly scarred, and, as it were, *chequered,* with the vestiges of severe floggings. Besides this, there are many large scars on other parts of her person, exhibiting an appearance as if the flesh had been deeply cut, or lacerated with *gashes,* by some instrument wielded by most unmerciful hands" (130).

That so much was made of Prince's marked body suggests a symbolic function that went beyond proof that enslaved persons were whipped, a fact readily admitted and considered justifiable by numerous enslavers.[25] The colonized body was supposed to be a blank page, something to be written on by the colonizing power, but that page was not supposed to reveal the cruelty and force behind the authorial gesture. While Prince's narrative can be read in one sense as sheer accusation, the focus on the skin offers a more complex reading as well.[26] By making much of its evidentiary potential, Prince and her supporters emphasized not only the visibility but also the vulnerability of skin, and in doing so suggested the vulnerability of the margin. Prince's skin made her visible in London, visible as a sign of colonial margins. The presence of that skin *in London* pulled the colonial margins back into the center, where they could not be ignored. Moreover, flayed skin provided a redoubled reminder of English vulnerability to deterioration at the margins of the margin. In the salt mines so important to Bermuda's economy and to the continued supply of salt to Londoners, Prince's skin was literally eaten away. At the hands of her owners, it received the permanent markers of the fissure that slavery presented to Englishness, of the tendency of Englishness to fray.

25. Even her most virulent attacker, James Macqueen, readily reported in *Blackwood's* that Prince had been horsewhipped by Wood "for quarreling with a fellow-servant, and being insolent to Mrs. Wood on her desiring her to be quiet" (749).

26. I rely here on Mary Douglas, who tells us that the body represents society and that its margins, including its skin, tend to control meaning: "All margins are dangerous. If they are pulled this way or that the shape of fundamental experience is altered. Any structure of ideas is vulnerable at its margins" (quoted in Sussman 50).

Prince's "chequered" skin offered a displaced image of the literalized fear that Englishness would be marked, frayed, and weakened, perhaps even destroyed, by slavery.

That even Prince's skin should become evidentiary material, pressed into service to authenticate her narrative, suggests that public displays of authenticity continued to play a role in national debates long after Johnson's attack on Macpherson and Ossian. As we shall see, the stories of enslaved persons were always subject to dispute by the West Indian plantocracy, engaged as it was throughout the 1820s and early 1830s in a credibility war with London abolitionists. But authentication served more than an immediate political purpose. Prioritizing authenticity aids national efforts because the discourses of authenticity can be manipulated to mark certain voices as those of insiders versus outsiders.[27] Efforts to authenticate Prince's story or alternatively to dismiss it as "inauthentic" began the moment it was published and continued until quite recently; indeed, some critics seem more than ready to insist that Prince could not possibly have told the story as Strickland recorded it, while others have taken equal pains to bolster the narrative with various other sorts of documentary evidence.[28] Such efforts are far from innocent, but instead intersect with the operations of empire to map, categorize, and evaluate its colonial possessions, in fact, to write them into existence.[29] That issues involving Prince's authenticity circulated around orality and literacy and take up the difficulties of translation inherent in any transcription suggests further continuities with my earlier discussion of Johnson's effort to undermine the Ossian project.[30] Like Macpherson's reproduction of Ossian, Prince's oral narrative was taken over and put to work in the service of various national and imperial interests.[31] Her words, no matter how accurately recorded, inevitably were integrated into the larger contexts of the abolition movement. Indeed, the problems with the "authenticity" of Prince's text were written into the work the moment Pringle and his literate circle of abolitionists decided to record the story. Well meaning as they

27. See Griffiths for a further elaboration of this argument.

28. Ferguson's investigations into external records in Bermuda have laid some questions to rest, but literary scholars still seem quite concerned with sorting out the different voices in Prince's narrative. See Bracks and Haynes.

29. Bhabha's *Location of Culture* underlies my argument here.

30. As Anne McClintock has argued, "The production of oral history is a technology of power under contest, which cannot be seen in isolation from the contexts of power from which it emerges" ("House of Difference" 226).

31. Given the dominance of print in Western culture, no oral account subsequently reduced to print is free from the problems presented by power relations. See McClintock, "House of Difference," for an analysis of the problem in relation to narratives emanating from South Africa.

were, Pringle's circle absorbed Prince's story: after Prince told it to Susannah Strickland, who tweaked it to an unknown extent, it was embedded in a complex hierarchy of power relations, the core narrative buried in layers of authenticity devices, contained within concentric circles of white editorial power. The dynamic was played out over Prince's body. Abolitionists relied on testimonies to the condition of that body to bring home the damage caused by beatings—a damage the enslavers repeatedly trivialized. Yet in doing so, they suggested their own status as insiders, "natural" citizens of Britain, in comparison to Prince's status as an outsider, always in need of authentication by those within the inner circle.

Yet the narrative's embedment in its elaborate paraphernalia tells two stories. While easily read as just one more example of white narrative cannibalism (the possibility that white masters might eat those they enslaved was noted in the case law as the limit case of the slave system),[32] it also suggests that Prince's story is internal to Englishness, that it cannot be expelled. Given this reading, the various formal qualities of the narrative, the way it was encased in its various authenticating meta-narratives, can be seen to trope the interiorized story. For it was the story of Prince's embeddedness in English culture, her internalization of Englishness and its internalization of her, that gave the narrative its transgressive power. Within the narrative, Prince emphasizes that embeddedness by dramatizing her ambivalent relationship with the Wood family, particularly after she has been brought to England. In England, Prince finds herself in captivity in London, despite a legal context in which, as she says, "I knew that I was free in England, but I did not know where to go, or how to get my living" (88). Prince's legal status was vexed by inconsistencies between English and colonial law. She may have been legally "free" in London, but this was a muddy issue that recent case law had left uncertain. Even if she were free in London though, she remained subject to slavery in the West Indies. In the end, the Woods returned to Antigua leaving Prince—at that time in her mid-forties—in London, but with no formal declaration that she was free. Therefore she was subject

32. This argument was not so far-fetched as one might think. In the *Zong* case of 1781, 133 enslaved Africans were forcibly drowned so that the ship's owners could collect under their insurance policy. In defense it was argued that they were simply chattel, "like goods" (quoted in Fryer 128). In the *Somerset* case, the enslaver's counsel seemed to suggest that even though he would not do it himself, under some views of the law, an enslaver could eat his property: "If it were necessary . . . that his master, even here, might kill, nay, might eat him, might sell [him] living or dead, might make him and his descendent property alienable, and this transmissible to posterity . . . I should only speak of it to testify my contempt and abhorrence." Even though one might claim them as property, "I will not . . . make a rigorous use of my power; I will neither sell them, eat them, nor part with them" (quoted in Michals 204).

to reenslavement should she attempt to return home. Thus, though supposedly already free, she attempted to buy her own freedom from the Woods. Each time they refused, at one point arguing that if they had sold her, they could have been charged with a crime, since she was free in London and could not legally be sold. Meanwhile, in an ironic reversal of the escaped slave narrative so well known in African-American history, the Wood family repeatedly tried to *evict* her. When they attempt to throw her out the door because she is too ill to do washing, she stays, saying, "I was a stranger, and did now know one door in the street from another, and was unwilling to go away" (77). Over a period of time, the scene was repeated again and again until she finally fled to the home of some fellow servants. Prince, like the slave system itself, became an embarrassment that refused to go away, one that claimed residence within the bounds of English culture.

Prince's narrative thus rejects the generic conventions of what eventually became the "classic" slave narrative. There is no escape, no arrival in the promised land, and certainly no upbeat conclusion. Like Prince's body, her story is "chequered"—marred, one might say, if one were enamored of the classic slave narrative, by her own refusal to leave. What are we to make of this unusual reversal—of the Woods' eviction of Prince and her refusal to be "free"? Moira Ferguson offers us a psychological and then a Hegelian explanation, blaming Prince's actions on her dependency, her unfamiliarity with London, her illness, and on her entrenchment in a master-slave relationship (*History* 17–23). But Prince's seeming rejection of freedom suggests a more complex story in which English identity is constantly reconfigured by the challenge Prince represented. By refusing to leave quietly, she underscored the Woods'—and ultimately England's—responsibility for her condition.

Prince's movements back and forth along the trajectory from slavery to freedom dramatized England's own ambivalence about the slave system, an ambivalence played out most legibly in what Peter Fryer has called the "pendulum" and James Walvin has called the "see-saw" of English law on slavery.[33] The ambivalence was as much rooted in English legal tradition as it was the result of a self-serving desire to continue profiting from colonial slavery. The feudal tradition of villenage[34]—occasionally invoked in the eighteenth century as a justification for slavery[35]—coexisted

33. Walvin offers clear descriptions of English legal developments related to slavery in *Black and White*. For another excellent summary, see Fryer 113–32. For a discussion by a legal historian who specializes in eighteenth-century studies, see Oldham.

34. See Michals for a fascinating discussion of feudal villenage and its impact on both Blackstone and Mansfield.

35. In 1749 Lord Hardwicke relied on villenage when he declared that slavery was legal

with the belief, expressed as early as 1569, that English air was "too pure—for slaves to breath in" (quoted in Woodard 138). Although the sentiment was later picked up by William Cowper and reiterated in *The Task* (Woodard 138), it was far from settled law. Case law and legal documents from 1677, 1694, and 1700 demonstrate that many believed enslaved people to be chattel whether they resided in England or not (Fryer 113). True, in 1706, Chief Justice John Holt (also responsible for almost single-handedly inventing seditious libel law) declared that "common law takes no notice of negroes being different from other men. By the common law no man can have property in another. . . . [T]here is no such thing as a slave by the laws of England" (quoted in Walvin, *Black and White* 111).[36] Given such pronouncements, by the late 1720s, West Indian owners were worried enough to request direction from English legal authorities. As a result, a proclamation from attorney general Sir Philip Yorke and solicitor general Charles Talbot reaffirmed slavery (Fryer 114). Nevertheless, in 1762 we again find juridical claims for freedom when Lord Chancellor Henley repeated the old argument that "as soon as a man sets foot on English ground he is free" (Walvin, *Black and White* 114).

Even the famous *Somerset* case which so many thought eliminated slavery in England was vexed by a commitment to the slave system. Decided by Chief Justice Mansfield in 1772, the case took up the efforts of an enslaved African, James Somerset, to escape a forced return to Jamaica. Given the conflicting decisions that governed the area as well as the unclear reports disseminated after the trial, it is not surprising that people were confused.[37] Mansfield's reluctance to decide *Somerset* was demonstrated by multiple postponements (at one point he adjourned for two weeks, at another for three months, at still another for a month) and pleas that the parties resolve the case for themselves. After squirming for months to disentangle himself from the case, Mansfield finally issued an equivocal ruling: "No master ever was allowed here to take a slave by force to be sold abroad because he deserted from his service, or for any other reason whatever—therefore the man must be discharged" (quoted in Walvin, *Black Ivory* 15). Perhaps one reason the case has been wrongly interpreted as establishing freedom in England is that the abolitionists wanted to see it that way. Although the various reports of the case are in

---

in England: "There were formerly villains [*sic*] or slaves in England . . . and although tenures are taken away, there are no laws that have destroyed servitude absolutely" (quoted in Fryer 114–15).

36. In one report of the case, Holt is quoted as saying that the law "looks on Negroes & Polacks as on the rest of mankind" (quoted in Oldham 49).

37. See Oldham for a legal historian's discussion of Mansfield's decision.

disarray, there is at least some evidence that Somerset himself as well as any number of abolitionists seized on it and advertised it as establishing freedom in England.[38] Meanwhile, Americans such as Benjamin Franklin mocked the decision, saying that England "piqued itself on its virtue, love of liberty, and the equity of its courts, in setting free a single negro." At best, *Somerset* established an uncertain tendency toward freedom that few could rely on.[39] Seven years later, Mansfield reportedly argued that it went "no further than that the master cannot by force compel [the slave] to go out of the kingdom" (Oldham 67). He further marked the decision's limitations by explicitly freeing his nephew's daughter, an enslaved woman of partial African descent, in his will in 1782. Long after Mansfield's death, the legal status of enslaved Africans brought to London was still undecided. In an 1822 case that illustrates the problems Prince faced, the enslaved Grace Jones was forcibly returned to Antigua from London, whereupon a customs officer seized her, claiming that having been in London, she must now be free. The court, mired in the inconsistencies between English and colonial law, held that her freedom had lasted only as long as she remained in England, no matter how she had ended up back in Antigua (Fryer 130–31). As the frustrated Justice Stowell remarked, "How the laws in respect of that trade made in England and enforced by our courts of law . . . can consist with any notion of its entire abolition here, is in my view of it, an utter impossibility" (Walvin, *Black and White* 137).

"Washing Tub Tales": Slaves, Laborers, and Domestics

Even Blackstone's supposedly magisterial *Commentaries* offered little help to those looking for an elegant solution to the problem of slavery. In the first edition of the *Commentaries,* Blackstone had written in support of those who believed that residence in England conferred freedom on enslaved Africans brought there: "This spirit of liberty is so deeply implanted in our constitution, and rooted even in our very soil, that a slave or a negro, the moment he lands in England, falls under the protection of the laws, and with regard to all natural rights becomes *eo instanti* a free-

38. Oldham offers a comparative analysis that illustrates the problem with trial reports of the period (56–58). He also reprints a letter that makes reference to Somerset's belief that Mansfield had freed Africans in England (66).

39. Oldham takes the unpopular position that Mansfield has been unfairly maligned for not seizing this opportunity to advance abolition. Instead, he sees Mansfield as operating within the bounds of precedent, and of finding that slavery was an institution "so odious as to require strict construction" (68).

man" (1:123). But in a localized demonstration of the "see-saw" of slavery law, Blackstone revised this finding in the next year's edition so as to render it meaningless, adding the words "though his master's right to his service may probably still continue" (quoted in Fryer 121). Although the revision may have been meant to bring the *Commentaries* into alignment with the Yorke-Talbot ruling, Blackstone seems also to have drawn on other references to slavery, such as those in Guy Miege's treatise *The New State of England Under Their Majesties K. William and Q. Mary*, published in 1691. In syntax similar enough to call Blackstone's originality into question, Miege declared that "a foreign Slave brought over into England is, upon Landing, *ipso facto* free from Slavery, though not from ordinary Service" (quoted in Fryer 113). That Miege and Blackstone could both bury forced labor in the afterthought of a tacked-on clause suggests not only a bit of juridical plagiarism but also a desire to emphasize slavery's peripheral qualities, its incompatibility with central tenets of English law. But the involuntary servitude "trailer" also suggests a continuum between slavery and servitude that the abolitionists' reductive notion of freedom tended to ignore. Even if Prince were realigned with servitude rather than slavery, she would not be "free." Despite the myths that circulated about English liberty, in English law only property owners experienced freedom in the sense that the abolitionists imagined it. Slaves, apprentices, most women, and all others without property experienced only a restricted version of freedom.

While Prince's narrative uses English liberty as a rallying cry, it also offers a more realistic, even pragmatic understanding of the nature of English freedom. She recognizes the vexed nature of servant "freedom" under English law, revealing liberty as a complex concept mired in conflicting race and class interests. The critique of class is so powerful here that it is no wonder the conservative racist and class-driven writer Macqueen derisively referred to Prince's narrative as her "Washing Tub Tales." True, in the rousing end to the narrative, Prince discriminates carefully between slavery and servitude: "They hire servants in England; and if they don't like them, they send them away: they can't lick them. Let them work ever so hard in England, they are far better off than slaves" (94). But throughout the narrative, we find Prince trying out two versions of personal identity, slipping back and forth between slave and servant, and demonstrating the constraints that confined both categories. Her vacillation along a number of different poles—from insider to outsider, from slave to free, from compliance to resistance—far from indicating a desire for slavery, suggests instead the uneasy relationship between institutional slavery and the servitude of the labor market. Neither Prince nor the

Woods represent the free market world of servitude as an easy one. Prince notes several times that she had nowhere to go in London. The fourth time Wood threatens Prince with eviction, he tells her, "If I wished to be free, I was free in England, and I might go and try what freedom would do for me, and be d——d" (78). As she leaves, she overhears her mistress say, "If she goes the people will rob her, and then turn her adrift" (79). Such remarks suggest that technical freedom in England would merely subject Prince to the tyranny of want experienced by any displaced, used-up laborer.

Macqueen's labeling of Prince's narrative as a "washtub tale" attempted to undermine Prince's combined critique of imperialism, the class structure, and English domesticity. Washing, far from being a trivial chore, had long been central to class disputes. Prince's critique expanded its metaphoric utility, demonstrating the relationship of washing to conversations about the empire on the one hand and about insular Englishness, as represented by the family, on the other. Although the infamous advertisements showing black children magically made white by Pears soap would be the work of future generations, there is little doubt that powerful associations between washing and colonialism drove Prince's narrative.[40] Prince's accusation that her "old master" in Bermuda "had an ugly fashion of stripping himself quite naked and ordering me then to wash him in a tub of water" (66) has resulted in much critical speculation concerning sexual abuse, but little has been said about the significance of the washtub as a sign of debilitating labor and tyranny. Imbricated in both the sexual "shame" she had experienced in Bermuda and the hardships of her work in the salt ponds of Turk's Island, washing comes to represent the abuses of slavery. Although washing her master in Bermuda "was worse to me than all the licks," washing linens, clothes, and other household items caused injury and disease. Prince tells us that washing for the Wood family was physically more difficult, more debilitating than salt mining on Turk's Island (69). With its hard physical demands, its exposure to extremes of temperature, and its use of caustic and no doubt bacteria-laden substances, washing stood in for the worst labor required of the enslaved.[41]

After her removal to England, washing takes on even greater weight in Prince's narrative. Washing was a pervasive problem in English culture:

40. See McClintock, *Imperial Leather* 210–13 for a further discussion of later implications of the British emphasis on cleanliness.

41. See Davidson for a discussion of the laundry products that preceded soap (142–43). They included lye derived from ashes, but also ammonia made from collected urine, a practice that continued in coal mining towns in England through the 1840s. Cow dung was also a popular cleanser.

the English themselves devoted any number of popular songs and rhymes to the fact that they hated doing the laundry (Davidson 150). Thus it provided a powerful symbol for slavery, one that ensured immediate recognition and sympathy. Usually saved up and done once a month or once every five or six weeks, the family laundry often took two or three people several fourteen-hour days to complete (Davidson 150–52). Significantly, Prince is ordered to wash clothes "the English way" almost upon landing in London, and she first protests the Woods' treatment of her when she is ordered to wash the "five bags of clothes which we had used at sea" (77). Prince located her refusal to wash the colonies out of the Woods' clothes in her physical condition. But such refusals, especially when made by enslaved women, engaged a politically resistant tradition that eventually made a real contribution to ending slavery in the British Caribbean in 1838.[42] In Prince's narrative, the refusal to work is met by increasingly oppressive measures. Like the work in the salt ponds, washing the dirt of the colonies out of the Woods' clothes is not negotiable. Prince's resistance to this hard work—work to which she was not originally assigned—prompts the first of several attempts to banish her from the house. Her repeated discussions of washing, coupled with the Woods' insistence that she do the wash or leave, show how a conflation of slavery, washing, and dirt had come to represent the ideological difficulty involved in absolving Englishness of responsibility for slavery.

Perhaps drawing on well-worn radical discourse, Prince presses washing into service as a metaphor for all wage labor, connecting her cause to that of the Reform movement. In her novel *Maria,* Wollstonecraft had relied on the washtub as a sign for the oppressive treatment accorded servants. Now Prince drew on the washtub to link slavery with servitude, replicating the slave-servant continuum that infected both English and colonial law and custom.[43] The Woods, too, drew on the elastic boundaries between servant and slave. When Prince's labor was necessary to the household, she was identified as a "slave"; when it became unnecessary or more of a burden than a help, she suddenly became a "servant" subject to immediate termination, to being cast out without resources on the London streets. In defense, Prince appropriates this fluidity at times to align herself with servitude. In England, other washerwomen help Prince with her work, and she compares their "pity" to the Woods' cold indifference. Showcasing her own entrepreneurial agency, Prince reveals herself to be taking in laundry on the side even while refusing to take responsibility for

42. See Morrissey, esp. 153.
43. Carole Barash points out that in Jamaica "the lines demarcating 'servants' from 'slaves' were in practice quite fluid" (409).

the Wood family laundry. At one point in the narrative, she even complains that she has no time to wash her own clothes and must send them out in order to keep up with the work the Woods have assigned her. Significantly, when Prince leaves the Wood household, she flees to the home of a fellow laundress (Midgley 87). Such displays of working-class agency and solidarity may have sparked a particularly high level of anxiety during this period of working-class reform. But such anxiety was not played out only on the national level; it infected every household that employed servants and, in an age in which much of the population experienced servitude at one time or another, many households that did not. What I can refer to only ironically as "the servant problem" is not a recent invention.[44] Retaining household servants willing, for subsistence wages, to do the dirty, difficult work that no one else wanted to do was at least as much a problem in the first third of the nineteenth century as it is said to be today. Thomas Carlyle's wife, Jane, for instance, went through thirty-four servants in the first thirty-two years of the nineteenth century, including one who, Prince-like, "refused to help with the laundry and accused Jane of treating her like a slave" (Davidson 164).

Because most household servants were young and in transition between their status as children and a future status as wives, they moved frequently to marry, to return to their families, or simply in search of better positions. Such mobility seems to have increased the political anxiety surrounding servitude, an anxiety often rearticulated through the charge that servants dressed above their station or, as we shall see later in this discussion, through accusations of hypersexuality.[45] Prince's possession of multiple sets of clothing indicates a high degree of independent agency in a world in which many poor people still owned only one set of clothes. As Margaret Hunt remarks, well into the eighteenth century, when poor people needed to wash their clothes "they went literally naked." Nakedness, later associated with colonized indigenous populations, including Africans, was, as Hunt says, "coded as 'One of Those Things "We" Are Not,' a boundary marker between middling respectability . . . and something else" (344). Precisely because clothes were a sign of independence, agency, and affluence, not to mention moral character, we find comments regarding Prince's dress. For instance, in Macqueen's attack on the narrative, he notes the testimony of Ann Todd, a "respectable female of colour," who said that "Molly had an abundance of clothes—could dress like a lady; indeed, more like the mistress than the servant. On some

---

44. As my argument demonstrates, the "servant problem" is one experienced in the first place by servants, not employers.

45. See Straub for a discussion of this form of rearticulation in the 1750s.

occasions she would be seen in silks" (749). Concerns with enslaved women's clothing surfaced repeatedly in the arguments over abolition. In 1832 the Select Committee on the Extinction of Slavery was both entertained and reassured by testimony that enslaved women liked "unnecessary finery" (Paton 167). On the one hand, such a superficial value system marked enslaved women's intellect as inferior, the occasion for low jokes. On the other, consumer desire demonstrated that enslaved people, once freed, could continue to be counted on as a labor force: they would work for more than mere subsistence. But the notion of overdressed African women also tapped into English anxieties about excess consumption and the destabilization of status. The repeated emphasis on Prince's clothes as well as the Woods' efforts to divest her of them (they argued that she carried off various items of clothing when she left them) suggest a struggle over Prince's claims to respectability, to the right to be treated as a person. Even Susannah Strickland made much of the fact that Prince outfitted herself in a new suit for Strickland's wedding, while Macqueen relied on the mere fact that Prince possessed clothes to undermine her claims of mistreatment.

Prince's narrative was deeply embedded in the larger national struggle for reform, in the realignment and restructuring of the class system that characterized the period.[46] As part of the larger antislavery movement, the reform movement helped build connections between workers and the political elite as well as between enslaved people and workers (Blackburn 443). The antislavery movement eventually took second place to the movement for reform, but it served an important function nevertheless, as it both metaphorically shadowed and directly supported reform. At times "slavery" served as the extreme example of worker oppression, while at other times "antislavery" operated as a sign of the goodwill and humanitarian spirit of the reform movement. Prince's effort to align enslaved people with servants reflected a trend in the abolitionist movement in which even supposedly apolitical groups such as domestic servants and women came together to support abolition (Blackburn 443). But it also entered into a confusing war of discourses, one in which the language of slavery was used to support all sorts of different causes. At some points during the abolition movement, working-class activists even disrupted abolitionist rallies with their claims that employers enslaved their workers in Britain and that Britain should put its own house in order before it dealt with the colonies (Turley, *Culture* 182–83). Although this did not reflect the majority view, from 1792 through the 1840s, comparisons to

46. See Blackburn for a full discussion of this issue.

slavery were often used to further the reform cause (Walvin, *England* 113). In this sense, one could almost say that slavery was necessary to the working-class effort for reform.

In comparing herself to working-class people, Prince drew on such language for her own purposes. But her efforts to associate herself with free laborers could cut both ways. Some planters tried to claim that enslaved people were just another sort of working-class group, that they were treated better in some respects than other sorts of servants (Ward, *Slavery* 2). In the *Somerset* case, such an association had been used as an argument *against* rather than *for* freeing the enslaved. There, rather perversely, the relationship between master and servant, the servant's servitude, was emphasized to suggest how very awkward it would be if masters were forced to free those they believed they owned. As the counsel for Somerset's owners argued: "It would be a great surprize, and some inconvenient, if a foreigner bringing over a servant, as soon as he got hither, must take care of his carriage, his horse, and himself in whatever method he might have the luck to invent. . . . Thus, neither superior, or inferior, both go without their dinner" (quoted in Fryer 123). This almost comic image of domestic disorder suggests that slavery's role as a model for other sorts of domestic servitude, its powerful relationship to domesticity, was already firmly in place more than fifty years before Prince drew on it. That slavery was seen as so directly related to a stable domestic life helps us understand why Prince's narrative posed such a threat on a domestic level. She reconstituted the harmonious domestic family, the site in which the Woods tried to naturalize slavery, as a site of political struggle and resistance.

Perhaps her narrative provoked so much juridical energy because it made a spectacle of what was supposed to be private and domestic. What Karen Chase and Michael Levenson have called the "spectacle of intimacy" may not have come into its own until the Victorians, but we can trace its beginnings in the intense, sometimes lascivious interest that Prince's account of her private life with the Woods evoked. By 1831, England was if anything more deeply invested in an understanding of the relationship between the peaceful and well-ordered domestic setting and a peaceful well-ordered nation than it had been at the time of the *Somerset* case. In clinging to home, albeit the Woods' home, Prince retained the ability to critique not only her own domestic situation but English domesticity as well. Her account of her experiences with the Woods amounts to an attack on the nature of the English home at large, a revelation that the English household on which so much of the English national fantasy relied was far from orderly, clean, and peaceful. Instead, she constructed English domesticity as dirty, chaotic, sexualized, and violent. Prince's narrative told the true story of domesticity, one of hierarchy rather than progress, of displacement and estrangement rather than homecoming.[47] We have already seen Prince's deconstruction of the domestic progress narrative, the way she revealed domestic education as an education in the variety of available beatings and whippings. But beatings did not tell all of the story. Prince's narrative made a spectacle of domesticity, revealing the Wood household, even when in London and thus away from the presumably degenerating effects of the colonies, to be a place of shouting and abuse, where woman threatened woman, and the solution to the problem presented by a sick worker was to put her out on the streets.

Mrs. Wood's virtue was at issue just as much as Prince's. The English abolitionists had made much of the connection between womanly virtue and the abolitionist cause in both their tracts and public displays of abolitionist support.[48] As Colley records, "By 1830, there were ladies' anti-slavery societies in almost every British town, the biggest in Birmingham distributing some 35,000 items of propaganda every year" (*Britons* 278). In turn, the plantocracy emphasized the virtue of their own women; they supposedly ran well-governed homes where enslaved people were lifted out of their "natural" depravity. But the expression of female virtue worked only so long as the English home remained insulated from signs of colonial oppression, from the violence and coercion that underwrote plantation life. Prince's narrative associated the unsavory details linked to colonial contamination of the English home with women as well as men, as she blamed her mistreatment on Mrs. Wood as much as on her husband. According to the narrative, it was Mrs. Wood who abandoned Prince in an outbuilding when she was ill; Mrs. Wood who "told me that if I did not mind what I was about, she would get my master to strip me and give me fifty lashes"; Mrs. Wood who ordered her put in "the Cage" overnight; and Mrs. Wood who "was always abusing and fretting after me," using "ill language" (80). The challenge was powerful because it consolidated English worries about the pernicious effects of the colonies on national identity and located those worries in civil domestic relations. In suggesting that the presence of colonial slavery could cause dissension

47. McClintock has suggested that violence and disorder characterized the reformulation of domestic life along Victorian lines. Victorian domestic life was "more often than not violent. . . . Animals, women and colonized peoples were wrested from their putatively 'natural' yet, ironically, 'unreasonable' state of 'savagery' and inducted through the domestic progress narrative into a hierarchical relation to white men" (*Imperial Leather* 35).

48. As Charlotte Sussman has shown, this was frequently emphasized in abolitionist tracts where "active female virtue is conjoined to a kind of national sensibility. . . . The compassion of British women symbolizes a specific national identity, a quality that distinguishes England from the rest of the world" (60).

in the family, Prince called into question domesticity's autonomy from national strife. Indeed, what prompted Wood's charges of libel was the suggestion that the Wood family did not exist in perfect domestic harmony.

Libeling the Nation: Prince and "Official" Juridical Culture

Given all that was at stake in Prince's story, it is not surprising that English libel law was pressed into service to remedy the destabilization the narrative attempted. Libel law, connected as it was to laws involving sedition and treason, functioned to protect deeply held convictions about national identity. Seditious libel law, familiar to literary critics as the law that put Defoe in the stocks, developed in concert with larger societal changes usually associated with the growth of a "public sphere" oriented toward identification with nation rather than kingdom. Before 1695, the government controlled the press through licensing laws which required printers to apply for and receive a license before printing a work. The system was hierarchical, reminding every printer at least metaphorically that the Crown controlled what would be published. Early efforts to do away with the licensing acts emerged directly from Protestant-Catholic tensions of the late 1670s, when the Crown attempted to use the licensing acts to control anti-Catholic exclusionist publications. Finding alternative ways to control a now unruly press led the Crown first to the treason laws, which ultimately proved procedurally unwieldy, and then to seditious libel law. Pre-1695 "seditious libel" cases were actually tried under the licensing statutes or sometimes under the law of *scandalum magnatum,* prohibiting criticism of the Crown and its officials. The case law, even when calling on supposed precedents, consistently confuses treason cases with cases for sedition and sedition cases with prosecutions for *scandalum magnatum.* As Philip Hamburger points out, although any number of different cases "went under the label of 'seditious libel,' they reveal nothing about the common law offense that eventually acquired that name" (682). As I have suggested earlier, prepublication licensing requirements finally lapsed in 1695, in part because they were associated with tyranny and Catholicism (Hamburger 670–716).[49] Thus, seditious libel law was a late English invention, largely written into being after 1695 by Chief Justice John Holt,

---

49. Hamburger argues at one point that the Crown allowed the licensing act to expire without renewal because it had discovered treason prosecution to offer a more effective way of controlling the press. It seems more likely, given even his evidence, that the Crown first allowed the act to expire for a number of different reasons and then turned to prosecutions for treason to control the press. As Hamburger points out, resort to treason laws involved

who worked over a period of fifteen years to create a body of flexible and powerful precedents aimed at increasing government control over oppositional writing.[50]

Although some historians have suggested that seditious libel law and private libel law have nothing in common, eighteenth-century legal experts clearly saw a connection (Slaughter 362, note 41). While seditious libel law arose from treason cases, and private libel law from the desire to control disputes between individuals, both assumed an integrated nation in which each citizen fully identified and was identified with the larger national cause. Seditious or "public" libel law most clearly protected the nation from public attack because it protected public officials and governing bodies, but all forms of defamation were considered potential national threats.[51] Individual reputations intersected with the national reputation in this view; the characters of individuals were not a private matter but instead were of public concern.[52] As Francis Holt asserted in his 1812 treatise *The Law of Libel*, public libel law protected "political persons of all kinds," but private libel law protected all of England's "subjects whatsoever."[53] Holt, like most commentators on libel, waxes patriotic as he explains the relationship: "No man can reasonably set his own character at a higher estimation than the law of England itself puts upon it. Acting in the same spirit, in which in all criminal cases [the law] presupposes the party innocent till proved to be guilty, it takes the honesty, morality, and sound religion of every member of the community, as a reasonable presumption" (160).

---

a number of different procedural and political problems, all of which resulted in the Treason Trials Act of 1696, meant to control and limit the excesses of such prosecutions.

50. John Holt (1642–1710) is usually represented as offering relief to historians who are looking for honesty and intelligence in the judiciary. As Edward Foss remarked, he was "erudite in law, independent in character, and just and firm in his decisions. In him we fix the commencement of a new era of judicial purity and freedom" (386). See Foss for a complete biographical entry.

51. "Defamation" is the umbrella term that includes slander (oral attacks on character) and libel (written attacks). In general, libel was considered the more serious of the two as it had the potential for greater distribution and thus for doing more damage to reputation. For work on slander in the early modern period, see M. Lindsay Kaplan and Gowing.

52. See Post and Slaughter for the development of common law defamation. Slaughter suggests that the shift in defamation law from a concern with honor to a concern with reputation reflects differences between a hierarchical society and a democratic one (352, note 2).

53. Francis Holt (1780–1844) does not seem to have been related to Chief Justice John Holt. He was a legal author and dramatist who may have had some interest in laws regarding printing and publication as he was the principal editor of *Bell's Weekly Messenger* throughout most of his life. He wrote at least two dramas, including a comedy, *The Land We Live In*, which went to three editions but was performed at Drury Lane only once in 1805. See *Dictionary of National Biography*.

Libel law reinforced national integrity by protecting the community from infighting and establishing community standards for speech. Libelous statements tended to create disharmony among individuals and within the community. As the court had argued in *Villars v. Monsley,* the problem involved the publication of words that tended "to hinder mankind from associating or having intercourse" with the injured party (quoted in Holt 196). Given the technicalities and big money verdicts of contemporary libel cases, we tend to forget that slander and libel law originated in an effort to reduce the number of public affrays. Libels, Holt argued, hold a man "up to scorn and ridicule . . . and impair him in the enjoyment of general society, and injure those imperfect rights of friendly intercourse, and mutual benevolence, which man has with respect to man" (161). Moreover, common ways of speaking, common boundaries between what could and what could not be said about others, were thought essential to national integration and unity. As John Borthwick remarked in 1830, to place limitations on speech through the use of libel law "involves the consideration of the habits, manners, and even fancies, and prejudices of the people, for whose government it is intended, and requires alternation of constant occurrence corresponding with the changes effected in the state of society by political emergencies, advancement in arts and civilization, and even by the changing habits, fashions, and propensities of private individuals" (12–13).

That it concerned itself with the "habits, manners, and even fancies" of the people suggests that libel law was intimately tied up with English ideals. Certainly the branch of libel law involving sedition, with its concern for authorial identity and authenticity, emerged from state efforts to control dissent, from the perceived need to attach libelous and seditious remarks to individual bodies that could be disciplined and controlled. But by the 1830s, such repression was met with intense resistance. As Francis Holt suggested, the very constitution of England was "the fruit of a free press" (40). Thus, "there is nothing, indeed, upon which Englishmen are justly more sensible than upon whatever has the appearance of affecting the freedom of the press" (46). No wonder then that Blackstone felt it necessary to append a paragraph to his section on seditious libel explaining at length why it was *not* an infringement on freedom of the press. Holt too seems almost defensive in his extensive efforts to explain libel's compatibility with the freedom of the press:

> This branch of the law of England contains nothing contradictory to the spirit of the constitution, but is, in every respect, in perfect conformity with the general criminal law of the country. It is unnecessary to say more, than

that it is an analogous part of a system, which, beyond any other code of laws in the civilized world, secures the interests of government and establishments at the least possible cost of personal restriction; and is thus a practical example of what has always been considered as the characteristic of a good and free government that of uniting the peace, order, and union of civilized life, with the greatest possible portion of the independent exercise and enjoyment of our natural faculties. (311)

Despite Holt's belief that it was "unnecessary to say more," most had a great deal to say about the tensions that Holt tries to ease here: between "the interests of government" and "the least possible personal restriction," between a "free government" and the "union of civilized life," in short, between restrictions on the press and the English constitution. Libel law, because of its relationship to English ideals, was at the heart of national life.

By the 1830s, libel law could be said to have a national history of unintended results and explosive outcomes. Considered "one of the most extraordinary transactions" of its time, the prosecution of the clergyman Henry Sacheverell in 1710 demonstrated just how out of control a government trial for seditious libel could become.[54] That Chief Justice John Holt, who had so carefully crafted seditious libel law in order to increase governmental control, died during this first great show trial of the century may have been a boon: he would have been appalled at the results of his tinkering with the law. Brought up for a sermon attacking the "false brethren" who he said had placed the Church of England in danger, Sacheverell entered Westminster[55] as a little-known man "with a very small measure of religions, virtue, learning, or good sense" and exited a national hero. The trial—which absorbed the whole of the government's energy and attention for over three weeks—transformed Sacheverell into a popular icon. "Great crowds ran about his coach, with many shouts, expressing their concern for him in a very rude and tumultuous manner. . . . [T]he multitudes that followed him, all the way as he came, and as he went back, shewed a great concern for him, pressing about him, and striving to kiss his hand: money was thrown among them; and they were animated to such a pitch of fury, that they went to pull down some Meeting houses" (Howell, *State Trials* 12–13). The publicity was intense, generating over three hundred publications, and by the end of the affair Sacheverell, ordered only to burn his offending sermon and pay a fine,

54. My discussion of Sacheverell's case is drawn from Geoffrey Holmes's account and from *The Tryal of Dr. Henry Sacheverell* (1710).
55. See Baker, *Common Law*, chap. 15, for a discussion of the use of Westminster as a law court.

had become a rich man. In hundreds of other cases throughout the century, those prosecuted may not have been as lucky.[56] But as John Barrell has pointed out in regard to the famous treason trials of the 1790s, such trials can be repressive, but they can also "mobilize and exploit a wide range of discourses whose very profusion made it impossible for the court to fix the meaning of the law on its own terms" (*Pandora* 119).

The history of libel is full of incidents in which the effort to contain subversion actually displays it, magnified and amplified. This dynamic of unpredictable results was still current in Prince's time. When William Cobbett, the editor of the notorious *Complete Collection of State Trials*, was tried for seditious libel in 1810 for publishing a critique of the British army that suggested it was less disciplined than Napoleon's armies, he too was fined. But the verdict had unintentional results: celebrated at dinners attended by hundreds of supporters and entertained by the ringing of church bells on his return home, Cobbett became a hero in radical circles (Thomas, *State Trials* 13). During the first three decades of the century, hundreds of radicals and radical sympathizers like Cobbett were prosecuted for criminal libel (Wickwar 17). Libel and sedition trials were used by both sides. On the one hand, the government drew on them at worst to stifle dissent, at best to try to establish the boundaries of public debate. On the other hand, public trials gave radicals a forum and forced the state to make its attitudes public. By the 1820s, the radicals had developed sophisticated methods for exploiting show trials and had high hopes for their political efficacy (Wood, *Radical Satire* 98–99). The radicals expected, for instance, that show trials would be well attended and covered by the press. Certainly earlier cases had drawn large audiences and street crowds including both black and white spectators. Although it is difficult to know how well attended the cases generated by Prince's narrative were, the newspaper reports record what seems to have been the laughter of the crowd. In any case, the spectacular functions of libel actions were well documented. Addison had long ago suggested that libels had a mysterious ability to attract attention.[57] And only a few years before the Prince case, Borthwick had argued that because it was "the nature of every case of libel to excite much general interest and in many instances to engage the attention if not excite the passions of the whole nation, a ready and extensive market is afforded, which not merely admits, but demands supply of mental food for the curiosity of the public" (8).

56. Wickwar's account, now dated, still contains the best survey of prosecutions during the age of reform.
57. "What shall we say of the pleasure which a man takes in the reading of a Defamatory libel?" Addison asked in *Spectator* 451 (4:89).

In the abolitionist controversy, both sides tried to capitalize on libel law. In a case that resonates with Pringle's later difficulties, John Hatchard, an abolitionist printer, was indicted for criminal seditious libel in 1816. The case, sensational enough to be included in *State Trials,* reveals libel law in use as a tool of the plantocracy. Hatchard, publisher of the annual report for the African Institution, an organization run by William Wilberforce, was prosecuted for publishing the *Tenth Annual Report of the Directors of the African Institution.* The report included the story of an Antiguan aide-de-camp to the governor, Sir James Leith, who had supposedly flogged a pregnant enslaved woman.[58] When she complained to the governor, the aide-de-camp was dismissed. As the story went, he retaliated by sending an enslaved boy dressed in uniform to the governor on a donkey. Supposedly, the outraged governor then presented an indictment to the grand jury, which unconscionably refused it. Unfortunately for the abolitionists, the story, chosen so carefully for its sympathetic—and no doubt for its sadomasochistic—appeal, was false.[59] The Antiguan colonial government, angered by its depiction as a body of tyrannical, malicious slavers, fought back, charging Hatchard with seditious libel on behalf of the aides-de-camp of Antigua and of "the administration of justice in the island" (Thomas, *State Trials* 204). They won on the argument that the report was based on "a false, scandalous, and malignant fabrication, invented for the wicked purpose of holding out to the British public . . . that those who in the situation of grand jurymen are called to administer justice, are so debased by the horrid tyranny in which a system of slavery allows them to indulge that no negro can, under any possible circumstances, obtain redress at their hands" (Thomas, *State Trials* 209).

The plantocracy seems to have wanted to make of Prince a similar example. In reaction to her narrative, James Macqueen attacked her furiously, meanwhile defending the Woods and colonial slavery in *Blackwood's.* Calling Prince's narrative a "blacker specimen" of "the hideous falsehoods and misrepresentations" commonly launched against the plantocracy, Macqueen realigned the relationship between slavery, liberty, and Englishness, pointing out that Prince came to England voluntarily and repeatedly citing her failure to flee the Woods. On issues of domesticity

58. See Wood, *Blind Memory,* and Paton for extended discussions of abolitionists' use of narratives detailing the sexual and physical torture of enslaved women. Such narratives seem to have been particularly prevalent during the 1830s.

59. Marcus Wood argues that the "confusion of suffering with desirability" characterized abolitionist images of beaten women (*Blind Memory* 236). The focus on beaten women seen in both the Hatchard and Prince cases probably also served to comfort those worried about organized revolts. To represent the "typical" enslaved person as a helpless beaten women suggested the unlikeliness of violent rebellion.

Macqueen was even harsher. He made no attempt to deny that Prince had been beaten, instead suggesting that as a well-known "type," the unruly and hypersexualized female slave, she deserved it. He accused Prince of prostitution (749) and Pringle not only of "secret closetings and labours with Mary," but also of corrupting his family by bringing her into the house (750–51). As Macqueen put it, Pringle and his friends spent their time "poking their noses into every scene of black filth" and contaminated their families by exposing them to inappropriate information. From Macqueen's point of view, Pringle's real fault was that he brought colonial issues home, right into the domestic space of the English house: his "continued labour by night and by day in the study, in the parlour, and in the drawing-room is to call for and to nestle amidst all kinds of colonial immorality and uncleanness . . . and on every occasion to lay all these before the eyes, and impress them upon the minds, of the females of his family!" (751). Macqueen referred in particular to Pringle's wife, noting that she provided Pringle "this legal British backing" to protect him from charges of immorality. According to Macqueen, Pringle's entire relationship with Prince was suspicious, possibly the result of Pringle's time in the colonies. "In London maidservants are not removed from the washing tub to the parlour without an object," sneered Macqueen (750). Pringle was at fault for having introduced Prince—who, despite her time at the English washtub, represented "black filth"—into the intimate space reserved for the English family. Macqueen apparently saw it as his duty to evict Prince from this space.

Perhaps fearing a Hatchard-type libel prosecution himself, perhaps simply eager to seize the first-strike advantage, Pringle filed suit against Macqueen, complaining not of Macqueen's attack on Prince, but of the attack on Pringle's and his wife's characters. Macqueen had not only "thought proper to impute intentional falsehood and gross misconduct to the plaintiff," but also had "attacked the ladies of his family" (Ferguson, *Mary Prince* 137).[60] Reflecting the general erasure of enslaved women from abolition debates, the trial made little of Prince's story. As Diane Paton has shown, abolition arguments "excluded women from consideration," by and large forcing enslaved women into the roles of sexual victims or consumers (163). What is most notable about the case is the way it evades both Prince herself and the issue of slavery. Pringle's attorney classified the difference between Pringle and Macqueen as one involving a "con-

60. The two legal cases were reported in the *London Times,* the first on February 21 and the second on March 1, 1833. Ferguson reprints these in appendixes 5 and 6 of her edition of Prince's narrative. Page references are to this more accessible reprint version rather than to the less available source.

siderable difference of opinion" between abolitionists and "a numerous and powerful party" from the West Indies "who left no measure untried either by intimidation, or oppression, or calumny, to prevent any correct information as to the state and condition of the slaves from being given to the public" (137). Cadell's attorney argued that abolition "had nothing to do with it in court of justice" (138). Prince was not named in the lawsuit. She testified, but only to the fact that she had told the story to Pringle. Since no further questions were asked, she had no opportunity to defend herself against the charges of prostitution, theft, and deceit. Although Pringle won, the jury trivialized his cause by awarding him only three pounds. Meanwhile, Prince had been written out of the story, her character seemingly immaterial to a dispute that was largely about attacks on English domesticity.

In response to Pringle's somewhat muted victory, John Wood filed his own suit. As in the first libel suit, the charges erased issues of slavery and freedom, reimagining the story of Prince's enslavement as a narrative of disrupted English domesticity. In this story, Prince represented the disruptive outsider, the thorn in the side of the Woods' domestic happiness. The Woods called a number of witnesses to present a "good owner" defense: as responsible slaveowners, they had taken good care of Prince. In contrast, she was represented as lazy, sexual, disruptive, and greedy, an exemplar of all forms of disorder.[61] In the second trial it was Prince—and the character of all enslaved people—rather than British slavery that was put to the question. The aim was to rewrite her to fit prevailing stereotypes about enslaved African women, stereotypes focusing on their laziness, consumer behavior, and sexuality.[62] Such a rewriting was not simply a matter of personal cruelty or a ploy to vindicate the Wood family. Rather it worked to mediate between abolition and the plantocracy. The suggestion that all English people, despite their differences over slavery, had a common "other" was meant to heal the division between England and the colonies by reintegrating the publicly reviled plantocracy into the community.

61. The case provides an apt illustration of Paul Gilroy's contention that "explanations of criminal behavior which make use of national and racial characteristics are probably as old as the modern juridical system itself. The identification of law with national interests, and of criminality with un-English qualities, dates from [the] process of state formation and has a long history which remains relevant to the analysis of 'race' and crime today" (*No Black* 74).

62. Paton suggests that these are three important categories for understanding British views of African women in other testimony of the period. That my own analysis of the trial records—records that Paton does not discuss—revealed these categories long before I read Paton's recent work not only confirms Paton's observation but also suggests the ubiquity of the categories.

Revising Prince's narrative to highlight her ungovernability, the Woods' witnesses testified that she was lazy. As if prepared beforehand, a number of witnesses testified that she showed "a disinclination to work," "appeared to perform her work very unwillingly," and was "very lazy" (143–44).[63] In truth, Prince seems to have been far from lazy. She was seriously entrepreneurial, having earned her own price and tried to purchase herself several times during the course of her life. But reinscribing her rejection of work as "laziness" rather than resistance to slavery seemed crucial to the attack on her story. A sign of resistant agency, such entrepreneurship had to be erased or at worst reinterpreted as something else. Predictably enough, the witnesses rearticulated her agency as sexuality, just as Macqueen had done in his *Blackwood's* piece. Whereas Macqueen had located Martha Wilcox, a woman Prince had criticized in the narrative, and got her to say that Prince "also made money *many, many* other ways by her badness; I mean, by allowing men to visit her and by selling****to worthless men" (749), the charges made in court were more subtle. On cross-examination Prince was asked about sexual details that Pringle and Strickland had presumably purged from the published narrative. Given the era, her testimony that she had "lived seven years" with the white Captain Abbot before marrying her present husband and been "made a fool of" by a second man who promised to free her may have been as damaging as charges of prostitution (147–48). Evidence of such sexual activity (a form of self-help under the circumstances) reframed her energy and initiative as immorality.

Meanwhile, the Woods made good use of the opportunity to reestablish their own home as a place of domestic harmony, marred only by Prince's disruptive presence. Prince had testified that Mr. Wood had beaten her both on his own initiative and at Mrs. Wood's request and that Mrs. Wood had called her "a devil, a black devil, and a spawn, and said that she wanted to be a lady" (Ferguson, *Mary Prince* 146). In response, the Woods brought witnesses to testify to their mildness. According to these witnesses, the family was "everything that was kind" (142), "very mild and gentle to their servants" (143), gave them "every comfort" (143). That two of these witnesses habitually beat their own servants was left for cross-examination to discover. Bringing in their own daughter to testify, the Woods represented themselves as a united family of kindly employers, made much of the fact that they had paid Prince a wage (which she denied), and emphasized their intention to free her when they returned

63. For an argument suggesting that "the rejection of work . . . has deep roots in the expressive culture of black Britain" (73) because it represented resistance to the slave system, see Gilroy, *No Black*.

to Antigua. Prince, by contrast, was revealed to be "a great deal of trouble," "very lazy," and in what were perhaps the most damaging charges, a woman who fought with other women when jealous of their position in the household (142–44).

The testimony reveals some debate over the circumstances under which Prince in fact fought with these other women. In the published narrative she discusses only a dispute over a stolen pig, a valuable commodity in Antigua but the fuel for low jokes in London courtrooms. Even Prince's desire to regulate her domestic life along English lines was rewritten as a sign of her low, sexual nature. In testimony that elicited repeated laughter from the audience, Prince seems to have been egged on to discuss an incident in which she beat another woman for sleeping with Captain Abbot. As Prince testified:

> One night she found another woman in bed with the Captain in her house. This woman had pretended to be a friend of witness. (Laughter). Witness licked her, and she was obliged to get out of bed. (A laugh). The captain laughed, and the woman said she done it to plague witness. Witness took her next day to the Moravian black leader, when she denied it, and witness then licked her again. (A laugh). (147)

That "laughter" was recorded in newspaper accounts of the trial suggests that the courtroom reduced Prince's story from tragedy to comedy, from a story of terrible mistreatment to one of carnivalesque disorder. Numerous prints in circulation during the period reveal the ludic power of miscegenation imagery, the laughter evoked by suggestions of sexual relations between black women and white men (Wood, *Blind Memory* 163). The laughter that greeted her story seems to have united the audience around a common understanding of African women's sexuality with its "low" comic violence, an understanding developed through decades of exposure to satirical cartoons and other popular representations of African women's behavior.[64] The resulting decision granting the Wood family twenty-five pounds in damages—an inexplicable decision given the weak evidence brought by the Woods' self-interested witnesses—suggests that the tactic worked. Prince's travails, including her dramatic account of beatings and torture, became instead comic material, a mock-epic of "washing tub tales" in which broadly drawn black women put on fisticuffs, fighting, perhaps over pigs, perhaps over white men, but in any case over little of consequence.

The legal cases thus rewrote Prince's story to make it more compatible

64. See Wood, *Blind Memory* 152–72, and Merians's discussion of the Hottentot Venus.

with Englishness and less of a threat to English domesticity. Whereas Prince's story had threatened to break the community apart as symbolized by the opening up of the Woods' domestic space to public scrutiny, the laughter evoked at the trial implied a community united around Prince's difference, able to come together around the easy shared laughter at Prince's expense. As I said at the beginning of this chapter, Prince's case offers a particularly interesting study in containment and resistance. The courts trivialized her cause, marked her as "other," and rescued English domesticity from the charges the narrative made against it. But in protecting the core of English ideals, they may have paved the way for gradual change. On the one hand, the law worked to contain Prince's resistance, repackaging it as comic and thus trivializing its impact. Perhaps, as most legal theorists believe, the very function of law is to contain resistance, or in less theoretical language, to provide a space in which conflicts can be "worked out," "reconciled," and "mediated." Certainly, postcolonial legal theory suggests the repressive operations of a juridical culture designed to absorb resistance.[65] On the other hand, such a reading of Prince neglects the equivocal ending to her story and the way that ending reflected all of England's equivocations regarding slavery. For the case was lost not on the evidence but by default: the loss was the result of Pringle's inability to bring witnesses from the West Indies to London. A default decision always suggests the possibility of a different result. What happened after the case was determined is consistent with all of the reversals detailed in Prince's narrative: the Woods went back to Antigua, while Prince was absorbed into London life. Meanwhile, the battle between abolition and the plantocracy ended equivocally as well with the Emancipation Act of 1833. Although the act is often trumpeted as a blow for freedom, it was a weak blow. It freed children under six as of August 1, 1834, but adults and older children were forced, in a system that resonates with Blackstone's waffling, to serve six years of "apprenticeship." Not until 1838 was the apprenticeship requirement dropped (Colley, *Britons* 356). With that Britain turned its energies to forcing other colonizers to meet their own recently adopted standards.

Prince's story, coming directly before abolition and right at the end of the "long" eighteenth century, may suggest a sort of neat closure to this project. But this project ends not neatly but equivocally itself. It stops at a moment of transition from the more localized print spectacle of mid- to late-eighteenth-century culture to the larger "spectacle of intimacy," that nationwide, highly publicized sort of scandal that redefined national life

65. See Boire for a restatement of this theory in the postcolonial context.

during the Victorian era. Prince's story, and others like it buried in the archives of abolitionist journals, formed a vital part of what might be argued to be the first nationwide or even empirewide public relations campaign. In Prince, and more largely in the abolition movement itself, we have thus seen the expansion of the print spectacle, its moment of emergence into modern culture's reliance on "public relations" to guide and mold group behavior. We have also seen how such movements, though they can effect change, maintained English identity categories. Through its complicated coalitions, legal show trials, and indefatigable public canvassing, the abolition movement accomplished Prince's purposes, to "let the English people know the truth . . . and call loud to the great King of England, till all the poor blacks be given free" (94), but in an ambivalent, ambiguous way that not only protected the core of English identity but also unified the community against difference. Yet Prince accomplished no small thing. She brought the disorderly and disordering speech of the people into the center of English juridical life and thus represents a moment in which the "other" speaks in public. While it is difficult to trace Prince's agency, buried as it is in layers of textuality, the machinations of her handlers, and our own suspicions of orality and transcription, that it involved a savvy attack on English domestic intimacy seems crucial to understanding its public impact.

Prince's physical presence in a London court, in the very center of official national culture, destabilizes the image with which I began this book. There, in the mid-1770s, Johnson sat in his bedroom brandishing an oak staff and staking a metaphorical claim for an emergent middle-class construction of English national authorship. Challenging almost every aspect of that identity category, Prince, authorized by the very claims to a unique identity that the English had themselves developed, appears in almost binary opposition to Johnson's version of authorship. An enslaved African rather than a patronage-adverse native, an illiterate rather than a highly educated producer of texts, a worker fully invested in the world of commercial exchange rather than a man whose leisure depended on it, Prince nevertheless spoke. In speaking, she offered a spectacular version of her story to her London observers, a view of the margin in the very act of interrupting the complacent center. Although the laughers in the courtroom may not have realized it, in Prince they had witnessed one possible version of their own postimperial future.

Epilogue

The Ends of National Scandal: Globalization

> Pirates never return home, as the act of piracy
> itself disassociates from territories, nations, essentialized
> identities, master narratives, homogenized places, a
> perpetual motion of moving booty across seas of images.
> PATRICIA R. ZIMMERMAN, *States of Emergency*

While writing this book, I had to struggle with my own loyalty to what copyright cases call "fixation," to the fixed text and its related ideas of closure, containment, and ownership. Tidying up the manuscript has also meant "fixing" the text, tying up its stories and imposing my own desire for closure on their inconsistencies and contingencies. This epilogue offers the opportunity to mess things up again, to destabilize some of the fixed meanings these stories tell. Through releasing rather than containing the central players in this book, through disclosure rather than closure, I want to suggest a different sort of ending, one in which those who operated outside the moral and monied economies of the eighteenth-century print industry—the Irish printers, Macpherson, Macaulay, and Prince—continued to do so long past the artificial endings I imposed on their stories. They acted as pirates, not in the destructive sense in which Richardson used the word, but in the sense that they appropriated mainstream discourses and distribution networks and put them to work in cultural fields far from where they originated.

The Irish printers, for example, were only partially "Englished" in 1800, when the Act of Union subjected them to English copyright law. Richardson's tracts represented an early move in what became a flurry of regulatory activity in the late 1750s. The London booksellers organized, raised funds, and threatened provincial English booksellers involved in the recirculation of Irish and Scottish reprints with organized prosecution under acts meant to control imports. But their plan, to send "riding officers" around the country to police the provincial trade, failed for want of practicality (Feather, *History* 79–80). Given the volume of pirated copies and their complex channels of dissemination, as well as the disruption of the trade effected by the *Donaldson* decision's creation of the public domain, the London center found it impossible to control the fringe. Not until after the Union of England and Ireland in 1800 was the Irish book trade placed under central control.[1] The Union, and with it copyright enforcement that now extended to Ireland, destroyed the Irish book trade, but not the traders themselves. Close to one hundred of them emigrated to the United States, where they were instrumental to setting up a trade in the new nation. During the next ninety years or so, until the passage of the Chace Act in 1891, they transformed the print industry in the United States, mostly by pirating the very English texts that remained under copyright in Great Britain.

Macpherson also upset popular understandings of how moral disapprobation ought to work. If he cowered before Johnson's oak staff, it was not for long. In 1771 he had published *An Introduction to the History of Great Britain and Ireland,* a pro-Celtic tract dismissed by most serious readers. But by 1775 things had changed. To David Hume's chagrin, Macpherson was selected to write the continuation to Hume's *History of England,* eventually selling his copyright in *The History of Great Britain* for £3,000. Hume had clearly not wanted to write the last volume of the *History* himself. But neither had he planned to be succeeded by Macpherson, whose poems he had denounced as a "ludicrous imposition" (quoted in deGategno, *James Macpherson* 107). Painted by Joshua Reynolds as an eighteenth-century gentleman, Macpherson had a successful career as an agent for an Indian prince, became a member of the House of Commons, and died a wealthy and respected Scottish gentleman of large estate.[2] He had successfully negotiated print and political economies, making a fortune from his shape-shifting ability to represent not only Britain but also the Indian interests it wished to dominate.

Macaulay too had an extranational career. Forced out of the center, she

---

1. See Richard Cole's account of the Irish trade at the turn of the century. It failed, Cole says, in part because of the growth of competing reprint industries in Britain and the United States and a prohibitive tax on paper imported into Ireland (the Irish authorities were trying to encourage Irish production of paper). But the Act of Union provided the death blow to the trade (148–55).

2. I rely on Paul deGategno's account of Macpherson's life.

adopted the margins as her own, traveling to France and to America, where she was thought "a Lady of most Extraordinary talent, a Commanding Genius" (quoted in Hill, *Virago* 127). Taken up by George Washington, who showed her around his estate, celebrated by Benjamin Franklin and Thomas Jefferson, she inspired Mercy Otis Warren to write a history of the American Revolution. Back in England, she wrote a proto-feminist tract that both preceded and influenced Wollstonecraft. A pirate in her own right, she took the English ideas of equality and the liberty of the subject and disseminated them throughout the new nation immediately after the American Revolution. At her death, her image was again placed in circulation. William Graham, the young husband who proved to be a loyal, companionate spouse, installed a medallion at Benfield Church to honor her. The image of her wreathed head in profile on the medallion, reminiscent of the frontispieces that decorated the volumes of the *History of England,* represented a return to the respectful treatment she had received during much of her career.

Prince's most transgressive act may have been the simple one of staying in London. But like the other pirates in this story, she put into circulation a resistant version of African identity, one that rejected dominant boundaries and economies, and created its own mini-worlds of alternative economic exchanges, alternative family systems, and alternative work ethics. Her account foreshadows the ways in which the empire would later bite back.[3] By refusing to stay in the colonies and infiltrating the center, challenging its own self-satisfied belief in its importance, she modeled behaviors currently celebrated by postimperial writers such as Rushdie and Naipaul.

These eighteenth-century figures upset English ideas about what authorship should be and how English authorship should represent itself to the world. In their movements, their appropriation of dominant discourses and channels of exchange to their own purposes, and their ability to shift the center, they functioned, if not like historical pirates, at least like the pirates of popular myth. They represent the mobility and fluidity of print, always escaping Britain's strenuous efforts to tie it to the single signifier of nation. Writing in 2002, I find it impossible not to see them as harbingers of globalization, now represented by an endless stream of text flowing through the Internet and by the piratical potential of digitalization. For a number of years I have wanted to relate something I observed in the late 1980s, an event crucial to understanding this project. In the

---

3. In this regard, see particularly Paul Gilroy's discussion of African labor and family life as forms of resistance in *There Ain't No Black in the Union Jack.*

spring of 1985 I hiked into an isolated village in Borneo with my brother, an agent of globalization himself in his role as a Shell Oil Company diver in the South China Sea. Eager to see an "authentic" tribal celebration, we had driven over roads that only barely resisted the encroaching jungle, in the end abandoning our mosquito-infested car for footpaths and swinging reed bridges. The temperature was, as always, about 90 degrees. The village had no electricity, no plumbing, no running water other than a stream. Its inhabitants were drinking rice wine from gourds and eating spiderlike creatures from communal bowls. But our search for an essentialized authenticity failed. Western culture intervened, not in the shape of McDonald's, the usual villain of the piece, but in the sound of Madonna, whose music blared from a battery-operated boom box hooked up to speakers suspended from bamboo posts. How ironic: Madonna, a pirate herself, pirated internationally; Madonna, the ultimate sign of performativity, performing the deconstruction of the very authenticity she had made a career of undermining. I found myself mourning Borneo's lost culture as Johnson had mourned what he could not find in the Hebrides. The infiltration of bootleg cassette tapes into every corner of Asia and Africa had "ruined" the tribe; American popular culture had debased even the heart of Borneo. But this story, like the other stories I have told in this book, offers more than just another model of Western control and domination, of a one-way acculturation. In appropriating Madonna's music (and refusing to pay for it), her Asian audience refused as well my Western effort to reduce them to the experience of the authentic. They refused to perform authenticity for me in the simple, soothing way I had expected, instead insisting on their own complex hybrid identity. By injecting contemporaneity into primitive time, they had played an elaborate joke on a naive Westerner.

By now this image of bootleg tapes, the product of Asian indifference to Western copyright protection, seems almost antique. Today's media pirates rely on digitalization and satellite transmissions and, if interested in Madonna at all, are as likely to "sample" her, incorporating her image and music into a larger compilation, as to copy her. Global culture, of course, suggests the global corporation. As Western culture has shattered into postmodern fragments, the global corporation has swept them up into its ever-enlarging conglomerates. Copyright battles now pitch not author against printer, or even printer against printer, but corporate conglomerate against corporate conglomerate. But while copyright regulation, fraud prosecutions for forgery, and libel suits all continue to attempt to control dissemination, the very complexity and proliferation offered by the Web and digitalization make piracy impossible to control. Meanwhile, in the interstices of corporate-owned technology, new systems of dissemination that bring artist and consumer into immediate contact offer new ways of doing business that cut out or at least reduce corporate influence. This is a world in which musicians can produce and sell a million copies of a compact disc without ever placing an ad or contracting with a music distributor. Consumers too have changed; "mindless" consumption co-exists with the consumer's ability to choose and mix different texts, songs, and images. If anyone with an on-line connection can become an author of sorts, then anyone can become a pirate as well. The globalization of culture effected by the digital revolution suggests the end of national authorship. In its place, one compelling model of authorship will be that of the transnational pirate, resistant to all localized loyalties, but also exerting a profoundly creative, even revolutionary force.

Works Cited

Abrams, Howard B. "Originality and Creativity in Copyright Law." *Law and Contemporary Problems* 55 (1998): 3–44.

"Account of the Life and Writings of Catharine Macaulay Graham." *European Magazine* 4 (1783): 330–34.

Adams, J. R. R. *The Printed Word and the Common Man: Popular Culture in Ulster, 1700–1900.* Belfast: Queen's University, Institute of Irish Studies, 1987.

Addison, Joseph, and Richard Steele. *The Spectator.* Vols. 1–5. Ed. Donald F. Bond. Oxford: Clarendon Press, 1965.

——. *The Tatler.* Vols. 1–3. Ed. Donald F. Bond. Oxford: Clarendon Press, 1987.

Ahmad, Aijaz. *In Theory: Classes, Nations, Literature.* London: Verso, 1992.

The Airs, Duets, Choruses, and Argument, of the New Ballet Pantomime, (Taken from Ossian) Called Oscar and Malvina; or, The Hall of Fingal. As performed at the Theatre-Royal, Covent Garden. 3d ed. London: W. Woodfall for T. Cadell, 1791.

Altman, Janet Gurkin. "Graffigny's Epistemology and the Emergence of Third-World Ideology." In *Writing the Female Voice: Essays on Epistolary Literature,* ed. Elizabeth Goldsmith. Boston: Northeastern University Press, 1989. 172–202.

Amodio, Mark C. "Contemporary Critical Approaches and Studies in Oral Tradition." In *Teaching Oral Traditions,* ed. John Miles Foley. New York: MLA, 1998. 95–105.

Amussen, Susan Dwyer. "The Gendering of Popular Culture in Early Modern England." In *Popular Culture in England, c. 1500–1850,* ed. Tim Harris. New York: St. Martin's Press, 1995. 48–68.

Anderson, Benedict. *Imagined Communities: Reflections on the Origin and Spread of Nationalism.* London: Verso, 1991.

——. Introduction to *Mapping the Nation,* ed. Gopal Balakrishnan. London: Verso, 1990. 1–16.

Anderson, Howard, et al., eds. *The Familiar Letter in the Eighteenth Century.* Lawrence: University of Kansas Press, 1966.

Appleby, John C. "A Nursery of Pirates: The English Pirate Community in Ireland in the Early Seventeenth Century." *International Journal of Maritime History* 2 (1990): 1–27.

Aravamudan, Srinivas. *Tropicopolitans: Colonialism and Agency, 1688–1804.* Durham: Duke University Press, 1999.

Armstrong, Nancy. *Desire and Domestic Fiction: A Political History of the Novel.* New York: Oxford University Press, 1987.

Austen, Jane. "Sir Charles Grandison." Ed. Brian Southam. Oxford: Clarendon Press, 1980.

Backscheider, Paula R., and John Richetti. *Popular Fiction by Women, 1660–1730: An Anthology.* Oxford: Clarendon Press, 1996.

Baer, Joel. "'The Complicated Plot of Piracy': Aspects of English Criminal Law and the Image of the Pirate in Defoe." *Studies in Eighteenth-Century Culture* 14 (1985): 3–28.

Baier, Annette. "Good Men's Women: Hume on Chastity and Trust." *Hume Studies* 5 (1979): 1–19.

———. "Hume: The Reflective Women's Epistemologist?" In *A Mind of One's Own: Feminist Essays on Reason and Objectivity*, ed. Louise M. Antony and Charlotte Witt. Boulder: Westview Press, 1993. 19–38.

———. "Hume, The Women's Moral Theorist?" In *Women and Moral Theory*, ed. Eva Feder Kittay and Diana T. Meyers. Totowa, N.J.: Rowman & Littlefield, 1987. 37–55.

Baines, Paul. *The House of Forgery in Eighteenth-Century Britain.* Aldershot, U.K.: Ashgate, 1999.

Baker, J. H. *The Common Law Tradition: Lawyers, Books, and the Law.* London: Hambledon Press, 2000.

———. *An Introduction to Legal History.* 3d ed. London: Butterworths, 1990.

Balibar, Etienne, and Immanuel Wallerstein. *Race, Nation, Class: Ambiguous Identities.* London: Verso 1991.

Barash, Carol. "The Character of Difference: The Creole Woman as Cultural Mediator in Narratives about Jamaica." *Eighteenth-Century Studies* 23 (1990): 406–24.

Barbauld, Anna. *The Correspondence of Samuel Richardson.* 6 vols. London: n.p., 1804.

Barker, Gerald A. *Grandison's Heirs: The Paragon's Progress in the Late-Eighteenth-Century English Novel.* Newark: University of Delaware Press, 1985.

Barrell, John. *The Birth of Pandora and the Division of Knowledge.* Philadelphia: University of Pennsylvania Press, 1992.

———. *English Literature in History, 1730–80: An Equal, Wide Survey.* New York: St. Martin's Press, 1983.

Barry, Jonathan. "Literacy and Literature in Popular Culture: Reading and Writing in Historical Perspective." In *Popular Culture in England, c. 1500–1850*, ed. Tim Harris. New York: St. Martin's Press, 1995. 69–94.

Bartlett, Thomas. *The Fall and Rise of the Irish Nation: The Catholic Question, 1690–1830.* Savage, Md.: Barnes and Noble Books, 1992.

———. "Protestant Nationalism in Eighteenth-Century Ireland." In *Nations and Nationalisms: France, Britain, Ireland, and the Eighteenth-Century Context*, ed. Michael O'Dea and Kevin Whelan. Oxford: Voltaire Foundation, 1995. 79–88.

Basker, James G. "Scotticisms and the Problem of Cultural Identity in Eighteenth-Century Britain." *Eighteenth-Century Life* 15 (1991): 81–95.

Bate, W. Jackson. *Samuel Johnson.* New York: Harcourt Brace Jovanovich, 1975.

Baucom, Ian. *Out of Place: Englishness, Empire, and the Locations of Identity.* Princeton: Princeton University Press, 1999.

Baumgartner, Barbara Ann. "Reading and Writing Bodily Violence in Nineteenth-Century American Women's Writing." Ph.D. diss., Northwestern University, 1998.

Beckett, J. C. "Literature in English, 1691–1800." In *A New History of Ireland*, vol. 4. Ed. W. E. Vaughn and T. W. Moody. Oxford: Clarendon Press, 1986. 424–70.

Beckwith, Mildred. "Catharine Macaulay: Eighteenth-Century Rebel." Ph.D. diss., Ohio State University, 1953.

Beebee, Thomas. *Clarissa on the Continent: Translation and Seduction.* University Park: Pennsylvania State University Press, 1990.

Bender, John. "A New History of the Enlightenment." In *The Profession of Eighteenth-Century Literature: Reflections on an Institution,* ed. Leo Damrosch. Madison: University of Wisconsin Press, 1992. 62–83.

Bender, Thomas. *The Antislavery Debate: Capitalism and Abolitionism as a Problem in Historical Interpretation.* Berkeley: University of California Press, 1992.

Benjamin, Walter. "The Work of Art in the Age of Mechanical Reproduction." In *Illuminations,* ed. Hannah Arendt. New York: Schocken Books, 1969. 217–51.

Benkler, Yochai. "Free as the Air to Common Use: First Amendment Constraints on Enclosure of the Public Domain." *NYU Law Review* 74 (1999): 354–446.

Berlant, Lauren. *The Anatomy of National Fantasy.* Chicago: University of Chicago Press, 1991.

Bhabha, Homi. "The Commitment to Theory." *New Formations* 5 (1988): 5–23.

——. *The Location of Culture.* London: Routledge, 1994.

——, ed. *Nation and Narration.* London: Routledge, 1990.

Black, Jeremy. *The British and the Grand Tour.* London: Croom Helm, 1985.

——. *The Grand Tour in the Eighteenth Century.* New York: St. Martin's Press, 1992.

Blackburn, Robin. *The Overthrow of Colonial Slavery.* London: Verso, 1988.

Blackstone, William. *The Commentaries on the Laws of England.* Chicago: University of Chicago Press, 1979.

Bogel, Fredric. *The Dream of My Brother: An Essay on Johnson's Authority.* Victoria, B.C.: University of Victoria Press, 1990.

——. "Johnson and the Role of Authority." In *The New Eighteenth Century: Theory, Politics, English Literature,* ed. Felicity Nussbaum and Laura Brown. New York: Methuen, 1987. 189–209.

Boire, Gary. "'Ratione officii': Representing Law in Postcolonial Cultures." *Mosaic* 27 (1994): 199–214.

Boker, Uwe. "The Marketing of Macpherson: The International Book Trade and the First Phase of German Ossian Reception." In *Ossian Revisited,* ed. Howard Gaskill. Edinburgh: Edinburgh University Press, 1991. 73–93.

Boos, Florence, and William Boos. "Catharine Macaulay: Historian and Political Reformer." *International Journal of Women's Studies* 3 (1983): 49–65.

Borthwick, John. *Observations upon the Modes of Prosecuting for Libel According to the Law of England.* London: James Ridgway, 1830.

Boswell, James. *Boswell's Journal of a Tour to the Hebrides with Samuel Johnson, LL.D. 1773.* Ed. Frederick A. Pottle and Charles H. Bennett. New York: McGraw Hill, 1961.

——. *The Decision of the Court of Session, upon the Question of Literary Property in the Cause of Hinton against Donaldson.* Edinburgh, 1774. Reprinted in *The Literary Property Debate: Six Tracts, 1764–1774,* ed. Stephen Parks. New York: Garland, 1975.

——. *Life of Johnson.* Ed. R. W. Chapman. Oxford: Oxford University Press, 1987.

Bourdieu, Pierre. "The Force of Law: Toward a Sociology of the Juridical Field." *Hastings Law Journal* 38 (1987): 805–24.

Boyce, D. George. *Nationalism in Ireland.* London: Routledge, 1991.

Bracks, Lean'tin LaVerne. "History, Language, and Image/Identity in Selected Works of Women of the Diaspora: Mary Prince a West Indian Slave, Toni Morrison, Alice Walker, and Paule Marshall." Ph.D. diss., University of Nebraska, 1996.

Bradshaw, Brendan. "Nationalism and Historical Scholarship in Modern Ireland." *Irish Historical Studies* 26 (1989): 329–51.

Bradshaw, Brendan, Andrew Hadfield, and Willy Maley, eds. *Representing Ireland:*

Literature and the Origins of Conflict, 1534–1660. Cambridge: Cambridge University Press, 1993.

Bradshaw, Brendan, and Peter Roberts, ed. *British Consciousness and Identity: The Making of Britain, 1533–1707.* Cambridge: Cambridge University Press, 1998.

Brant, Clare. "Speaking of Women: Scandal and the Law in the Mid-Eighteenth Century." In *Women, Texts, and History, 1575–1760,* ed. Clare Brant and Diane Purkiss. New York: Routledge, 1992. 242–70.

A Bridal Ode on the Marriage of Catherine and Petruchio. London: J. Bew, 1779.

Brooks, Christopher. "Johnson's Insular Mind and the Analogy of Travel: *A Journey to the Western Islands of Scotland.*" *Essays in Literature* 18 (1991): 21–36.

Brophy, Elizabeth. *Samuel Richardson: The Triumph of Craft.* Knoxville: University of Tennessee Press, 1977.

Brown, Homer Obed. *Institutions of the English Novel: From Defoe to Scott.* Philadelphia: University of Pennsylvania Press, 1976.

——. "Tom Jones: The Bastard of History." *Boundary* 7 (1979): 201–33.

Brown, Laura. "Reading Race and Gender: Jonathan Swift." *Eighteenth-Century Studies* 23 (1990): 425–43.

Burg, B. R. *Sodomy and the Perception of Evil: English Sea Rovers in the Seventeenth-Century Caribbean.* New York: New York University Press, 1983.

Bysveen, Josef. *Epic Tradition and Innovation in James Macpherson's Fingal.* Stockholm: Uppsala, 1982.

"A Candid Examination of the History of Sir Charles Grandison." London: Dodsley, 1754. Reprinted in *Three Criticisms of Richardson's Fiction, 1749–1754.* New York: Garland, 1974.

Carroll, John, ed. *Selected Letters of Samuel Richardson.* Oxford: Clarendon Press, 1964.

Carter-Ruck, P. F. *Libel and Slander.* London: Faber and Faber, 1972.

The Cases of the Appellants and Respondents in the Cause of Literary Property, Before the House of Lords. London, 1774. Reprinted in *The Literary Property Debate: Six Tracts, 1764–1774,* ed. Stephen Parks. New York: Garland, 1975.

Casey, Lee A. "Pirate Constitutionalism: An Essay in Self-Government." *Journal of Law and Politics* 8 (1992): 447–537.

Castle, Terry. *Masquerade and Civilization.* Stanford: Stanford University Press, 1986.

Chaber, Lois. "*Sir Charles Grandison* and the Human Prospect." In *New Essays on Samuel Richardson,* ed. Albert J. Rivero. New York: St. Martin's Press, 1996. 193–208.

Chaney, Edward. *The Evolution of the Grand Tour: Anglo-Italian Cultural Relations since the Renaissance.* London: Frank Cass, 1998.

Chase, Karen, and Michael Levenson. *The Spectacle of Intimacy: A Public Life for the Victorian Family.* Princeton: Princeton University Press, 2000.

Chatten, Elizabeth N. *Samuel Foote.* Boston: Twayne, 1980.

Christensen, Jerome. *Practicing Enlightenment: Hume and the Formation of a Literary Career,* Madison: University of Wisconsin Press, 1987.

Chung, Ewha. *Samuel Richardson's New Nation: Paragons of the Domestic Sphere and "Native" Virtue.* New York: Peter Lang, 1998.

Clark, J. C. D. *The Language of Liberty, 1660–1832.* Cambridge: Cambridge University Press, 1994.

Cole, Richard Cargill. *Irish Booksellers and English Writers, 1740–1800,* London: Mansell Publishing, 1986.

Colley, Linda. *Britons Forging the Nation, 1707–1837.* New Haven: Yale University Press, 1992.

——. "Radical Patriotism in Eighteenth-Century England." In *Patriotism: The Making and Unmaking of British National Identity,* ed. Raphael Samuel. Vol. 1: *History and Politics.* London: Routledge, 1989. 169–87.

Collins, A. S. *Authorship in the Days of Johnson.* 1927. Clifton, N.J.: Augustus M. Kelley, 1973.

Connolly, S. J. "Eighteenth-Century Ireland: Colony or *Ancien Regime*?" In *The Making of Modern Irish History: Revisionism and the Revisionist Controversy,* ed. D. George Boyce and Alan O'Day. London: Routledge, 1996. 15–33.

Cook, Elizabeth Heckendorn. *Epistolary Bodies: Gender and Genre in the Eighteenth-Century Republic of Letters.* Stanford: Stanford University Press, 1996.

Corbett, Mary Jean. "Another Tale to Tell: Postcolonial Theory and the Case of *Castle Rackrent.*" *Criticism* 36 (1994): 383–400.

Cowper, William. *The Poems of William Cowper.* Ed. John D. Baird and Charles Ryskamp. Vol. 1. Oxford: Clarendon Press, 1980.

Cressy, David. *Literacy and the Social Order: Reading and Writing in Tudor and Stuart England.* Cambridge: Cambridge University Press, 1980.

"Critical Remarks on Sir Charles Grandison, Clarissa, and Pamela." London: J. Dowse, 1754. Reprinted in *Three Criticisms of Richardson's Fiction, 1749–1754.* New York: Garland, 1974.

Critical Review 55 (1783): 212–16.

Cullen, L. M. "Economic Development, 1691–1750." In *A New History of Ireland.* Vol. 4. Ed. T. W. Moody and W. E. Vaughan. Oxford: Clarendon Press, 1986. 151–58.

Curley, Thomas. "Johnson's Last Word on Ossian: Ghostwriting for William Shaw." In *Aberdeen and the Enlightenment,* ed. Jennifer J. Carter and Joan H. Pittock. Aberdeen: Aberdeen University Press, 1987. 375–433.

Dabydeen, David. "Eighteenth-Century English Literature on Commerce and Slavery." In *The Black Presence in English Literature,* ed. David Dabydeen. Manchester: Manchester University Press, 1985. 26–49.

Davidson, Caroline. *A Woman's Work Is Never Done: A History of Housework in the British Isles, 1650–1950.* London: Chatto and Windus, 1982.

Davis, Leith. *Acts of Union: Scotland and the Literary Negotiation of the British Nation, 1707–1830.* Stanford: Stanford University Press, 1998.

Davis, Natalie Zemon. "Gender and Genre: Women as Historical Writers, 1400–1820." In *Beyond Their Sex: Learned Women of the European Past,* ed. Patricia H. Labalme. New York: New York University Press, 1980. 153–82.

——. "History's Two Bodies." *American Historical Review* 93 (1988): 1–30.

Deane, Seamus. "Imperialism/Nationalism." In *Critical Terms for Literary Study.* 2d ed. Ed. Frank Lentricchia and Thomas McLaughlin. Chicago: University of Chicago Press, 1995. 354–68.

Defoe, Daniel. *A General History of the Pirates.* Ed. Manuel Schonhorn. Columbia: University of South Carolina Press, 1972.

deGategno, Paul. *James Macpherson.* Boston: G. K. Hall, 1989.

——. "'The Source of Daily and Exalted Pleasure': Jefferson Reads the Poems of Ossian." In *Ossian Revisited,* ed. Howard Gaskill. Edinburgh: Edinburgh University Press, 1991. 94–108.

Deutsch, Karl W. *Nationalism and Social Communication: An Inquiry into the Foundations of Nationality.* 2d ed. Cambridge: MIT Press, 1996.

Dickinson, H. T. *Caricatures and the Constitution, 1760–1832.* Cambridge: Chadwyck-Healey, 1986.

Dimock, Wai Chee. "Criminal Law, Female Virtue, and the Rise of Liberalism." *Yale Journal of Law and Humanities* 41 (1992): 209–48.

Works Cited

Ditchfield, G. M. "Some Literary and Political Views of Catherine Macaulay." *American Notes and Queries* 12 (1974): 70–76.

Dolan, John C. "James Macpherson and Hugh Blair: The Expropriation and Foreign Transfer of Third-World Literary Property." Paper presented at Conference on Intellectual Property and the Construction of Authorship, April 18–21, 1991, Case Western Reserve University.

Donald, Diana. *The Age of Caricature: Satirical Prints in the Reign of George III.* New Haven: Yale University Press, 1996.

Donaldson v. Becket. 98 Eng. Rep. 257, 1776.

Donnelly, Lucy Martin. "The Celebrated Mrs. Macaulay." *William and Mary Quarterly,* 3d ser., 6 (1949): 172–207.

Doody, Margaret Anne. *A Natural Passion: A Study of the Novels of Samuel Richardson.* Oxford: Clarendon Press, 1974.

——. "Richardson's Politics." *Eighteenth-Century Fiction* 2 (1990). 113–26.

——. *The True Story of the Novel.* New Brunswick: Rutgers University Press, 1997.

Dorn, Judith. "Reading Women Reading History: The Philosophy of Periodical Form in Charlotte Lennox's *The Lady's Museum.*" *Historical Reflections/Réflexions Historiques* 18 (1992): 7–27.

Doyle, John Robert, Jr. *Thomas Pringle.* New York: Twayne Publishers, 1972.

Drescher, Seymour. *Capitalism and Antislavery: British Mobilization in Comparative Perspective.* New York: Oxford University Press, 1987.

——. "Public Opinion and the Destruction of British Colonial Slavery." In *Slavery and British Society, 1776–1846.* Ed. James Walvin. Baton Rouge: Louisiana State University Press, 1982. 22–48.

——. "Whose Abolition? Popular Pressure and the Ending of the British Slave Trade" *Past and Present* 143 (1994). 136–66.

Dresser, Madge. "Britannia." In *Patriotism: The Making and Unmaking of British National Identity.* Vol. 3. Ed. Raphael Samuel. London: Routledge, 1989. 26–49.

Duncan, Douglas. "Scholarship and Politeness in the Early Eighteenth Century." In *The History of Scottish Literature.* Vol. 2. Ed. Andrew Hook. Aberdeen: Aberdeen University Press, 1987. 51–64.

Dussinger, John A. "Masters and Servants: Political Discourse in Richardson's *A Collection of Moral Sentiments.*" *Eighteenth-Century Fiction* 5 (1993): 239–52.

Eagleton, Terry. *The Rape of Clarissa.* Minneapolis: University of Minnesota Press, 1982.

Earle, Edward. "The Effect of Romanticism on the Nineteenth-Century Development of Copyright Law." *Intellectual Property Journal* 6 (September 1991): 269–90.

Eaves, T. C. Duncan, and Ben D. Kimpel. *Samuel Richardson: A Biography.* Oxford: Clarendon Press, 1971.

Edwards, Viv, and Thomas J. Sienkewicz, eds. *Oral Cultures Past and Present.* Oxford: Basil Blackwell, 1991.

Eley, Geoff, and Ronald Grigor Suny, eds. *Becoming National: A Reader.* New York: Oxford University Press, 1996.

Equiano, Olaudah. *The Interesting Narrative of the Life of Olaudah Equiano.* Ed. Werner Sollors. New York: Norton, 2001.

Evans, Eric. "Englishness and Britishness: National Identities, c. 1790–c. 1870." In *Uniting the Kingdom? The Making of British History.* Ed. Alexander Grant and Keith J. Stringer. London: Routledge, 1995. 223–43.

Favret, Mary A. *Romantic Correspondence: Women, Politics, and the Fiction of Letters.* Cambridge: Cambridge University Press, 1993.

Feather, Jane. *The Least Likely Bride.* New York: Random House, 2000.

Feather, John. *A History of British Publishing*. London: Croom Helm, 1988.

——. *Publishing, Piracy, and Politics: An Historical Study of Copyright in Britain*. London: Mansell Publishing, 1994.

The Female Patriot, An Epistle from C——t——e M——c——y to the Reverend Dr. W——l——n ON *her late Marriage*. London: J. Bew, 1779.

Ferguson, Moira. *Colonialism and Gender Relations from Mary Wollstonecraft to Jamaica Kincaid*. New York: Columbia University Press, 1993.

——. *Subject to Others: British Women Writers and Colonial Slavery, 1670–1834*. New York: Routledge, 1992.

——, ed. *The History of Mary Prince*. Ann Arbor: University of Michigan Press, 1997.

Ferguson, William. *Scotland 1689 to the Present*. New York: Frederick A. Praeger, 1968.

Finlay, Richard. "Keeping the Covenant: Scottish National Identity." In *Eighteenth-Century Scotland: New Perspectives*, ed. T. M. Devine and J. R. Young. East Lothian, Scotland: Tuckwell Press, 1999. 122–33.

Flynn, Carol. *Samuel Richardson: A Man of Letters*. Princeton: Princeton University Press, 1982.

Folkenflik, Robert. "Macpherson, Chatterton, Blake, and the Great Age of Literary Forgery." *Centennial Review* 18 (1974): 378–91.

Foote, Samuel. *The Devil on Two Sticks: A Comedy in Three Acts*. London: Sherlock for T. Cadell, 1778.

Foss, Edward. *Judges of England with Sketches of Their Lives*. Vol. 7. London: John Murray, 1864. Reprint, New York: AMS Press, 1966.

Foucault, Michel. "What Is an Author?" In *The Foucault Reader*, ed. Paul Rabinow. New York: Pantheon Books, 1984. 101–20.

Fowler, Alastair. "Calling a Spade a Spade: A to Z via PC." *TLS*, February 16, 2001. 4–6.

Fox, Claire Gilbride. "Catharine Macaulay, An Eighteenth-Century Clio." *Winterthur Portfolio* 4 (1968): 129–42.

French Painting, 1774–1830: The Age of Revolution. Detroit: Wayne State University Press, 1975.

Frow, John. "Public Domain and Collective Rights in Culture." *Intellectual Property Journal* 13 (1998): 39–52.

Fryer, Peter. *Staying Power: The History of Black People in Britain*. London: Pluto Press, 1984.

Fysh, Stephanie. *The Work(s) of Samuel Richardson*. Newark: University of Delaware Press, 1997.

Gaines, Jane. *Contested Culture: The Image, the Voice, and the Law*. Chapel Hill: University of North Carolina Press, 1991.

Galinsky, Karl. *The Herakles Theme: The Adaptations of the Hero in Literature from Homer to the Twentieth Century*. Totowa, N.J.: Rowman and Littlefield, 1972.

Garber, Marjorie. *Vested Interests: Cross-Dressing and Cultural Anxiety*. New York: Routledge, 1997.

Gaskill, Howard. "Ossian in Europe." *Canadian Review of Comparative Literature* 21 (1994): 643–75.

——. "'Ossian' Macpherson: Towards a Rehabilitation." *Comparative Criticism* 8 (1986): 113–48.

——, ed. *Ossian Revisited*. Edinburgh: Edinburgh University Press, 1991.

Gates, Henry Louis, Jr. *Figures in Black: Words, Signs, and the "Racial" Self*. Oxford: Oxford University Press, 1987.

Geiger, Marianne. "Mercy Otis Warren and Catharine Sawbridge Macaulay: Historians in the Transatlantic Republican Tradition." Ph.D. diss., New York University, 1986.

Gellner, Ernest. *Nations and Nationalism since 1780*. Cambridge: Cambridge University Press, 1990.

Gikandi, Simon. *Maps of Englishness: Writing Identity in the Culture of Colonialism*. New York: Columbia University Press, 1996.

Gilbert, Helen. "De-scribing Orality: Performance and the Recuperation of Voice." In *De-scribing Empire: Post-colonialism and Textuality*, ed. Chris Tiffin and Alan Lawson. London: Routledge, 1994. 98–111.

Gilroy, Paul. *The Black Atlantic: Modernity and Double Consciousness*. Cambridge: Harvard University Press, 1993.

——. *"There Ain't No Black in the Union Jack"*: *The Cultural Politics of Race and Nation*. Chicago: University of Chicago Press, 1987, 1991.

Godard, Barbara. "Intertextuality." In *Encyclopedia of Contemporary Literary Theory: Approaches, Scholars, Terms*, ed. Irena R. Makaryk. Toronto: University of Toronto Press, 1995. 568–72.

Goldsmith, Elizabeth, ed. *Writing the Female Voice: Essays on Epistolary Literature*. Boston: Northeastern University Press, 1989.

Goodrich, Peter. *Law in the Courts of Love: Literature and Other Minor Jurisprudences*. London: Routledge, 1996.

——. *Oedipus Lex: Psychoanalysis, History, Law*. Berkeley: University of California Press, 1995.

——. "Poor Illiterate Reason: History, Nationalism, and Common Law." *Social and Legal Studies* 1 (1992): 7–28.

Goody, Jack. "Alternative Paths to Knowledge in Oral and Literate Cultures." In *Spoken and Written Language: Exploring Orality and Literacy*, ed. Deborah Tannen. Norwood, N.J.: Ablex Publishing, 1982. 201–15.

Gowing, Laura. *Domestic Dangers: Women, Words, and Sex in Early Modern London*. Oxford: Clarendon Press, 1998.

Grafton, Anthony. *The Footnote: A Curious History*. Cambridge: Harvard University Press, 1997.

——. *Forgers and Critics: Creativity and Duplicity in Western Scholarship*. Princeton: Princeton University Press, 1990.

Graham, Patrick. *Essay on the Authenticity of the Poems of Ossian*. Edinburgh: James Ballantyne, 1805.

Gray's Inn Journal, October 13, 1753.

Greaves, Tom, ed. *Intellectual Property Rights for Indigenous Peoples: A Sourcebook*. Oklahoma City: Society for Applied Anthropology, 1994.

Green, Thomas A. "The Jury, Seditious Libel, and the Criminal Law." In *Juries, Libel, and Justice: The Role of English Juries in Seventeenth- and Eighteenth-Century Trials for Libel and Slander*. Los Angeles: William Andrews Clark Memorial Library, 1984. 38–91.

Greene, Donald J. "Johnson and the Great War for Empire." In *English Writers of the Eighteenth Century*, ed. John H. Middendorf. New York: Columbia University Press, 1971. 37–65.

Griffin, Robert A. "Anonymity and Authorship." *New Literary History* 30, 4 (autumn 1999): 877–95.

Griffiths, Gareth. "The Myth of Authenticity." In *De-scribing Empire*, ed. Chris Tiffin and Alan Lawson. London: Routledge, 1994. 70–85.

Grigor, Iain Fraser. *Highland Resistance: the Radical Tradition in the Scottish North*. Edinburgh: Mainstream Publishing, 2000.

Groom, Nick. "Celts, Goths, and the Nature of the Literary Source." In *Tradition in Transition: Women Writers, Marginal Texts, and the Eighteenth-Century Canon,* ed. Alvaro Ribeiro, S. J., and James G. Basker. Oxford: Clarendon Press, 1996. 275–96.

Guest, Harriet. *Small Change: Women, Learning, Patriotism, 1750–1810.* Chicago: University of Chicago Press, 2000.

Gunderloch, Anja. "Eighteenth-Century Fraud and Oral Tradition." In *Orality, Literacy, and Modern Media,* ed. Dietrich Scheunemann. Columbia, S.C.: Camden House, 1966. 44–63.

Gutwirth, Madelyn. *The Twilight of the Goddesses: Women and Representation in the French Revolutionary Era.* New Brunswick: Rutgers University Press, 1992.

Gwilliam, Tassie. *Samuel Richardson's Fictions of Gender.* Stanford: Stanford University Press, 1993.

Hadas, Moses, ed. *Heliodorus: An Ethiopian Romance.* Philadelphia: University of Pennsylvania Press, 1999.

Hadfield, Andrew, and Willy Maley. "Introduction: Irish Representations and English Alternatives." In *Representing Ireland: Literature and the Origins of Conflict, 1534–1660,* ed. Brendan Bradshaw et al. London: Cambridge University Press, 1993. 1–23.

Hall, Kim. "Culinary Spaces, Colonial Spaces: The Gendering of Sugar in the Seventeenth Century." In *Feminist Readings of Early Modern Culture,* ed. Valerie Traub et al. Cambridge: Cambridge University Press, 1996. 168–90.

Hall, Rodney Bruce. *National Collective Identity: Social Constructs and International Systems.* New York: Columbia University Press, 1998.

Hamburger, Philip. "The Development of the Law of Seditious Libel and the Control of the Press." *Stanford Law Review* 37 (1985): 661–765.

Harding, Alan. *A Social History of English Law.* Gloucester, Mass.: Peter Smith, 1973.

Hardinge, George. *Rowley and Chatterton in the Shades.* London: T. Becket, 1788.

Hardt, Michael, and Antonio Negri. *Empire.* Cambridge: Harvard University Press, 2000.

Hargrave, Francis. *An Argument in Defence of Literary Property.* 2d ed. London: n.p., 1774. Reprint, *An Argument in Defence of Literary Property, 1774, Francis Hargrave; Four Tracts on Freedom of the Press, 1790–1821.* Ed. Stephen Parks. New York: Garland, 1974.

Harris, Jocelyn. "The Reviser Observed: The Last Volume of *Sir Charles Grandison.*" *Studies in Bibliography* 29 (1976): 1–31.

——. *Samuel Richardson.* Cambridge: Cambridge University Press, 1987.

Harris, Michael. "Paper Pirates: The Alternative Book Trade in Mid-Eighteenth-Century London." In *Fakes and Frauds: Varieties of Deception in Print and Manuscript,* ed. Robin Myers and Michael Harris. Winchester, Del.: Oak Knoll Press, 1996. 47–69.

Harris, Tim, ed. *Popular Culture in England, 1500–1850.* New York: St. Martin's Press, 1995.

Hart, Kevin. "Economic Acts: Johnson in Scotland. *Eighteenth-Century Life* 16 (1992): 94–110.

——. *Samuel Johnson and the Culture of Property.* Cambridge: Cambridge University Press, 1999.

Harvie, Christopher. "Anglo-Saxons into Celts: The Scottish Intellectuals, 1760–1930." In *Celticism,* ed. Terence Brown. Amsterdam: Rodopi, 1996. 231–56.

——. *Scotland and Nationalism.* London: George Allen & Unwin, 1977.

Hawkins, John. *The Life of Samuel Johnson.* London: n.p., 1789.

Hay, Carla H. "Catharine Macaulay and the American Revolution." *The Historian 56* (1994): 301–16.

Haydon, Colin. *Anti-Catholicism in Eighteenth-Century England, c. 1714–80.* Manchester: Manchester University Press, 1993.

Haynes, Rosetta R. "Voice, Body, and Collaboration: Constructions of Authority in *The History of Mary Prince.*" *The Literary Griot* 11 (1999): 18–32.

Hechter, Michael. *Internal Colonialism: The Celtic Fringe in British National Development, 1536–1966.* Berkeley: University of California Press, 1975.

Helgerson, Richard. *Forms of Nationhood: The Elizabethan Writing of England.* Chicago: University of Chicago Press, 1992.

Helmholz, R. H., and Thomas A. Green. *Juries, Libel, and Justice: The Role of English Juries in Seventeenth- and Eighteenth-Century Trials for Libel and Slander.* Los Angeles: William Andrews Clark Memorial Library, 1984.

Hercules and Omphale: A Grand Pantomimic Spectacle in Two Parts. Composed by Mr. Byrn. London: Macleish, 1794.

Hertz, Neil. "Medusa's Head: Male Hysteria under Political Pressure." *Representations* 4 (1983): 27–54.

Hesse, Carla. "Enlightenment Epistemology and the Laws of Authorship in Revolutionary France, 1777–1793." *Representations* 30 (1990): 109–37.

Heward, Edmund. *Lord Mansfield.* Chichester B. Rose, 1979.

Hickey, Alison. "'Extensive Views' in Johnson's *Journey to the Western Islands of Scotland.*" *Studies in English Literature, 1500–1900* 32 (1992): 537–54.

Hicks, Philip. *Neoclassical History and English Culture: From Clarendon to Hume.* New York: St. Martin's Press, 1996.

Higgins, Patricia. "The Reactions of Women with Special Reference to Women Petitioners." In *Politics, Religion, and the English Civil War,* ed. Brian Manning. New York: St. Martin's Press, 1973. 177–222.

Hill, Bridget. "The Links between Mary Wollstonecraft and Catharine Macaulay: New Evidence." *Women's History Review* 4 (1995): 177–92.

——. *The Republican Virago: The Life and Times of Catharine Macaulay, Historian.* Oxford: Clarendon Press, 1992.

Hill, Christopher. "Radical Pirates." In *The Collected Essays of Christopher Hill.* Vol. 3. Amherst: University of Massachusetts Press, 1984. 161–87.

Hobsbawm, Eric, and Terence Ranger, eds. *The Invention of Tradition.* Cambridge: Cambridge University Press, 1983.

Holliday, John. *The Life of William, Late Earl of Mansfield.* London: Printed for P. Elmsly, 1797.

Holmes, Geoffrey. *The Trial of Doctor Sacheverell.* London: Eyre Methuen, 1973.

Holt, Francis. *The law of libel: which is contained, a general history of this law in the ancient codes, and of its introduction, and successive alterations, in the law of England.* London: Printed for W. Reed, 1812. Reprint, New York: Garland Publishing, 1978.

Home, Stewart, ed. *Plagiarism: Art as Commodity and Strategies for Its Negation.* London: Aporia, 1987.

Houston, R. A. *Scottish Literacy and the Scottish Identity.* Cambridge: Cambridge University Press, 1985.

Howell, T. B. *A Complete Collection of State Trials.* Vol. 15. London: T. C. Hansard, 1812.

Hudson, Nicholas. "'Oral Tradition': The Evolution of an Eighteenth-Century Concept." In *Tradition in Transition: Women Writers, Marginal Texts, and the Eighteenth-Century Canon,* ed. Alvaro Ribeiro, S. J., and James G. Basker. Oxford: Clarendon Press, 1996. 160–76.

Hume, David. *Essays Moral, Political, and Literary.* Rev. ed. Ed. Eugene F. Miller. Indianapolis: Liberty Classics, 1987.

——. *The History of England.* 6 vols. Indianapolis: Liberty Classics, 1985.

——. *The Letters of David Hume.* Ed. J. Y. T. Grieg. Vol. 1. Oxford: Clarendon Press, 1932.

——. *A Treatise of Human Nature.* Ed. L. A. Selby-Bigge. 2d ed. Rev. P. H. Nidditch. Oxford: Clarendon Press, 1978.

Hunt, Margaret. *The Middling Sort: Commerce, Gender, and the Family in England, 1680–1780.* Berkeley: University of California Press, 1996.

——. "Racism, Imperialism, and the Traveler's Gaze in Eighteenth-Century England." *Journal of British Studies* 32 (1993): 333–57.

Hutchinson, John. *The Dynamics of Cultural Nationalism: The Gaelic Revival and the Creation of the Irish Nation State.* London: Allen and Unwin, 1987.

Hutchinson, John, and Anthony D. Smith, eds. *Nationalism.* Oxford: Oxford University Press, 1994.

Ingamells, John. "Discovering Italy: British Travelers in the Eighteenth-Century." In *Grand Tour: The Lure of Italy in the Eighteenth Century,* ed. Andrew Wilton and Ilaria Bignamini. London: Tate Gallery Publishing, 1996. 21–30.

Irigaray, Luce. *This Sex Which Is Not One.* Trans. Catherine Porter. Ithaca: Cornell University Press, 1985.

Ishay, Micheline R., ed. *The National Reader.* Atlantic Highlands, N.J.: Humanities Press International, 1995.

Jameson, Fredric. "Third-World Literature in the Era of Multinational Capitalism." *Social Text* 15 (1986): 65–88.

Jaszi, Peter. "Toward a Theory of Copyright: The Metamorphoses of 'Authorship.'" *Duke Law Journal* (1991): 455–502.

Jodrell, Paul. *A Widow and No Widow.* London: n.p., 1780.

Johns, Adrian. *The Nature of the Book.* Chicago: University of Chicago Press, 1998.

Johnson, Claudia. *Equivocal Beings: Politics, Gender, and Sentimentality in the 1790s.* Chicago: University of Chicago Press, 1995.

Johnson, Samuel. *The History of Rasselas, Prince of Abyssinia.* In *Samuel Johnson: Selected Poetry and Prose,* ed. Frank Brady and W. K. Wimsatt. Berkeley: University of California Press, 1977. 73–153.

——. *A Journey to the Western Islands of Scotland.* Ed. Mary Lascelles. New Haven: Yale University Press, 1971.

——. *Letters of Samuel Johnson.* Vol. 2. Ed. Bruce Redford. Princeton, N.J.: Princeton University Press, 1992–1994.

——. Preface to *A Dictionary of the English Language.* In *Selected Poetry and Prose: Samuel Johnson,* ed. Frank Brady and W. K. Wimsatt. Berkeley: University of California Press, 1977. 277–98.

——. Preface to *The Plays of William Shakespeare.* In *Selected Poetry and Prose: Samuel Johnson,* ed. Frank Brady and W. K. Wimsatt. Berkeley: University of California Press, 1977. 299–336.

Kampen, Natalie Boymel. "Omphale and the Instability of Gender." In *Sexuality in Ancient Art: Near East, Egypt, Greece, and Italy,* ed. Natalie Boymel Kampen. Cambridge: Cambridge University Press, 1996. 233–46.

Kaplan, Louise J. *The Family Romance of the Imposter-Poet Thomas Chatterton.* New York: Atheneum, 1988.

Kaplan, M. Lindsay. *The Culture of Slander in Early Modern England.* Cambridge: Cambridge University Press, 1997.

Works Cited

Kauffman, Linda S. *Discourses of Desire: Gender, Genre, and Epistolary Fictions.* Ithaca: Cornell University Press, 1986.

Kelly, James. "The Abduction of Women of Fortune in Eighteenth-Century Ireland." *Eighteenth-Century Ireland* 9 (1994): 7–43.

Kenyon, John. *The History Men: The Historical Profession in England since the Renaissance.* London: Weidenfeld and Nicolson, 1993.

Kernan, Alvin. *Samuel Johnson and the Impact of Print.* Princeton: Princeton University Press, 1989.

Kewes, Paulina. *Authorship and Appropriation: Writing for the Stage in England, 1660–1710.* Oxford: Clarendon Press, 1998.

Knights, Mark. "London's 'Monster' Petition of 1680." *Historical Journal* 36 (1993): 39–67.

——. "Petitioning and the Political Theorists." *Past and Present* 138 (1993): 94–111.

Kristeva, Julia. *Strangers to Ourselves.* Trans. Leon S. Roudiez. New York: Columbia University Press, 1991.

Kucich, Greg. "'The Horrid Theatre of Human Sufferings': Gendering the Stages of History in Catharine Macaulay and Percy Bysshe Shelley." In *Lessons of Romanticism: A Critical Companion* ed. Thomas Pfau and Robert F. Gleckner. Durham: Duke University Press, 1998. 448–65.

Lacan, Jacques. *Ecrits.* New York: Norton, 1976.

Laing, Malcolm, ed. *The Poems of Ossian.* Edinburgh: Archibald Constable, 1805.

Landon, Michael de L. *Erin and Britannia: The Historical Background to a Modern Tragedy.* Chicago: Nelson-Hall, 1981.

Lange, David. "Recognizing the Public Domain." *Law and Contemporary Problems* 44 (1981): 147–78.

Laqueur, Thomas. "Bodies, Details, and the Humanitarian Narrative." In *The New Cultural History,* ed. Lynn Hunt. Berkeley: University of California Press, 1989. 176–204.

Laughlin, Corinna. "The Lawless Language of Macpherson's *Ossian.*" *Studies in English Literature, 1500–1900* 40, 3 (2000): 511–37.

Leerssen, Joep. *Mere Irish and Fíor-Ghael.* Notre Dame: University of Notre Dame Press, 1997.

——. "Ossianic Liminality: Between Native Tradition and Preromantic Taste." In *From Gaelic to Romantic Ossianic Translation.* ed. Fiona Stafford and Howard Gaskill. Amsterdam: Rodopi, 1998. 1–16.

Leighton, C. D. A. *Catholicism in a Protestant Kingdom: A Study of the Irish Ancien Regime.* New York: St. Martin's Press, 1994.

Leneman, Leah. "The Effects of Ossian in Lowland Scotland." In *Aberdeen and the Enlightenment,* ed. Jennifer Carter and Joan H. Pittock. Aberdeen: Aberdeen University Press, 1987. 257–362.

Lerer, Seth. "'Representyed now in yower syght': The Culture of Spectatorship in Late-Fifteenth-Century England." In *Bodies and Disciplines.* Vol. 9. Ed. Barbara A. Hanawalt and David Wallace. Minneapolis: University of Minnesota Press, 1996. 29–62.

Levine, Joseph M. *The Battle of the Books: History and Literature in the Augustan Age.* Ithaca: Cornell University Press, 1991.

——. *Humanism and History: Origins of Modern English Historiography.* Ithaca: Cornell University Press, 1987.

Levinson, Brett. "The Limits of Postcolonial Theory after Said/Bhabha, or: Is Latin America a Postcolonial Site." *Journal for the Psychoanalysis of Culture and Society* 1 (1996): 145–58.

Lindey, Alexander. *Plagiarism and Originality*. New York: Harper, 1952.

Lipking, Lawrence. "Samuel Johnson and the Canon." In *Interpretation and Cultural History*, ed. Joan Pittock. New York: St. Martin's Press, 1991. 153–74.

Litman, Jessica. "The Public Domain." *Emory Law Journal* 39 (1990): 965–1023.

Looser, Devoney. *British Women Writers and the Writing of History, 1670–1820*. Baltimore: Johns Hopkins University Press, 2000.

Lury, Celia. *Cultural Rights: Technology, Legality, and Personality*. London: Routledge, 1993.

Lynch, Deidre. "Beating the Track of the Alphabet: Samuel Johnson, Tourism, and the ABCs of Modern Authority." *ELH*. 57 (1990): 357–405.

——. *The Economy of Character: Novels, Market Culture, and the Business of Inner Meaning*. Chicago: University of Chicago Press, 1998.

Macaulay, Catharine. *The History of England from the Accession of James I to That of the Brunswick Line*. 8 vols. London: n.p., 1763–83.

——. *The History of England from the Revolution to the Present Time in a Series of Letters to a Friend*. Bath: n.p., 1778.

——. *Letters on Education with Observations on Religious and Metaphysical Subjects*. 1790. New York: Garland Publishing, 1974.

——. *A Modest Plea for the Property of Copyright*. Bath: n.p., 1774.

——. *Observations on the Reflections of the Right Hon. Edmund Burke on the Revolution in France, in a Letter to the Right Hon. The Earl of Stanhope*. Boston: Thomas & Andrews, 1791.

Mack, Maynard. *Alexander Pope: A Life*. New York: Norton, 1985.

Mackenzie, Henry, ed. *Report of the Committee of the Highland Society of Scotland*. Edinburgh: Edinburgh University Press, 1805.

Mackie, Erin. *Market à la Mode: Fashion, Commodity, and Gender in The Tatler and The Spectator*. Baltimore: Johns Hopkins University Press, 1997.

Macpherson, James. *Fragments of Ancient Poetry*. 1760. Los Angeles: University of California Press, 1966.

——. *The Poems of Ossian, Containing the Poetical Works of James Macpherson, Esq. in Prose and Rhyme: With Notes and Illustrations*. Ed. Malcolm Laing. 2 vols. 1805. New York: AMS Press, 1974.

——. *The Poems of Ossian and Related Works*. Ed. Howard Gaskill. Edinburgh: Edinburgh University Press, 1996.

Macqueen, James. "The Colonial Empire of Great Britain." *Blackwood's Edinburgh Magazine* 30 (1831): 705–64.

Malcolmson, Patricia E. *English Laundresses: A Social History, 1850–1930*. Urbana: University of Illinois Press, 1986.

Marks, Sylvia Kasey. *Sir Charles Grandison: The Compleat Conduct Book*. Lewisburg: Bucknell University Press, 1986.

Matteo, Sante. "Ossian and *Risorgimento*: The Poetics of Nationalism." In *Romanticism across the Disciplines*, ed. Larry H. Peer. Lanham, N.Y.: University Press of America, 1998. 27–40.

Mayer, Robert. *History and the Early English Novel*. Cambridge: Cambridge University Press, 1997.

Mazzucco-Than, Cecile. "'As Easy as a Chimney Pot to Blacken': Catharine Macaulay 'the Celebrated Female Historian.'" *Prose Studies* 18 (1995): 78–104.

McAdam, E. L. *Dr. Johnson and the English Law*. Syracuse: University of Syracuse Press, 1951.

McClintock, Anne. "Family Feuds: Gender, Nationalism, and the Family." Special issue, "Nationalism and National Identities." *Feminist Review* 44 (1993): 61–80.

——. *Imperial Leather.* New York: Routledge, 1997.

——. "'The Very House of Difference': Race, Gender, and the Politics of South African Women's Narrative in *Poppie Nongena.*" In *The Bounds of Race: Perspectives on Hegemony and Resistance,* ed. Dominick LaCapra. Ithaca: Cornell University Press, 1991. 196–230.

McDowell, Paula. "Consuming Women: The Life of the 'Literary Lady' as Popular Culture in Eighteenth-Century England." *Genre* 26 (1993): 219–52.

McFarlane, Cameron. *The Sodomite in Fiction and Satire, 1660–1750.* New York: Columbia University Press, 1997.

McGowan, Ian. "Boswell's *Journal of a Tour to the Hebrides.*" In *Tradition in Transition: Women Writers, Marginal Texts, and the Eighteenth-Century Canon,* ed. Alvaro Ribeiro, S. J., and James G. Basker. Oxford: Clarendon Press, 1996. 127–43.

McKenzie, Henry, ed. *Report of the Committee of the Highland Society of Scotland.* Edinburgh: n.p., 1805.

McKeon, Michael. *The Origins of the English Novel, 1600–1740.* Baltimore: Johns Hopkins University Press, 1987.

McKillop, Alan Dugold. "On Sir Charles Grandison." In *Samuel Richardson: A Collection of Critical Essays,* Ed. John Carrol. Englewood Cliffs, N.J.: Prentice-Hall, 1969. 124–38.

——. *Samuel Richardson: Printer and Novelist.* 1936. Hamden, Conn.: Shoe String Press, 1960.

McLaughlin, Jack, ed. *To His Excellency Thomas Jefferson: Letters to a President.* New York: Avon Books, 1993.

McLynn, F. J. *Charles Edward Stuart: A Tragedy in Many Acts.* London: Routledge, 1988.

——. *Crime and Punishment in Eighteenth-Century England.* Oxford: Oxford University Press, 1991.

McMaster, Juliet. "*Sir Charles Grandison:* Richardson on Body and Character." *Eighteenth-Century Fiction* 1 (1989): 83–102.

Meiring, Jane. *Thomas Pringle: His Life and Times.* Cape Town: Balkema, 1968.

Meltzer, Françoise. *The Stakes and Claims of Literary Originality.* Chicago: University of Chicago Press, 1994.

Merians, Linda E. "What They Are, Who We Are: Representations of the 'Hottentot' in Eighteenth-Century Britain." *Eighteenth-Century Life* 17 (1993): 14–39.

Metzdorf, Robert F. "M'Nicol, Macpherson, and Johnson." In *Eighteenth-Century Studies in Honor of Donald F. Hyde,* ed. W. H. Bond. New York: Grolier Club, 1970. 45–61.

Michals, Teresa. "'That Sole and Despotic Dominion': Slaves, Wives, and Game in Blackstone's *Commentaries.*" *Eighteenth-Century Studies* 27 (1993–94): 195–216.

Midgley, Clare. *Women against Slavery: The British Campaigns, 1780–1870.* London: Routledge, 1992.

Millar v. Taylor. 98 Eng. Rep. 201, 1769.

Moore, Dafydd. "Heroic Incoherence in James Macpherson's *The Poems of Ossian.*" *Eighteenth-Century Studies* 34 (2000): 43–59.

Moretti, Franco. *Modern Epic: The World-System from Goethe to Garcia Marquez.* Trans. Quintin Hoare. London: Verso, 1996.

Morrissey, Marietta. *Slave Women in the New World: Gender Stratification in the Caribbean.* Lawrence: University Press of Kansas, 1989.

Mossner, E. C. *The Life of David Hume.* Austin: University of Texas Press, 1954.

Mossner, George. *Nationalism and Sexuality: Respectability and Abnormal Sexuality in Modern Europe.* New York: Howard Fertig, 1985.

Munns, Jessica, ed. *The Clothes That Wear Us: Essays on Dressing and Transgressing in Eighteenth-Century Culture.* Newark: University of Delaware Press, 1999.

Munter, Robert. *A Dictionary of the Print Trade in Ireland, 1550–1775.* New York: Fordham University Press, 1988.

Murdoch, Alexander. *British History, 1660–1832: National Identity and Local Culture.* New York: St. Martin's Press, 1998.

——. "Scotland and the Idea of Britain in the Eighteenth Century." In *Eighteenth-Century Scotland: New Perspectives,* ed. T. M. Devine and J. R. Young. East Lothian, Scotland: Tuckwell Press, 1999. 106–21.

Murphy, Peter. "Fool's Gold: The Highland Treasures of Macpherson's Ossian." *ELH* 53 (1986): 576–91.

——. *Poetry as an Occupation and an Art in Britain, 1760–1830.* Cambridge: Cambridge University Press, 1993.

Murry, Dian H. *Pirates of the South China Coast, 1790–1810.* Stanford: Stanford University Press, 1987.

Nairn, Tom. *The Break-up of Britain: Crisis and Neo-nationalism.* 2d ed. London: NLB and Verso, 1981.

Newman, Gerald. *The Rise of English Nationalism: A Cultural History, 1740–1830.* Rev. ed. New York: St. Martin's Press, 1997.

Norton, David Fate, and Richard H. Popkin. *David Hume: Philosophical Historian.* Indianapolis: Bobbs-Merrill, 1965.

Nussbaum, Felicity. "Heteroclites: The Gender of Character in the Scandalous Memoirs." In *The New Eighteenth Century: Theory, Politics, English Literature,* ed. Felicity Nussbaum and Laura Brown. New York: Methuen, 1987. 144–67.

Oates, J. C. T. "Cambridge and the Copyright Act of Queen Anne (1710–1814)." In *Quick Springs of Sense: Studies in the Eighteenth Century,* ed. Larry S. Champion. Athens: University of Georgia Press, 1974. 61–73.

O'Brien, Karen. "Johnson's View of the Scottish Enlightenment in *A Journey to the Western Islands of Scotland.*" *Age of Johnson* 4 (1991): 59–82.

O'Connor, Maura. *The Romance of Italy and the English Political Imagination.* New York: St. Martin's Press, 1998.

O'Conor, Charles. *Dissertations on the antient history of ireland wherein an account is given of the origin, government, letters, sciences, religion, manners, customs, of the antient inhabitants.* Dublin: James Hoey, 1753.

——. *Letters of Charles O'Conor of Belanagare: A Catholic Voice in Eighteenth-Century Ireland.* Ed. Robert E. Ward, John F. Wrynne, and Catherine Coogan Ward. Washington, D. C.: Catholic University of America Press, 1988.

O'Donovan, Declan. "The Money Bill Dispute of 1753." In *Penal Era and Golden Age: Essays in Irish History, 1690–1800,* ed. Thomas Bartlett and D. W. Hayton. Belfast: Ulsten Historical foundation, 1979. 55–87.

Okie, Laird. *Augustan Historical Writing: Histories of England in the English Enlightenment.* Lanham, N.Y.: University Press of America, 1991.

Okun, Henry. "Ossian in Painting." *Journal of the Warburg and Courtauld Institutes* 30 (1967): 327–56.

Oldfield, J. R. *Popular Politics and British Anti-slavery: The Mobilization of Public Opinion against the Slave Trade, 1787–1807.* Manchester: Manchester University Press, 1995.

Oldham, James. "New Light on Mansfield and Slavery." *Journal of British Studies* 27 (1988): 45–68.

Ong, Walter. *Orality and Literacy: The Technologizing of the Word.* London: Routledge, 1982.

Outram, Dorinda. *The Body and the French Revolution.* New Haven: Yale University Press, 1989.

Owen, John B. *The Eighteenth Century.* New York: Norton, 1977.

Paquet, Sandra Pouchet. "The Heartbeat of a West Indian Slave: The History of Mary Prince." *African American Review* 26 (1992): 131–46.

Parker, Andrew. Introduction to *Nationalisms and Sexualities.* Ed. Andrew Parker, Mary Russo, Doris Sommer, and Patricia Yaeger. New York: Routledge, 1992. 1–18.

Pask, Amanda. "Cultural Appropriation and the Law: An Analysis of the Legal Regimes Concerning Culture." *Intellectual Property Journal* 8 (1993–94): 57–86.

Paton, Diane. "Decency, Dependence, and the Lash: Gender and the British Debate on Slave Emancipation, 1830–34." *Slavery and Abolition* 17 (1996): 163–84.

The Patriot Divine to the Female Historian. London: n.p., 1779.

Pattanayak, D. P. "Literacy: An Instrument of Oppression." In *Literacy and Orality,* ed. David R. Olson and Nancy Torrance. Cambridge: Cambridge University Press, 1991. 105–8.

Patterson, L. Ray. *Copyright in Historical Perspective.* Nashville: Vanderbilt University Press, 1968.

Patterson, L. Ray, and Stanley W. Lindberg. *The Nature of Copyright: A Law of User's Rights.* Athens: University of Georgia Press, 1991.

Paull, H. M. *Literary Ethics: A Study in the Growth of the Literary Conscience.* New York: E. P. Dutton, 1929.

Peardon, Thomas Preston. *The Transition in English Historical Writing, 1760–1830.* New York: Columbia University Press, 1933.

Perry, Ruth. *Women, Letters, and the Novel.* New York: AMS Press, 1980.

Pettit, Henry, ed. *The Correspondence of Edward Young: 1683–1765.* Oxford: Clarendon Press, 1971.

Phillips, Mark Salber. "Adam Smith and the History of Private Life: Social and Sentimental Narratives in Eighteenth-Century Historiography." In *The Historical Imagination in Early Modern Britain,* ed. Donald R. Kelley and David Harris Sacks. Cambridge: Cambridge University Press, 1997. 318–42.

———. *Society and Sentiment: Genres of Historical Writing in Britain, 1740–1820.* Princeton: Princeton University Press, 2000.

Phillipson, Nicholas. "Politics, Politeness, and the Anglicisation of Early Eighteenth-Century Scottish Culture." In *Scotland and England: 1286–1815.* Ed. Roger A. Mason. Edinburgh: John Donald Publishers, 1987. 226–46.

Pierson, Robert Craig. "The Revisions of Richardson's *Sir Charles Grandison.*" *Studies in Bibliography* 21 (1968): 163–89.

Pittock, Murry G. H. *Inventing and Resisting Britain: Cultural Identities in Britain and Ireland, 1685–1789.* New York: St. Martin's Press, 1997.

The Pleadings of the Counsel before the House of Lords in the Great Cause Concerning Literary Property. London: n.p., n.d. Reprinted in *The Literary Property Debate: Six Tracts, 1764–1774,* ed. Stephen Parks. New York: Garland, 1975.

Pocock, J. G. A. *Barbarism and Religion.* 2 vols. Cambridge: Cambridge University Press, 2000.

———. "Catharine Macaulay: Patriot Historian." In *Women Writers and the Early Modern British Political Tradition,* ed. Hilda L. Smith. Cambridge: Cambridge University Press, 1998. 243–58.

———. *The Machiavellian Moment: Florentine Political Thought and the Atlantic Republican Tradition.* Princeton: Princeton University Press, 1975.

Pollard, Mary. *Dublin's Trade in Books, 1550–1800.* Oxford: Clarendon Press, 1989.

Poovey, Mary. "Curing the 'Social Body' in 1832: James Phillips Kay and the Irish in Manchester." *Gender and History* 5 (1993): 196–211.

Pope v. Curll. 26 Eng. Rep. 608, 1741.

Porter, Roy. *The Creation of the Modern World.* New York: W. W. Norton, 2000.

——. *English Society in the Eighteenth Century.* New York: Penguin, 1986.

Post, Robert C. "The Social Foundations of Defamation Law: Reputation and the Constitution." *California Law Review* 74 (1986): 691.

Pratt, Mary Louise. "Linguistic Utopias." In *The Linguistics of Writing: Arguments between Language and Literature,* ed. Nigel Fabb, Derek Atridge, Alan Durant, and Colin MacCabe. New York: Methuen, 1987. 48–66.

Price, John Valdimir. *David Hume.* Boston: Twayne Publishers, 1991.

"Pringle v. Cadell." *The Times,* February 21, 1833, 4.

Prophecy of Queen Emma: An Ancient Ballad lately Discovered, Written by Johannes Turgotus, Prior of Durham, in the Reign of William Rufus. To which is added by the Editor, An Account of the Discovery, and Hints Towards a Vindication of the Authenticity of the Poems of Ossian And Rowley. London: n.p., 1782.

[Ralph, James.] "Case of Authors by Profession or Trade, Stated with Regard to Booksellers, the Stage, and the Public." No Matter by Whom. London: R. Griffiths, 1758. Reprinted in *Freedom of the Press and the Literary Property Debate, 1755–1700.* New York: Garland, 1974.

Ransom, Harry. *The First Copyright Statute.* Austin: University of Texas Press, 1956.

Reddick, Allen. *The Making of Johnson's Dictionary, 1746–1773.* Cambridge: Cambridge University Press, 1990.

Redford, Bruce. *The Converse of the Pen: Acts of Intimacy in the Eighteenth-Century Familiar Letter.* Chicago: University of Chicago Press, 1986.

Rediker, Marcus. *Between the Devil and the Deep Blue Sea: Merchant Seamen, Pirates, and the Anglo-American Maritime World, 1700–1750.* New York: Cambridge University Press, 1987.

Reinert, Thomas. *Regulating Confusion: Samuel Johnson and the Crowd.* Durham: Duke University Press, 1996.

"A Remarkable Moving Letter, which was Suggested by an Extraordinary Epistle Sent by Her on her Second Marriage to Her Clerical Admirer." London: n.p., 1779.

Review of *The History of England from the Accession of the James the First to that of the Brunswick Line. Monthly Review* 29 (1763): 372–82.

Richardson, Samuel. "An Address to the Public, on the Treatment which the Editor of . . . Grandison has met with." London: n.p., 1754.

——. "The Case of Samuel Richardson, of London, Printer; with regard to the Invasion of his Property in The History of Sir Charles Grandison, before publication by certain booksellers in Dublin." London 1753.

——. *Pamela.* Ed. T. C. Duncan Eaves and Ben D. Kimpel. Boston: Houghton Mifflin, 1971.

——. *Sir Charles Grandison.* Ed. Jocelyn Harris. Oxford: Oxford University Press, 1986.

Richetti, John. *Popular Fiction before Richardson: Narrative Patterns, 1700–1739.* Oxford: Clarendon Press, 1969.

Ritchie, Robert C. *Captain Kidd and the War against the Pirates.* Cambridge: Harvard University Press, 1986.

Rogers, Pat. *Johnson and Boswell: The Transit of Caledonia.* Oxford: Clarendon Press, 1995.

——. "The Noblest Savage of Them All: Johnson, Omai, and Other Primitives." *Age of Johnson* 5 (1992): 281–301.

Rose, Jacqueline. *States of Fantasy.* Oxford: Clarendon Press, 1996.

Rose, Mark. "The Author as Proprietor: *Donaldson v. Becket* and the Geneology of Modern Authorship." *Representations* 23 (1988): 51–85.

——. "The Author in Court: Pope v. Curll 1741." *Cardozo Arts and Entertainment Law Journal* 10 (1992): 475–93.

——. *Authors and Owners: The Invention of Copyright.* Cambridge: Harvard University Press, 1993.

Rosenblum, Robert, and H. W. Janson. *Nineteenth-Century Art.* Englewood Cliffs, N.J.: Prentice-Hall, 1984.

Rosenthal, Laura J. *Playwrights and Plagiarists in Early Modern England: Gender, Authorship, Literary Property.* Ithaca: Cornell University Press, 1996.

Ross, Richard J. "The Commoning of the Common Law: The Renaissance Debate over Printing English Law, 1520–1640." *University of Pennsylvania Law Review* 146 (1998): 323–461.

——. "The Memorial Culture of Early Modern English Lawyers: Memory as Keyword, Shelter, and Identity, 1560–1640." *Yale Journal of Law and the Humanities* 10 (1998): 229–326.

Sabor, Peter. "A Safe Bridge over the Narrow Seas": Crossing the Channel with Samuel Richardson." Ed. John McVeagh. *All Before Them: Attitudes to Abroad in English Literature, 1660–1780.* London: Ashfield Press, 1989. 159–70.

Sale, William Merritt. *Samuel Richardson: A Bibliographical Record of His Literary Career with Historical Notes.* New Haven: Yale University Press, 1936.

——. *Samuel Richardson: Master Printer.* Ithaca: Cornell University Press, 1950.

Saunders, David. *Authorship and Copyright.* London: Routledge, 1992.

Saunders, David, and Ian Hunter. "Lessons from the 'Literatory': How to Historicise Authorship." *Critical Inquiry* 17 (1991): 479–509.

Schama, Simon. *Landscape and Memory.* New York: Alfred A. Knopf, 1995.

Scherwatzky, Steven. "Johnson, *Rasselas,* and the Politics of Empire." *Eighteenth-Century Life* 16 (1992): 102–13.

Schlereth, Thomas J. *The Cosmopolitan Ideal in Enlightenment Thought: Its Form and Function in the Ideas of Franklin, Hume, and Voltaire, 1694–1790.* Notre Dame: University of Notre Dame Press, 1977.

Schnorrenberg, Barbara B. "The Brood-Hen of Faction: Mrs. Macaulay and Radical Politics, 1765–75." *Albion* 11 (1979): 33–45.

——. "Challenging Eighteenth-Century Boundaries: Catharine Macaulay Graham, Female Historian." Paper presented at the Southeastern American Society for Eighteenth-Century Studies conference, Chapel Hill, N.C., March 2002.

——. "An Opportunity Missed: Catherine Macaulay on the Revolution of 1688." *Studies in Eighteenth-Century Culture* 20 (1990): 231–40.

——. "A True Relation of the Life and Career of James Graham, 1745–1794." *Eighteenth-Century Life* 15 (1991): 58–75.

Scott, Sir Walter. Review of *The Report of the Committee of the Highland Society* and *The Poems of Ossian,* ed. Malcolm Laing. *Edinburgh Review, or Critical Journal* (April–July 1805). Vol. 6. New York: Eastburn, Kirk, 1815.

Scudéry, Madeliene de. *Artamène, ou Le Grand Cyrus.* 10 vols. Paris: A Covrbé, 1650–55.

——. *Artamenes, or The Grand Cyrus, that Excellent Romance.* Trans. F. G. Esq. London: J. Darby et al., 1691.

——. *Clélie, histoire romaine.* 10 vols. Paris: Covrbé, 1658–62.

Sharpe, James A. "The People and the Law." In *Popular Culture in Seventeenth-Century England,* ed. Barry Reay. London: Croom Helm, 1985. 244–70.

Sharpe, Jenny. "'Something Akin to Freedom': The Case of Mary Prince." *Differences: A Journal of Feminist Cultural Studies* 8 (1996): 31–56.

Sharpe, Kevin, and Steven N. Zwicker, eds. Introduction to *Refiguring Revolutions: Aesthetics and Politics from the English Revolution to the Romantic Revolution.* Berkeley: University of California Press, 1998. 1–21.

Shaw, William. Appendix to "An Inquiry into the Authenticity of the Poems Ascribed to Ossian With a Reply to Mr. Clark's Answer." Reprinted in *Aberdeen and the Enlightenment* ed. Jennifer J. Carter and Joan H. Pittock. Aberdeen: Aberdeen University Press, 1987.

Sher, Richard B. "Percy, Shaw, and the Ferguson 'Cheat." In *Ossian Revisited.* Edinburgh: Edinburgh University Press, 1991. 207–45.

———. "'Those Scotch Imposters and Their Cabal': Ossian and the Scottish Enlightenment." In *Man and Nature,* ed. R. L. Emerson, Gilles Girard. London, Ontario: University of Western Ontario Press, 1982. 55–63.

Sher, Richard B., and Dafydd Moore. "Select Bibliography: James Macpherson and Ossian." *http://www.c18.rutgers.edu/biblio/macpherson.html.* 1999.

Sherman, Brad. "From the Non-original to the Ab-original: A History." In *Of Authors and Origins: Essays on Copyright Law,* ed. Brad Shermand and Alain Strowel. Oxford: Clarendon Press, 1994. 111–30.

Sherry, Frank. *Raiders and Rebels: The Golden Age of Piracy.* New York: Hearst Marine Books, 1986.

Simpson, Kenneth. *The Protean Scot: The Crisis of Identity in Eighteenth-Century Scottish Literature.* Aberdeen: Aberdeen University Press: 1988.

Siskin, Clifford. "Epilogue: The Rise of Novelism." In *Cultural Institutions of the Novel,* ed. Deidre Lynch and William B. Warner. Durham: Duke University Press, 1996. 423–40.

Slattery, William C., ed. *The Richardson-Stinstra Correspondence and Stinstra's Prefaces to Clarissa.* Carbondale: Southern Illinois University Press, 1969.

Slaughter, M. M. "The Development of Common Law Defamation Privileges: From Communitarian Society to Market Society." *Cardozo Law Review* 14 (1992): 351–406.

The Slave's Narrative. Ed. Charles T. Davis and Henry Louis Gates Jr. Oxford: Oxford University Press, 1985.

Smith, Anthony D. Introduction to *Nationalist Movements.* Ed. Anthony D. Smith. New York: St. Martin's Press, 1977. 1–30.

———. "Neo-classicist and Romantic Elements and the Emergence of Nationalist Conceptions." In *Nationalist Movements,* ed. Anthony D. Smith. New York: St. Martin's Press, 1977.

Smith, Bonnie. *The Gender of History: Men, Women, and Historical Practice.* Cambridge: Harvard University Press, 1998.

Smith, Bruce. *The Acoustic World of Modern England: Attending to the O-Factor.* Chicago: University of Chicago Press, 1999.

Smith-Rosenberg, Carroll. "Coquettes and Revolutionaries in Young America." In *Literature and the Body: Essays on Populations and Persons,* ed. Elaine Scarry. Baltimore: Johns Hopkins University Press, 1986. 160–84.

Smout, T. C. *A History of the Scottish People: 1560–1830.* New York: Charles Scribner's Sons, 1970.

Snyder, Edward D. "The Wild Irish: A Study of Some English Satires against the Irish, Scots, and Welsh." *Modern Philology* 17 (1920): 147–85.

Solow, Barbara L., and Stanley L. Engerman, eds. *British Capitalism and Caribbean Slavery: The Legacy of Eric Williams.* Cambridge: Cambridge University Press, 1987.

Sorensen, Janet. *The Grammar of Empire.* Cambridge: Cambridge University Press, 2000.

Spacks, Patricia. "Forgotten Genres." *Modern Language Studies* 18 (1988): 47–56.

Stafford, Fiona J. "'Dangerous Success': Ossian, Wordsworth, and English Romantic Literature." In *Ossian Revisited,* ed. Howard Gaskill. Edinburgh: Edinburgh University Press, 1991. 49–72.

——. *The Sublime Savage: A Study of James Macpherson and the Poems of Ossian.* Edinburgh: Edinburgh University Press, 1988.

Stallybrass, Peter, and Allon White. *The Politics and Poetics of Transgression.* London: Methuen, 1986.

State Law: Or, The Doctrine of Libels, Discussed and Examined. 2d ed. Reprinted in *Freedom of the Press: Six Tracts, 1712–1730.* New York: Garland, 1974.

Staves, Susan. "'The Liberty of a She-Subject of England': Rights Rhetoric and the Female Thucydides." *Cardozo Studies in Law and Literature* 5 (fall 1989): 161–84.

Stevenson, David R. "David Hume, Historicist." *Historian* 52 (1990): 209–18.

Stewart, Susan. *Crimes of Writing: Problems in the Containment of Representation.* Durham: Duke University Press, 1994.

——. *On Longing: Narratives of the Miniature, the Gigantic, the Souvenir, the Collection.* Durham: Duke University Press, 1993.

Stillinger, Jack. *Multiple Authorship and the Myth of Solitary Genius.* New York: Oxford University Press, 1991.

Straub, Kristina. "Heteroanxiety and the Case of Elizabeth Canning." *Eighteenth-Century Studies* 30 (1997): 296–304.

Sussman, Charlotte. "Women and the Politics of Sugar, 1792." *Representations,* 48 (1994): 48–69.

Sutherland, Lucy S., ed. *The Correspondence of Edmund Burke.* Vol. 2, Chicago: University of Chicago Press, 1960.

Tannen, Deborah. "The Oral/Literate Continuum in Discourse." In *Spoken and Written Language: Exploring Orality and Literacy,* ed. Deborah Tannen. Norwood, N.J.: Ablex Publishing, 1982.

Thomas, Donald., ed. *State Trials* London: Routledge and Kegan Paul, 1972.

Thomas, Peter D. G. *Johns Wilkes: A Friend to Liberty.* Oxford: Clarendon Press, 1996.

Thompson v. Stanhope. 27 Eng. Rep. 476, 1774.

Thompson, E. P. *Customs in Common: Studies in Traditional Popular Culture.* New York: New Press, 1991.

Thompson, Eva M. "Mary Prince, and Contexts for 'The History of Mary Prince, A West Indian Slave, Related by Herself.'" Ph.D. diss. Ohio State University, 1998.

Thomson, Derick. *The Gaelic Sources of Macpherson's "Ossian."* 1952. Edinburgh: Oliver and Boyd, 1982.

——. "James Macpherson." In *The Companion to Gaelic Scotland,* ed. Derick S. Thomson. Oxford: Basil Blackwell, 1983. 189–90.

Thomson, Janice E. *Mercenaries, Pirates, and Sovereigns: State-Building and Extraterritorial Violence in Early Modern Europe.* Princeton: Princeton University Press, 1994.

Tierney, James E. "Eighteenth-Century Dublin-London Publishing Relations: The Case of George Faulkner." In *The Book Trade and Its Customers, 1450–1900.* ed. Arnold Hunt, Giles Mandelbrote, and Alison Shell. New Castle, Del.: Oak Knoll Press, 1997. 133–40.

Tombo, Rudolf. *Ossian in Germany.* 1901. New York: AMS Press, 1966.

Tompson, Richard C. "Scottish Judges and the Birth of British Copyright." *Juridical Review* (1992): 18–42.

Toohey, Robert E. *Liberty and Empire: British Radical Solutions to the American Problem, 1774–1776.* Lexington: University Press of Kentucky, 1978.

Trevor-Roper, Hugh. "The Invention of Tradition: The Highland Tradition of Scotland." In *The Invention of Tradition,* ed. Eric Hobsbawm and Terence Ranger. Cambridge: Cambridge University Press, 1983. 15–41.

Trumpener, Katie. *Bardic Nationalism: The Romantic Novel and the British Empire.* Princeton: Princeton University Press, 1997.

The Tryal of Dr. Henry Sacheverell, Before the House of Peers, for High Crimes and Misdemeanors. London: Jacob Tonson, 1710.

Tumbleson, Raymond. *Catholicism in the English Protestant Imagination: Nationalism, Religion, and Literature 1660–1745.* Cambridge: Cambridge University Press, 1998.

Turley, David. *The Culture of English Antislavery, 1780–1860.* London: Routledge, 1991.

Turley, Hans. "Piracy, Identity, and Desire in *Captain Singleton.*" *Eighteenth-Century Studies* 31 (1997–98): 199–214.

——. *Rum, Sodomy, and the Lash: Piracy, Sexuality, and Masculine Identity.* New York: New York University Press, 1999.

Van Tiegham, Paul. *Ossian en France.* 2 vols. Paris: n.p., 1917.

Verdery, Katherine. "Whither 'Nation' and 'Nationalism'"? In *Mapping the Nation,* ed. Gopal Balakrishna. London: Verso, 1996. 226–34.

Vincent, David. *Literacy and Popular Culture, 1750–1914.* Cambridge: Cambridge University Press, 1989.

Walker, Brian. *Dancing to History's Tune: History, Myth, and Politics in Ireland.* Belfast: Queen's University of Belfast, 1996.

Wall, Wendy. *The Imprint of Gender.* Ithaca: Cornell University Press, 1993.

Wallerstein, Immanuel. *The Modern World System.* New York: Academic Press, 1974.

Walpole, Horace. *Letters of Horace Walpole.* Ed. Peter Cunningham. Edinburgh: John Grant, 1906.

Walvin, James. *Black and White: The Negro and English Society, 1555–1945.* London: Penguin, 1973.

——. *Black Ivory: A History of British Slavery.* Washington, D.C.: Howard University Press, 1994.

——. *England, Slaves, and Freedom, 1776–1838.* London: Macmillan, 1986.

——. "The Propaganda of Anti-slavery." In *Slavery and British Society, 1776–1846,* ed. James Walvin. Baton Rouge: Louisiana State University Press, 1982. 49–68.

Ward, J. R. *British West Indian Slavery, 1750–1834.* Oxford: Clarendon Press, 1988.

Ward, Robert E. *Prince of Dublin Printers: The Letters of George Faulkner.* Lexington: University Press of Kentucky, 1972.

Warner, William B. "Formulating Fiction: Romancing the General Reader in Early Modern Britain." In *Cultural Institutions of the Novel,* ed. Deidre Lynch and William B. Warner. Durham: Duke University Press, 1996. 279–305.

——. "The Institutionalization of Authorship: Richardson's Battle with the Irish Bookseller." Paper presented at 1991 conference of the Society for Critical Exchange at Case Western University, April 18–21, 1991.

——. *Licensing Entertainment: The Elevation of Novel Reading in Britain, 1684–1750.* Berkeley: University of California Press, 1998.

Wechselblatt, Martin. "Finding Mr. Boswell: Rhetoric, Authority, and National Identity in Johnson's *A Journey to the Western Islands of Scotland. ELH* 60 (1993): 117–48.

Weinbrot, Howard D. *Britannia's Issue: The Rise of British Literature from Dryden to Ossian.* Cambridge: Cambridge University Press, 1993.

Works Cited

Wexler, Victor G. *David Hume and the History of England*. Philadelphia: American Philosophical Society 1979.

Whalley, Peter. *An Essay on the Manner of Writing History*. 1746. Ed. Keith Stewart. Los Angeles: University of California, William Andrews Clark Memorial Library, 1960.

Wheeler, Roxann. "The Complexion of Desire: Racial Ideology and Mid-Eighteenth-Century British Novels." *Eighteenth-Century Studies* 32, 3 (spring 1999): 309–32.

White, Harold Ogden. *Plagiarism and Imitation during the English Renaissance: A Study in Critical Distinctions*. Cambridge: Harvard University Press, 1935.

Whitford, Margaret, ed. *The Irigaray Reader*. Oxford: Blackwell, 1993.

Whitlock, Gillian. "The Silent Scribe: Susanna and 'Black Mary.'" *International Journal of Canadian Studies* (spring 1995): 249–60.

Wickwar, W. Hardy. *The Struggle for Freedom of the Press 1819–1832*. New York: Johnson Reprint, 1972.

Williams, Eric. *Capitalism and Slavery*. Chapel Hill: University of North Carolinia Press, 1944.

Williamson, Margaret. "The Greek Romance." In *The Progress of Romance: The Politics of Popular Fiction*, ed. Jean Radford. London: Routledge, 1986. 23–45.

Wilton, Andrew, and Ilaria Bignamini, eds. *The Grand Tour: The Lure of Italy in the Eighteenth Century*, London: Tate Gallery Publishing, 1996.

Withey, Lynne E. "Catharine Macaulay and the Uses of History: Ancient Rights, Perfectionism, and Propaganda," *Journal of British Studies* 16 (1976): 59–83.

Wood, Marcus. *Blind Memory: Visual Representations of Slavery in England and America, 1780–1865*. New York: Routledge, 2000.

———. *Radical Satire and Print Culture, 1790–1822*. Oxford: Clarendon Press, 1994.

Woodard, Helena. *African-British Writings in the Eighteenth Century: The Politics of Race and Reason*. Westport, Conn.: Greenwood Press, 1999.

Woodmansee, Martha. "The Genius and the Copyright: Economic and Legal Conditions of the Emergence of the 'Author.'" *Eighteenth-Century Studies* 17 (1984): 425–48.

Woodmansee, Martha, and Peter Jaszi, eds. *The Construction of Authorship: Textual Appropriation in Law and Literature*. Durham: Duke University Press, 1991.

"Wood v. Pringle." *The Times*, March 1, 1833, 6–7.

Woolf, D. R. "A Feminine Past? Gender, Genre, and Historical Knowledge in England, 1500–1800." *American Historical Review* 102 (1997): 645–79.

Young, Edward. "Conjectures on Original Composition," In *Late Augustan Prose*, ed. Patricia Meyer Spacks. Englewood Cliffs, N.J.: Prentice-Hall, 1973. 47–85.

Young, Robert. *White Mythologies: Writing History and the West*. London: Routledge, 1990.

Zach, Wolfgang. "Mrs. Aubin and Richardson's Earliest Literary Manifesto (1739)." *English Studies* 62 (1981): 271–85.

Zaczek, Barbara Maria. *Censored Sentiments: Letters and Censorship in Epistolary Novels and Conduct Material*. Newark: University of Delaware Press, 1997.

Zimmerman, Everett. *The Boundaries of Fiction: History and the Eighteenth-Century British Novel*. Ithaca: Cornell University Press, 1996.

Zimmerman, Patricia R. *States of Emergency: Documentaries, Wars, Democracies*. Minneapolis: University of Minnesota Press, 2000.

Žižek, Slavoj. *For They Know Not What They Do: Enjoyment as a Political Factor*. London: Verso, 1991.

Zumwalt, Rosemary Levy. "A Historical Glossary of Critical Approaches." In *Teaching Oral Traditions*, ed. John Miles Foley. New York: MLA, 1998. 75–94.

Index

of Mary Prince, 183, 189; and Johnson, 91; and scandalous print spectacles, 175; and *Sir Charles Grandison,* 21; and tolerance, 24, 72. *See also* Colonialism; Internal colonialism

Englishness: and authorship, 10, 25, 209; and empire, 3, 71, 181; and *History of England,* 126; and *The History of Mary Prince,* 177, 178, 181, 182, 184, 189, 190, 200, 205; and Hume, 136; international export of, 5–6, 16, 21; and Johnson, 79, 88–89, 94, 108, 178; and law, 11; and liberty, 16, 25, 25n. 12, 126, 170; and Macaulay, 143–44, 145, 157; and Macpherson, 79; meaning of, 4; and national history, 124; and nationalism, 5; and reliance on slavery, 179; and Richardson, 28, 29, 62–63, 67–68, 71; and scandalous print spectacles, 16; and *Sir Charles Grandison,* 22, 23, 24, 25, 28, 33–34, 35, 37–38, 41; threats to, 3, 23, 67–68, 119. *See also* Britishness

Enlightenment, 7–8

Equiano, Olaudah, 177, 178, 180

Faulkner, George, 42, 46, 54, 55–56, 58–61, 127

Favret, Mary, 124, 141, 142

Ferguson, Moira, 185

Fielding, Sarah, 66, 67

Foote, Samuel, 146–47

Foucault, Michel, 50, 97

Fowler, Alastair, 93

Franklin, Benjamin, 187, 209

Freedom of the press, 120, 197–98

Fryer, Peter, 185

Gates, Henry Louis, 177

Gender: and attacks on women intellectuals, 124; England's relationship with, 3; and Hume, 130, 132, 134; and law, 126, 171; and literary property law, 126, 127, 158–71; and Macaulay, 138, 142, 143, 144–47, 144n. 33, 158, 169; and multiple identities, 17; and national history, 129–33, 143, 167, 169; and piracy, 56; and secret history genre, 127–35; and *Sir Charles Grandison,* 34. *See also* Women

Gibbon, Edward, 138, 139

Gikandi, Simon, 6, 20, 22

Girodet-Trioson, Anne-Louis, *Ossian and*

His Warriors Receiving the Dead Heroes of the French Army, 75–77, 76, 85, 120

Globalization, 209–10, 211

Goodrich, Peter, 109, 171

Grafton, Anthony, 9–10, 139n. 24

Graham, James, 122, 151n. 45, 152n. 47, 154, 158, 168, *168*

Graham, William, 122, 154, 158, 159, 165, 169, 209

Hargrave, Francis, 115, 116–17

Harris, Jocelyn, 33, 64

Hatchard, John, 200, 201

Hawkins, John, 1–2

Highland Society of Scotland, 78, 79, 111–12

Hill, Urania, 67

Hinton v. Donaldson, 118, 119

Historiography: and gender, 127–35; and Macaulay, 135–43, 135n. 19; and Macpherson, 100; and secret history, 124–26

History (Moore), 152, *153*

History of England (Macaulay): and Englishness, 126; and gender, 127, 136–37; and Hume, 129, 134, 139, 140; and Jefferson, 9; popularity of, 122, 135–36, 157; and private letters, 123, 139–43; and republican principles, 138, 147–48; and secret history genre, 17–18, 124, 139–43; and textual networks, 8

History of Mary Prince, The (Prince): as challenge to English norms, 176–87; and class issues, 177, 178, 180, 187–95; and cultural issues, 174, 175, 178, 185; and domesticity, 18, 177, 189, 193–95, 200–201, 202, 203–5, 206; and libel suits, 175, 175–76n. 10, 177, 195, 199, 200–206; publishing of, 173; and textual networks, 8

Hogarth, William, 48, 57

Hok-Sze Leung, Helen, 15

Holt, Francis, 196, 197–98

Holt, John, 186, 195, 198

Home, John, 85–86

Homer, 73, 74, 99, 118

Hume, David: and Baxter, 49; and Englishness, 136; and gender, 130, 132, 134; and Macaulay, 122, 125, 138, 139, 140, 147; and Macpherson, 84, 208; and petitioning, 149, 150; on women, 129–33, 164

Hutchinson, John, 45, 46

Index